Performing Shakespeare in Japan

Shakespeare has an astonishingly rich and varied performance tradition in Japan, stretching from the westernizing and modernizing ferment of the nineteenth-century Meiji era to the postmodern performance culture of today.

How has the tradition evolved? Where is it going? How is it to be accounted for in theatrical and cultural terms? What does it mean to do Shakespeare in Japan? Such questions are raised in the book's introduction and pursued in fourteen essays on key aspects, moments, and personalities in the performance tradition. These are followed by provocative interviews with four leading directors (Deguchi Norio, Suzuki Tadashi, Ninagawa Yukio, and Noda Hideki) and with one leading performer (Hira Mikijirô).

Unlike the very few existing books on Japanese Shakespeare, this book concentrates on modern and postmodern theatre, roughly from the 1970s, and contains contributions from both Japanese and Western scholars and theatre practitioners.

MINAMI RYUTA is Associate Professor of English at Kobe City University of Foreign Studies. He has co-edited, with Ian Carruthers and John Gillies, a CD-ROM on Deguchi Norio's productions of *A Midsummer Night's Dream* for the Department of Theatre and Drama, La Trobe University. He also compiled a chronology of Shakespearean performances in Japan for *Shakespeare and the Japanese Stage* published by Cambridge University Press in 1999.

IAN CARRUTHERS is Lecturer at La Trobe University, Melbourne. As Visiting Professor at Kansai Gaidai University in Japan, he taught traditional Japanese theatre and in 1994 won a Japan Foundation Fellowship to research the theatre of Suzuki Tadashi. He is currently writing a book, with Takahashi Yasunari, entitled *The Theatre of Suzuki Tadashi* for Cambridge University Press.

JOHN GILLIES is an Australian Research Council Research Fellow at the School of Arts & Media, La Trobe University, Melbourne. He has published numerous articles and book chapters. He is also the author of *Shakespeare and the Geography of Difference* published by Cambridge University Press in 1994 and editor, with Virginia Mason Vaughan, of *Playing the Globe* (1998).

Performing Shakespeare in Japan

EDITED BY

MINAMI RYUTA, IAN CARRUTHERS, JOHN GILLIES

CAMBRIDGE
UNIVERSITY PRESS

PUBLISHED BY THE PRESS SYNDICATE OF THE UNIVERSITY OF CAMBRIDGE
The Pitt Building, Trumpington Street, Cambridge, United Kingdom

CAMBRIDGE UNIVERSITY PRESS
The Edinburgh Building, Cambridge CB2 2RU, UK   www.cup.cam.ac.uk
40 West 20th Street, New York, NY 10011-4211, USA   www.cup.org
10 Stamford Road, Oakleigh, Melbourne 3166, Australia
Ruiz de Alarcón 13, 28014 Madrid, Spain

First published 2001

Printed in the United Kingdom at the University Press, Cambridge

Typeface Quadraat 10.5/14 pt.   *System* QuarkXPress™ [SE]

A catalogue record for this book is available from the British Library

ISBN 0 521 78244 9 hardback

CONTENTS

ILLUSTRATIONS

Colour

Between pages 114 and 115

Black and white

CONTRIBUTORS

MINAMI RYUTA is Associate Professor of English at Kobe City University of Foreign Studies

IAN CARRUTHERS is Lecturer at La Trobe University, Melbourne and was Visiting Professor at Kansai Gaidai University in Japan where he taught traditional Japanese theatre

JOHN GILLIES is an Australian Research Council Fellow at the School of Arts and Media, La Trobe University, Melbourne

ANZAI TETSUO is Professor of English at Sophia University, Tokyo

YOSHIHARA YUKARI is Associate Professor of English at Chikushi Jogakuen University for Women

JAMES R. BRANDON is Professor of Asian Theatre at the University of Hawai'i at Manoa where he has translated and directed Japanese plays in English for the past thirty years. He is editor of *The Cambridge Guide to Asian Theatre*

MATSUMOTO SHINKO, a researcher of modern Japanese Drama, taught Japanese drama at Waseda University Tokyo

UEDA MUNAKATA KUNIYOSHI is Emeritus Professor of English at Shizuoka University

MICHAEL SHAPIRO is Professor of English at the University of Illinois Urbana-Champaign where he is also Director of the Drobny Program in Jewish Culture and Society

PAULA VON LOEWENFELDT has taught Shakespeare and film studies at Purdue University where she is currently completing her doctorate in medieval and early modern literature and drama

SUEMATSU MICHIKO is Associate Professor of English at Gunma University

TAKAHASHI YASUNARI, the former President of the Shakespeare Society of Japan and the Vice-President of the International Shakespeare Society, is Professor of English at Showa Women's University, Tokyo

SUZUKI MASAE is Associate Professor of English at Kyoto Sangyô University

OHTANI TOMOKO teaches English at Tokyo Gakugei University, Meiji Gakuin University and Japan Women's University

TED MOTOHASHI is Associate Professor of English at Tokyo Metropolitan University

PREFACE

TAKAHASHI YASUNARI

The Fifth World Shakespeare Congress (Tokyo 1991), with the general theme of "Shakespeare and Cultural Traditions," significantly stressed the need for an inter-cultural viewpoint in Shakespeare studies, or, to put it more bluntly, a heightened awareness of Shakespeare's foreign consumability. One of the after-effects was a seminar on "Japanese Shakespeare Productions: Problems of Stylization and Localization" held at the Sixth World Shakespeare Congress (Los Angeles 1996). As a co-chair (with Ian Carruthers) of the seminar, I vividly remember the enthusiasm with which scholars from Japan and other countries discussed the "sea changes" (be they ravishing or estranging) undergone by the English Renaissance dramatist at the hands of Far Eastern directors after the passage of three to four centuries.

It is a great pleasure to me to know that the seminar has now been re-born into a new life. Extensive re-organizing by the editors, intensive re-thinking by the speakers, and participation of new members have produced what I expect will prove a new step in the history of Shakespeare studies.

ACKNOWLEDGEMENTS

Debts incurred in the process of bringing this book to press are many and various. We owe particular debts of gratitude to Professor Takahashi Yasunari for his expertise in setting up the research project in Japan and for his wise mentoring throughout; to Ted Motohashi for so efficiently and cheerfully coordinating an arduous research seminar at the Sixth "International Shakespeare Association" congress at Los Angeles in 1996; and to Matsuoka Kazuko for organizing the interviews with prominent directors and actors. Her deep knowledge of the field, as translator, critic and dramaturge, as well as her unfailing perspicacity and generosity have substantially contributed to the success of this project. Professors Anzai Tetsuo and James Brandon have also given valuable advice, and made invaluable contributions to the interview process. We deeply regret that, for reasons of space, we were not able to include James Brandon's article "Some Shakespeare(s) in Some Asia(s)," but are pleased that this magisterial survey of the whole field is available in print in the *Asian Studies Journal* (Journal of the Asian Studies Association of Australia) Vol.20, No.3, April 1997, 1–26.

Other scholars and friends have assisted us with help and advice along the way, particularly Dennis Bartholomeusz, co-editor (with Dr. Poonam Trivedi) of a forthcoming volume from a related "Shakespeare in Asia" conference (on "Shakespeare and India") in New Delhi, 1998. We also thank Professor J. R. Mulryne and Dr. Margaret Shewring who, after participating in our 1996 seminar in Los Angeles, kindly allowed us to see the proofs of their own *Shakespeare on the Japanese Stage* (Cambridge, 1998), co-edited with Professor Sasayama Takashi.

We are also beholden to all those who assisted with the transcription and translation of interviews, in particular: Inazawa Shôko (for transcription of tape-recordings), Hashimoto Kayoko, Yoshida Masako, Suzuki Masae and Chiba Shôko (for help with translation of, respectively: Deguchi and Suzuki, Ninagawa, Noda, and Hira). Hatta Genji and Yanagisawa Kayoko generously translated several articles which we were eventually forced to cut for reasons of economy. Paula von Loewenfeldt earns a particular debt of gratitude for taking on the exacting job of typing, formatting and collating the first draft of our typescript, as does Ann Philpott for indexing. We have a separate attribution sheet for photographers, but would like to thank particularly, Rei Zunde in Australia, and the offices of the directors and actors we interviewed for supplying such superb photographs.

We acknowledge a generous large grant from the Australia Research Council to Ian Carruthers, John Gillies and Dennis Bartholomeusz for a project on "Shakespeare in Asia" (1996–98) which underwrote a large part of our research into "Shakespeare in Japan," as also into "Shakespeare in China" and "Shakespeare in India."

For her expert guidance and patient practical help at all stages of the preparation of this book, we thank our editor, Sarah Stanton.

Note
Japanese names in this book follow conventional Japanese usage: the surname first, followed by the given name (except in the event that the given name is not Japanese).

A macron (ˆ) over a Japanese vowel indicates that the vowel is long. The macron is not used in the case of familiar names such as "Tokyo," "Osaka" and "Kyoto."

Introduction

MINAMI RYUTA, IAN CARRUTHERS, AND JOHN GILLIES

In her book *The Taming of the Samurai: Honorific Individualism and the Making of Modern Japan*, Ikegami Eiko asks how Meiji Japan could have reconstructed its society so quickly in response to the threat of the west. She rejects the notion that Japan was "simply a passive recipient of Western influence" in favor of the argument that "it was transformed from within by the determination and ambition of a number of individuals . . . who undertook significant social, psychological and physical risks."[1] Ikegami's argument provides a useful point of departure for discussion of the Japanese encounter with Shakespeare. This volume provides continuing evidence of theatre artists, from the Meiji period to the present, who extend our expectations of what it means to do Shakespeare through the adventurousness of their responses to the question of what it means to be Japanese.

Traditional Japanese theatre has been extensively studied this century by a long list of western scholars, but modern Japanese theatre, despite its richness and variety, and the fact that it has undergone an astonishing renaissance in the last thirty years, has so far attracted relatively little scholarly attention. In the field of Shakespeare as performance, much the same holds true. Studies of the literary or monocultural object prevail over studies of the theatrical or intercultural object. While the relative lack of attention paid to modern Japanese theatre (in which we include productions of Shakespeare) may seem an anomaly of western scholarship, it is also true of Japanese scholarship. Modern Japanese theatre is a subject rarely taught in Japanese universities, and though Shakespeare is ubiquitous (there are well over 800 members of The Shakespeare Society of Japan), his plays are generally not discussed in terms of their local theatrical manifestations. "Shakespeare in Japan" is currently as marginalized a topic of Japanese academic discourse as it is abroad.

In *Hamlet in Japan*, edited by Ueno Yoshiko (New York: AMS Press, 1995), actual productions are considered in three out of fifteen articles. Yet, anywhere between fifty to one hundred productions of Shakespeare can be seen in Tokyo every year. In *Shakespeare East and West*, edited by Fujita Minoru and Leonard Pronko (Tokyo: Japan Library, 1996), performance is entirely ignored.

Excellent as this work is in proposing alternative models of comparable stature to Shakespeare in Zeami and Chikamatsu, the book as a whole nevertheless runs the risk of unconsciously orientalizing modern Japanese production of Shakespeare by over-emphasizing comparisons between Shakespeare, Noh, and Kabuki, and largely ignoring the important contributions made by modern theatre producers. Fortunately, *Shakespeare and the Japanese Stage*, edited by Sasayama Takashi, J. R. Mulryne, and Margaret Shewring (Cambridge, 1998) has now gone some way towards rectifying that imbalance since it not only includes seven articles on "Shakespeare and the Japanese Stage" but a further seven on "Shakespeare our Japanese Contemporary."

This volume seeks further to extend such pioneering work in two ways: by including articles on a wider variety of individual Japanese theatre artists who have negotiated modernity and postmodernity in terms of tradition, and by offering in-depth interviews with four major theatre directors (Deguchi, Ninagawa, Suzuki, Noda) and a major actor (Hira), as well as separate studies of their individual work. Unlike the earlier studies, we concentrate far more extensively on the modern and postmodern period. Thus, nine out of our fifteen essays, and all five interviews, are concerned with postwar Shakespeare performances.

Before profiling the essays and interviews in detail, it might be helpful to outline their broad cultural and theatrical context. The Shakespeare of the Japanese theatre may be thought of as defined by a number of interlocking cultural modalities and theatrical forces:

(1) translation and adaptation
(2) the rise of Shingeki (New Drama) in the 1900s and the so-called "Shôgekijô Undô" (Little Theatre Movement) of the late 1960s
(3) international theatrical contact, Western and Asian

(1) Translation and adaptation

Translating Shakespeare has always been culturally complicated in Japan. Tsubouchi Shôyô's 1884 translation of *Julius Caesar* should be seen primarily as an extension of Kabuki, rather than as a linguistic and cultural importation of Shakespeare. However, his translations of *The Merchant of Venice* and *Hamlet* early in the new century were aimed at his own Bungei Kyôkai (Literary Association) thus helping to stimulate the rise of "Shingeki Shakespeare," in which performance is more closely linked to the authority of translation on the one hand and the act of reading on the other. To some extent this priority followed that of Shingeki (New Drama) per se, a movement dedicated to the performance of western drama in translation.[2] In the 1920s, Shakespeare came to be read and studied rather than performed. It was in this atmosphere that Tsubouchi's translations of Shakespeare's Complete Works were published in pocket editions in 1933–35 and widely read.[3] Ironically thereby, Shakespeare first took root in Japanese culture in the slightly archaic image of Kabuki – still detectable in Tsubouchi, the predominant translation until 1955.[4]

Since then, the translations of Fukuda Tsuneari, Odashima Yûshi, and Matsuoka Kazuko have followed – at shorter intervals and with a corresponding dispersal of cultural authority. These have all attempted to reinvent "Shakespeare" by keying him to different cultural registers, including that of performance. In 1955, Fukuda Tsuneari (playwright, director, and scholar of English literature) produced his own translation of *Hamlet* for the Bungaku-za company in a flawed attempt to find a way out of the Shingeki impasse (the production was virtually a reproduction of the 1953 Old Vic production he had seen in England). Distinctive features of Fukuda's rendering were his brisk, rhythmical, and dramatic style designed to release actors from conventional realistic acting.[5] Its impact is attested by the fact that Shakespeare performances by Shingeki companies in the late 1950s and 1960s were mostly done in Fukuda's rendering.

Odashima's translation (pub. 1973–80) represents the major breakthrough in the history of Shakespeare translation in Japan. The Shakespeare Theatre's staging of Odashima's translation of *The Complete Works* successfully served to popularize Shakespeare by attracting younger readers and audiences.[6] Like Fukuda's, Odashima's translation has a crisp and rhythmical style, yet what distinguishes his work is its phraseology, the use of colloquialisms, and abundant word-play. Unlike earlier translators, Odashima gave up trying to create an equivalent for blank verse and instead introduced the rapid tempo of daily conversation, which had been accelerating since the mid-1950s, prioritizing dramatic and theatrical effects over poetic ones.[7]

Since 1995, Odashima's dominance has in turn been challenged by Matsuoka Kazuko, the first female translator of Shakespeare in Japan. A strong point of Matsuoka's translations is that they are written for and revised during rehearsals with specific directors, such as David Leveaux. Another is her use of language to foreground gender issues. As a Shakespeare scholar and drama critic with strong sympathy for works of the Shôgekijô (Little Theatre) movement, Matsuoka's work is more closely linked to performance process.

Even on so summary a view, it should be clear that translation is always keyed to wider cultural effects and strategies, and either draws heavily from or bears heavily upon performance culture and practice.

While to a western eye, adaptation (considered as taking liberties with and thus challenging the cultural authority of the text) may appear a kind of antithesis to translation, the phenomenon is not quite so clear cut in Japan. Crucial here is the question of cultural motive. Shakespeare can be assimilated to the conventional world of an indigenous performance genre – as in the Noh Shakespeares of Ueda Munakata Kuniyoshi. Alternatively, Shakespeare may be adapted towards an indigenous performance genre in order to meet a perceived need to modernize – as in *Sakuradoki Zeni no yononaka* (Life is as fragile as cherry blossoms in a world of money), a pioneering Kabuki adaptation of *The Merchant of Venice* (Osaka, 1885). Takahashi Yasunari's Kyogen *Merry Wives of Windsor* (1991) also fits this category. Again, Shakespeare may be adapted in accord with an entirely new theatrical form (based on a fusion of Japanese performance traditions and western dramaturgy) as in the work of Suzuki Tadashi. This leads to a consideration of "new" theatre movements.

(2) The rise of Shingeki (New Drama) in the 1900s and the Shôgekijô Undô (Little Theatre Movement) in the sixties

While *Sakuradoki Zeni no yononaka* (hereafter, *Zeni*) was commercially successful as well as conceptually bold, Kabuki's theatrical and dramaturgical limitations appear to have prevented it from accommodating Shakespeare.[8] For a brief time, Shimpa became the host that Kabuki did not. From its origins in the first two decades of this century as amateur performance for the purpose of political propaganda, Shimpa was unrestrained by Kabuki conventions or by a Shingeki ethic of fidelity to the text.[9] Shimpa Shakespeare was inaugurated with a partial production of *Julius Caesar* in 1901, followed by Kawakami Otojirô's monumental stagings of *Othello*, *The Merchant of Venice*, and *Hamlet* in 1903. Anticipating Jan Kott by over half a century, Shimpa productions of Shakespeare were set in contemporary Meiji Japan (as were other plays in the repertoire). Shimpa's adaptive, experimental and modernizing spirit was however superseded by Shingeki Shakespeare. Increasing familiarity with western culture (through for example the influx of silent films from the 1910s) and a greater respect for textual authenticity appear to have led to a corresponding loss of confidence in the Shimpa hybrids.

The Shingeki (New Drama) Movement started with the foundation of the first Bungei Kyôkai (The Literary Society) in 1906, and that of the Jiyû Gekijô (The Liberal Theatre) in 1909. Shingeki, which principally mounted translations of modern western plays in their original western styles, aimed at creating a modern realist theatre in Japan to "enlighten the public." Although modern realist plays by Ibsen, Chekhov, and Gorky were preferred, Shingeki started with the production of Shakespeare's plays. The Bungei Kyôkai's *Hamlet* of 1911 was the first Japanese production of a western play in which female roles were uniformly played by actresses of a recognizably western type.[10] Yet, with the increasing popularity of modern European playwrights in the early 1920s, Shingeki companies came to stage Shakespeare less frequently than modern drama, and (in the 1930s) turned increasingly to socialist realism. With the rise of militarism in Japan, most Shingeki companies, and the foreign drama they represented, were inevitably repressed by the government.

The first two decades after World War II saw the re-emergence of Shingeki under the Occupation; ironically as the more violent (and "undemocratic") elements of Kabuki were repressed and western drama encouraged. Yet, as Shingeki established itself as mainstream and came to neglect its political and experimental commitments in the late 1950s, a new generation rose in opposition. The rebellion against Shingeki was first stirred up in conjunction with the leftist movement against the renewal of the US–Japan Security Treaty in 1960, and led to a wider theatre movement at the time of the next renewal in 1970. This movement, the "Shôgekijô Undô" [Little Theatre Movement] or "Angura Engeki" [Underground Theatre], has continued for the following three decades, producing such eminent theatre practitioners as Terayama Shûji, Kara Jûrô, Suzuki Tadashi, Ninagawa Yukio (those Senda Akihiko calls the first generation), and Ryûzanji Shô, Kisaragi Koharu, Noda Hideki, Kawamura Takeshi, and Iijima Sanae (in later generations).[11]

The Little Theatre Movement took shape as a denial of Shingeki, turning its back upon western plays.[12] The distinctive but general features of this Little Theatre movement can be summarized as follows:

1 denial of the modern idea of realism, or the invisible fourth-wall dividing audience and proscenium stage
2 denial of the supremacy of the dramatic text
3 re-evaluation of traditional Japanese theatre forms and popular entertainment.

It would seem self-evident that no one in this Movement would want to work on Shakespeare; and, initially, most did not.[13] Yet, as the Shôgekijô movement began to lose its original energy and creativity in the 1980s and 1990s, its practitioners increasingly turned to Shakespeare as a resource for their own creativity, thus creating new Shakespeares.[14]

(3) International theatrical contact, western and Asian

The first opportunity for Japanese to see a foreign production on home soil –
and a complete performance of a Shakespeare play – was in 1891, when a
touring American theatre troupe entertained the foreign residents in
Yokohama.[15] Shakespearean productions by British/American touring companies at the Gaiety Theatre in Yokohama came to exert considerable influence upon Japanese intellectuals such as Tsubouchi Shôyô, Osanai Kaoru,
and other advocates of early Shingeki. The significance of such touring companies can be surmised from a short essay written by Tsubouchi Shôyô.
About the Miln Company he maintains: ". . . I saw only *Hamlet* and *The
Merchant of Venice*. As they were presented rather conservatively, a few performances were enough for me to imagine how dozens of other Shakespeare
plays might be presented. They were useful not only when I read the Bard's
plays but also when I later produced *Hamlet* and *The Merchant of Venice*."[16] In
reference to Mrs. Janet Waldorf's performance of Shakespearean extracts at
the Gaiety in Yokohama, Tsubouchi observed:

I learnt the differences in gesture, facial expression and elocution between the
Japanese theatre and its Western counterpart. Particularly I became clearly aware
for the first time that there was a great difference between naturalistic and artistic
expression of laughter and sighs. Of course, in preparation for my lectures, I had
already extensively read foreign books and records on drama and learned how
leading British and American actors performed Shakespeare. As far as artistic
details went, I found seeing was believing. (*Works*, XII, 376)

Such first-hand experiences of Shakespeare and other modern western plays
at the Gaiety were a vital influence on the formation of Shingeki.

Foreign troupes would again vitally influence Japanese performance with
the visits of leading international companies such as the RSC from the
1970s.[17] In this case, however, the foreign influence would be (paradoxically)
in the direction of performative inventiveness and self-reliance rather than
imitativeness. This can be safely inferred from comments made by Suzuki
Tadashi in interview with Trevor Nunn at that time: "Now that I have seen
your *Winter's Tale*, all Shakespeare performances by our Shingeki companies
seem nothing but dull and shoddy imitations of Western productions. Since
such imitations can never surpass the originals, I think we have no choice but
to start tackling Shakespeare with our uniquely Japanese sense of theatre."[18]
Suzuki's recognition of the pointlessness of imitating British Shakespeare
was ubiquitous among Japanese theatre practitioners in the Little Theatre
Movement in the early 1970s.

Perhaps more in the tradition of the earlier, more ministerial, model of foreign influence are the sojourns of British directors with mainstream Japanese companies.[19] One of the earliest "visiting" directors was Michael Benthol, whose 1953 production of *Hamlet* at the Aldwich Fukuda Tsuneari had tried to imitate in 1955. Benthol was invited to direct *Romeo and Juliet* for the Kumo Theatre Company in Fukuda's translation as early as 1965. In the 1970s, several Shingeki companies and commercial theatres such as Tôhô and Shôchiku invited British directors such as Jeffrey Leavis (1974) and John David (1972, 1973, and 1975). Some directors worked with Japanese actors in almost the same way as with British actors, though in translation. This was, and still is, probably what the Japanese companies expected such directors to do, for, with a British director, their productions could claim a greater measure of "authenticity." A twist is provided by visiting directors who have tried to localize Shakespeare for Japanese actors and audiences. One of the earliest examples was Jeffrey Leavis who, in collaboration with Deguchi Norio and the Bungaku-za Company, set *Troilus and Cressida* in ancient Japan.[20]

The Japanese theatre scene has been greatly changed by the opening of the Tokyo Globe in 1988. Its opening season included The English Shakespeare Company's *The Wars of the Roses* and the National Theatre's productions of Peter Hall's *Cymbeline*, *The Winter's Tale*, and *The Tempest*. The Tokyo Globe has not only provided Japanese audiences with many opportunities to see British and other foreign productions of Shakespeare, but also afforded chances for young actors from the Shôgekijô movement to work with foreign directors. The success of such productions at the Tokyo Globe has encouraged other commercial theatres such as Theatre Cocoon and Ginza Saison Theatre to invite companies and directors from abroad.

One of the most important changes that the Tokyo Globe has brought about is its policy of inviting Shakespeare productions not only from Britain but from other countries as well. Such productions have included Ingmar Bergman's *Hamlet* (Sweden), Silviu Purcarete's *Titus Andronicus* (Romania), Robert Lepage's *The Tempest* and *Coriolanus* (Canada), and Lin Zhaohua's *Hamlet* (China). These non-British productions have encouraged Japanese audiences to question the "authenticity" and "canonicity" of British Shakespeare performance, and paved the way for new developments.

An important recent development in Shakespearean production is the collaboration of artists from different Asian countries and theatres (possibly inspired by innovative collaborations between Japanese actors from Kabuki, Noh, Shingeki and Shôgekijô in the sixties). The point to be registered here perhaps is that the more deeply localized Japanese Shakespeare productions of the 1980s and 1990s have become a medium for pan-Asian communication. Notable examples are Korean director Kim Johng Oku's

King Lear, staged with actors from six different countries in 1997; and Filipino director Nonon Padilla's 1998 *Romeo and Juliet*, which included a Kyogen actor and Shôgekijô actress. Among Asian Shakespeares, Ong Ken Sen's production of *Lear*, in Kishida Rio's adaptation, can be seen as epoch-making in several ways. In this production, actors from five countries (China, Thailand, Singapore, Malaysia, and Japan) teamed up to create an "Asian *Lear*" under a Singapore director. This was more than mere cultural exchange. Actors spoke their lines in their respective languages, and the Noh and Beijing Opera actors in the cast retained their own acting styles throughout performance, thus intentionally creating "discords" on various levels. In the program for this performance, Ong Ken Sen maintains:

In this production of *Lear*, I have attempted to search for a new world, a new Asia. This new Asia will continue to have a dialogue with the old, with traditions, with history. But its spirit should contain the youth and freshness that the present world so desperately needs as it progresses into the new millennium. Harmony is not what I seek but discord. A discord which will be symbolic of the complexity of the new millennium. There are no simple answers anymore. We have to deal with difference as we face the new millennium. We can no longer hold onto simple visions of the outside world and "the other."[21]

The essays: early modern and traditional theatre productions

What, then, "do we mean by Japanese Shakespeare?" The question posed by Anzai Tetsuo's provocative essay is a root problematic to which many essays in this volume return. In one sense, only plural answers are possible. "Shakespeare production in Japan," Anzai remarks, "has its own history now as long as a century"; in all of which time Shakespeare has been a radically divergent or unstable cultural and theatrical quantity.

The tentative cultural negotiations between Kabuki and Shakespeare are richly documented in James Brandon's "Shakespeare in Kabuki." To begin with, in the Meiji period, these were strictly on Kabuki's terms. In order to feature in Kabuki at all, Shakespearean content had to be assimilated into a Kabuki "world." In such a "world," Shakespeare was culturally invisible, surviving only in the form of plot trace or motif. Complete translation – as distinct from adaptation – of a Shakespeare play denied the actors the improvisation that was integral to their performances. Accordingly, the meeting between Shakespeare and Kabuki did not produce lasting results.

Zeni, the early Kabuki *Merchant of Venice*, is the exclusive focus of Yoshihara Yukari's avowedly postcolonial "Japan as 'Half Civilized.'" In this nationalistic 1885 adaptation, Shakespeare's play is not merely Japanized – the characters given Japanese names and the situation transposed into a Japan of the Edo era – but turned into a parable of the western money economy that Meiji Japan was struggling to accommodate. A later stage of the encounter between Shakespeare, Kabuki, and Shimpa is described by Matsumoto Shinko, who sees Osanai Kaoru's 1904 production of *Romeo and Juliet* as intermediate between audacious Kabuki adaptations such as *Zeni* and bold Shimpa adaptations such as Kawakami Otojirô's *Othello* (1903). Osanai eventually discovered that Kabuki actors could play Shakespeare as long as they spoke rather than chanted, and walked rather than danced (or, in other words, as long as they refrained from Kabuki acting). Matsumoto argues that this helped pave the way for canonic or Shingeki Shakespeare in 1918, when *Romeo and Juliet* was staged in Tsubouchi Shôyô's translation by the Bungei-za Company.

If Kabuki has tended to resist Shakespeare, so (to an even greater degree) has Noh. Ueda Munakata Kuniyoshi follows Zeami in insisting that Noh cannot be considered Noh unless it retains its traditional song, dance, and tripartite-role structure (warrior, old person, woman). His own contemporary adaptations are accordingly attentive to the stylistic needs of Noh. A contrasting kind of generic encounter is described by Michael Shapiro's essay on *The Braggart Samurai*, a Kyogen version of *The Merry Wives of Windsor*. In the words of its author Takahashi Yasunari: "You cannot kyogenize Shakespeare without Shakespeareanizing kyogen." Less formalized and more plebeian than Noh, Kyogen has perhaps proven more supple than its more aristocratic counterpart in adapting to contemporary democratic tastes.

The essays: post World War II productions

As the first Japanese director (albeit of film) to produce internationally acclaimed interpretations of Shakespeare, Kurosawa Akira fittingly heads this section. Paula von Loewenfeldt's close analysis of *Kumonosu-jô* (*Throne of Blood*) exposes the Eurocentrism of an earlier generation of western appreciations by stressing Kurosawa's interpretative sophistication equally with his Japanization (particularly the use of Noh conventions). Kurosawa's development of the role of his Banquo inaugurates a distinctive post-Meiji type of adaptation in which close textual attention is balanced by a deeply personal (almost autobiographical) inspiration.

We have already noted the theatrical revolution effected by the combination of Odashima's demotic translation of the canon with the "contemporary" and urbanized Shakespeare of Deguchi Norio. Deguchi's work with the

Shakespeare Company is surveyed by Suematsu Michiko. While the importance of Deguchi's early contribution at the JeanJean Little Theatre is properly stressed, so too is the harder-won theatrical self-reinvention of his later period, that of the three parallel productions of A *Midsummer Night's Dream* at the Globe-za (1994).

Intercultural adaptation is also the hallmark of Suzuki Tadashi. In one of two papers on this important director, Takahashi Yasunari discusses *The Tale of Lear*, Suzuki's first work to "build . . . itself 'single-mindedly' upon a Shakespearean play." Fidelity to the original is not, however, an end in itself. Shakespeare's play is not merely Japanized but recontextualized as the daydreaming of an old man in a mental home. More is at issue here than relevance or even localization. Shakespeare's tragic aesthetic is cited within an absurdist framing action. The effect, argues Takahashi, is to lead us to ask fundamental questions of the tragic experience, as of the place of the "classic" in postmodern culture. Ian Carruthers considers Suzuki's *The Chronicle of Macbeth*, produced in Australia and toured to Tokyo in 1992. He focuses on Suzuki's rehearsal interactions with Australian actors (and one American) as they negotiate his postmodern adaptation and stylized method of acting with varying degrees of success.

Of a later generation than Suzuki, Noda Hideki adapts Shakespeare more in the sense of rewriting than of cultural reframing. Suzuki Masae unpacks *Sandaime Richâdo*, perhaps Noda's most radical rewriting of a Shakespeare play (*Richard III*). At the conclusion of this extended dramatic dialogue (indeed argument), Shakespeare is completely dismantled and re-edified. Noda himself, however, is contextualized by Minami Ryuta, who reads Noda's earlier adaptations of *Twelfth Night* and A *Midsummer Night's Dream* against Iijima Sanae's *Arigachina Hanashi* (an adaptation of *Romeo and Juliet*). Noda's attitude of treating Shakespeare as source material rather than as authority is thereby seen as representative of the younger generation of Shôgekijô playwrights to which both Noda and Iijima belong.

No collection could be complete without mention of Takarazuka, the all-female theatre company. Founded in 1913, it is one of the oldest of modern theatre companies in Japan and, to western critics at least, one of the hardest to categorize conceptually. Reading Takarazuka's *Romeo and Juliet* against the horizon of *shôjo* (young girls) culture, Ohtani Tomoko finds Takarazuka both deconstructing the premodern Japanese form of patriarchy within which it had originally arisen as a theatre institution, and yet reconstructing it in the form of the postmodern Japanese consumerist image of the "cute."

In the context of these progressively more radical destabilizations of Shakespeare, Ted Motohashi's article on Gerard Murphy's production of *The*

Merchant of Venice for the Globe-za returns us to a recognizably "canonic" form of Shakespeare production. In Motohashi, however, the process whereby an English-speaking director "interacts" with Japanese-speaking actors is treated with enlarging skepticism.

Interviews with theatre artists

Part of the original plan devised in 1994 for the research seminar on "Shakespeare in Japan" (presented at the Sixth World Shakespeare Congress in Los Angeles) was not only to survey the whole field of performative production, from Meiji to the present, but also to counter the continuing literary bias of much scholarship on Shakespeare in Japan by the inclusion of interviews with major directors and actors.

Because of his standing as the first Japanese director to produce all thirty-seven of Shakespeare's plays, Deguchi Norio of the Shakespeare Theatre was the logical first choice for interview. Like his contemporaries Ninagawa Yukio and Suzuki Tadashi, Deguchi began his directing career in the late 1960s. It was a time of massive student protests: against the Vietnam War, and against a conservative establishment's complicity with America in allowing a foreign nuclear presence on Japanese soil. Deguchi's response to the Japanese manifestation of this worldwide "Youth Revolution" was the most direct and spontaneous, as his interview reveals, and it was one that would be recognizable to many theatre workers in other cultures who also came of age in the Little Theatre Movements of the time. Jan Kott's *Shakespeare Our Contemporary* and Peter Brook's *The Empty Space* were widely read and applied in Japan as in Europe, America, and Australia. "Shakespeare in jeans" became Deguchi's early artistic signature. In this sense, Deguchi's work may be the easiest for westerners to read; regrettably, his work has not yet been seen abroad.

Suzuki Tadashi, Ninagawa Yukio, and Noda Hideki, on the other hand, are well known for their international productions, and for that reason their discussion of their own work, and each other's, both in a national and international context, will be a welcome addition to the current state of knowledge about the differential artistic and political logics of performing Shakespeare in Japan and "Japanese Shakespeare" abroad. All reacted against the tendency of a previous generation of theatre workers to imitate British and European models (notably in the Haiyû-za and Bungaku-za), and all wanted to experiment theatrically, localize their productions, and interrogate Japanese traditions and recent history in different and personal ways. While Deguchi has remained with the Shakespeare Theatre all his professional life,

Suzuki and Ninagawa have moved from directing Little Theatre productions of new playwrights (Betsuyaku Minoru and Shimizu Kunio respectively) to productions of foreign classics on the international circuit in the 1980s. In Ninagawa's case this was with a commercial company (though in 1999 he worked with Sir Nigel Hawthorne and the RSC on a production of *King Lear*). The achievements of Suzuki's company with foreign classics on the other hand have won recognition for a method of actor training now in use around the world, most notably in America, Australia, Brazil, Argentina, and Denmark.

Noda Hideki is different again, belonging to a later generation untroubled by economic hardship and political unrest. Starting at Tokyo University in 1976, his Yume no Yûminsha Company (The Dream Wanderers) sprang to fame in 1983 as the voice of the young and affluent seeking to live out their *manga*-style fantasies of remaining forever young and uncommitted to the salary-man rat race. A remarkable actor and director, Noda is also a talented playwright whose "Shakespearean" love of intertextuality is enhanced by breathtaking athletic skills, spectacular speed, and imaginative/performative inventiveness. It is no accident that when he disbanded his company in 1991 he should have worked for a year with kindred spirits at Theatre de Complicite in London before returning to Tokyo to found NODA MAP.

Hira Mikijirô closes our account in the Interview section because, like Deguchi who opened it, he has made a personal commitment to playing the Shakespeare canon. He is, of course, famous abroad, principally for his leading roles in Ninagawa productions such as *Macbeth* and *The Tempest*, and for his female impersonation of Medea. However, this should not be taken to mean that we see him as somehow "representative."

Afterword

By way of conclusion, John Gillies, who, with Dennis Bartholomeusz, was a respondent at our "Shakespeare in Japan" seminar in Los Angeles, ties together the papers and interviews in a theoretical Afterword in which he measures "localized Shakespeare" as a paradigm in its own right – against the more familiar paradigm of "Shakespeare our contemporary."

NOTES

1 Ikegami Eiko, *The Taming of the Samurai: Honorific Individualism and the Making of Modern Japan* (Cambridge, Mass.: Harvard University Press, 1995), 365.

2 For Shingeki, see Donald Keene's *Dawn to the West: Japanese Literature in the Modern Era* (New York: Henry Holt, 1984), 399–488.

3 Tsubouchi finished his translations of Shakespeare's complete works in 1928, revising them again for re-publication between 1933 and 1935.

4 A notable exception is the collaboration of Senda Koreya, an actor and director, with Mikami Isao, a Shakespearean scholar. Their collaboration started with a production of *The Merry Wives of Windsor* by Shin Tsukiji Gekidan in 1937, followed by *Hamlet* in 1938. After World War II, Senda directed *The Merry Wives of Windsor* (1952) and *Antony and Cleopatra* (1979) in Mikami's translation for the Haiyû-za Company.

5 See Akutagawa Hiroshi, *Kimerareta igaino serifu* (Tokyo: Shinchôsha, 1972), 182. Akutagawa played Hamlet in Fukuda's production in 1955. Fukuda also translated and directed *Macbeth* (1958), *Othello* (1960), *Julius Caesar* (1961), and translated as many as fifteen of Shakespeare's plays.

6 The staging of Odashima's translations started with *Romeo and Juliet* in December 1968 by a company called "Teatoro Q" in Osaka. Yet, it was with the Bungaku-za Company's "Shakespeare Festival" in 1972 that Odashima's translations first drew the attention of theatre practitioners and audiences.

7 See Odashima Yûshi, *Shakespeare yori aiwo komete* (From Shakespeare with Love), (Tokyo: Shôbunsha, 1976), 48–49.

8 See James Brandon's article below.

9 For the rise and fall of Shimpa, see Benito Ortolani's *The Japanese Theatre: from Shamanistic Ritual to Contemporary Pluralism*, rev. edn. (Leiden: E. J. Brill, 1990), 233–42.

10 Actresses had appeared onstage before this but were quite unlike the Shingeki actresses trained by the Bungei Kyôkai. The first Japanese actresses were Ichikawa Kumeyachi, a woman with Kabuki training, and Sadayakko, an ex-geisha ('gei' performing arts, 'sha' person). Probably the best-known actress of the turn of the century, Sadayakko (the wife of Kawakami Otojirô) was compared favorably by western critics with Sarah Bernhardt and Eleanora Duse. As a Shimpa actress she appeared regularly alongside female impersonators, a not uncommon practice. The Bungei Kyôkai's first production of *Hamlet* in 1909 had used both actresses and female impersonators. All the female parts in the Jiyû Gekijô's *John Gabriel Borkman* in 1909 had been played by men.

11 For the Little Theatre Movement, see Takahashi Yasunari, "Alternative Japanese drama: a brief overview" in Robert T. Rolf and John K. Gillespie, *Alternative Japanese Drama* (Honolulu: Hawaii University Press, 1992), 1–9. Except for Terayama and Kara, all the other theatre practitioners cited here have worked on Shakespeare as a director, adaptor, or both, and some of them are discussed in this book.

12 Proponents of the Little Theatre Movement were however under the considerable influence of avant-garde dramatists and directors such as Samuel Beckett, Peter Brook, and Jerzy Grotowski.

13 Suzuki Tadashi is one exception, creating bold adaptations such as *Don Hamlet* in 1972 and *Yoru to Tokei* (*Macbeth*) in 1975 in his usual collage method.

14 Ninagawa Yukio started directing Shakespeare for the commercial theatre company Tôhô Ltd. as early as 1974, soon after dissolving his own company. On the other hand, Kishida Rio, a colleague of Terayama Shûji, has turned to Shakespeare only recently, in 1997. Other examples are Ryûzanji Shô's *Ryûzanji Macbeth*, Kawamura Takeshi's *A Man Called Macbeth*, Uesugi Shôzô's *Broken Hamlet*, and Kisaragi Koharu's *A Dining Table with Romeo and Freesias*.

15 The Miln Company presented *Hamlet*, *The Merchant of Venice*, *Macbeth*, *Othello*, *Romeo and Juliet*, *Julius Caesar*, and *Richard III* at the Gaiety Theatre in Yokohama in May 1891. George C. Miln was a British actor-manager who formed his own touring company in the United States. The Miln Company and the Allan Wilkie Company (British) visited the Gaiety Theatre at the turn of the century and staged Shakespeare plays, which several Japanese intellectuals attended. Concerning the touring companies at the Gaiety, see Masumoto Masahiko, *Yokohama Gête-za: Meiji Taishô no Seiyô Gekijô* (The Yokohama Gaiety Theatre: the Western-Style Theatre in the Meiji and Taishô Eras), 2nd edn. (Yokohama: Iwasaki Kinen Press, 1989).

16 "Naichi de Hajimete Mita Gaikoku Haiyû no Shakespeare-geki no Inshô" (Impressions of foreign actors' Shakespeare production that I have seen for the first time in Japan), in *Shôyô Senshû* (Collected Works of Tsubouchi Shôyô), 15 vols. (Tokyo, 1987), XII: 375–78; 376.

17 The Royal Shakespeare Company brought Trevor Nunn's *Winter's Tale* and Terry Hands' *Merry Wives of Windsor* in 1970, John Barton's *Othello*, *Twelfth Night*, and *Henry V* in 1972, and Peter Brook's *A Midsummer Night's Dream* in 1973. It is interesting to note that the first foreign company that produced Shakespeare after the War was a French one, Théâtre de France, which staged *Hamlet* under the direction of Jean-Louis Barrault in 1960.

18 "Table talk with Trevor Nunn," *The Asahi*, January 23, 1970.

19 Directors invited to produce Shakespeare for Japanese Shingeki and commercial companies include Michael Bogdanov (1983), Glen Walford (1986, 1987, and 1988), Adrian Noble (1982), and Giles Brock (1982).

20 Another notable example is Terence Knap's production of *Much Ado About Nothing* for the Theatre Troupe En in 1979. In this production, Knap set the play in Meiji Japan.

21 Ong Ken Sen, "*Lear*: linking night and day," The program for *Lear*, page 5. Takahashi Yasunari refers to this production in the postscript to his paper in this volume.

PART I

EARLY MODERN AND TRADITIONAL
THEATRE PRODUCTIONS

What do we mean by "Japanese" Shakespeare?

ANZAI TETSUO

If we want to discuss "Japanese Shakespeare" in any meaningful way, we have first of all to pause and try to answer the question, what do we really mean by the epithet "Japanese"? Unless we are content with a purely geographical sense of being produced in Japan, or unless we simply mean some exotic, quaint Japanesque touches, is it really possible to point out any distinctively Japanese features shared in common by all Japanese productions of Shakespeare? The question is of course a rhetorical one. There are no such Japanese characteristics – at least not in terms of visible, easily distinguishable stylistic features.

Ninagawa's *Macbeth* will provide us with an appropriate instance to begin with, in that it is no doubt the best known to the west, and also in that its Japanese features are, frankly, sometimes even aggressively conspicuous. Even if the end product may appear to be a lucky amalgamation of Shakespeare and the Japanese tradition, it would have been by no means possible by merely combining the two, by superimposing one on the other. It would have been impossible without Ninagawa's imagination working as a catalyst in the most private, innermost depths of his mind. In this sense, it is not necessarily appropriate to call the production a "Japanese Shakespeare"; in the same sense, Peter Brook's *A Midsummer Night's Dream* is a Brook Shakespeare and not an "English Shakespeare." The two directors both tried hard to relate the world of Shakespeare to the worlds they live in, and their success in the endeavor was achieved by delving into their own individual psyches deeply enough to reach the point where the two worlds meet. And this is, of course, not peculiar to Ninagawa and Peter Brook; it is basically true of all directors, of whatever nationality and cultural background, when creating their own unique, genuine Shakespeare. They are all faced with essentially the same problem, which could be overcome basically by the same means.

Needless to say, Ninagawa's productions represent only a fraction of the innumerable Shakespeares performed in Japan today, widely different from each other. Suzuki Tadashi's *King Lear*, for example, is obviously different from Ninagawa's *Macbeth*. Suzuki's *Lear* is far more formal and stylized in its acting idiom, strongly reminiscent of the traditional Japanese theatres, Noh in particular; whereas the acting style of Ninagawa is basically realistic or psychological – at least more eclectic. Moreover, while Ninagawa makes a point of keeping the text intact, Suzuki quite drastically cuts it short, sternly concentrating on the particular aspect of the play that interests him without hesitating to sacrifice all the rest. In short, Suzuki's Shakespeare is part of his endeavor to discover and realize what he believes to be the quintessence of the theatre, that which he has been pursuing throughout his career as a direc-tor, and his *Lear* is, so to speak, a dramatic essay on his metaphysics of the dramatic. The so-called "Suzuki method," for all its apparent Japanese fea-tures, is not a straightforward appropriation of the established conventions; rather, as he himself says, it is a highly personal, unique version of the Japanese theatrical tradition re-discovered, re-interpreted, re-defined, and re-organized by Suzuki's individual aesthetic sensibility and critical awareness.

To take another example from the productions of the directors with whom we had interviews, and who, incidentally, all belong to more or less the same generation: Deguchi Norio's works, again as widely different from Ninagawa's as from Suzuki's, are more straightforward, closer to the western style, exhibit little gesture of Japanization, and seem a little more cosmopolitan. But this again reflects his own personal idea of the theatre in general and Shakespeare in particular, as is clear from what he had to say in the interview. What led him initially to direct Shakespeare was his keen awareness of the suffocatingly restrictive limitations of the modern realistic theatre and his persistent urge to break through the limitations and discover a freer, more dynamic, exuberant, and imaginative kind of theatre. What makes his Shakespeare different from those of Ninagawa and Suzuki is, thus, not so much his particular understand-ing of Shakespeare as his characteristic mode of expression. Instead of turning to the traditional theatres as the source of inspiration, he has chosen the theat-rical idiom most easily accessible to the young audience of Tokyo today; he has, thus, been trying to make Shakespeare a frankly entertaining theatre, with a powerful, absorbing story-line, bold, clear-cut characters, a good deal of excitement, and a sense of wonder that is immediately appealing to contempo-rary young people.

There is yet another matter we have to take into account: that is, the histori-cal perspective. Shakespeare production in Japan has its own history now, as long as a century, in the course of which its basic approach to Shakespeare, along with the attitude towards Japanization (including the policy of anti-Japanization), has undergone radical changes more than once or twice. And in this respect, too, the situation is fundamentally the same as in England. If there is little meaning in labeling work as "Japanese Shakespeare" or "English Shakespeare," it is not simply because we find so much divergence in so many contemporary productions; it is also because we have had such a great variety in past productions in both England and Japan. This, in turn, means in effect that Shakespeare production in Japan is not necessarily an exotic, eccentric, exceptional case; rather, it forms an integral part of the worldwide process of realizing the inexhaustible potentialities latent in Shakespeare – or rather potentialities latent in the interaction between Shakespeare and each age, each culture, each director, each actor, and each audience. True, the distance Japanese directors have to travel may be greater than that English-speaking directors have to cover, but the nature of the problems they are faced with is essentially the same. The very peripherality of our position might give us a vantage point from which we might command a better view.

But now we have to go back to the question raised at the beginning: Is it possible to point out any distinctively Japanese features held in common by Japanese productions of Shakespeare? The answer is already clear enough; so far as visible, readily recognizable style is concerned, the answer is obviously "no." And yet, it is nonetheless possible, I believe, to point out one common element shared at least by all the three directors we have discussed; they all approach Shakespeare basically as an archetype of the theatre, in which they expect to re-discover and explore what is quintessential to the theatre. And this common attitude, in turn, may well be related to their acute historical awareness. In the Japanese theatrical scene, we have a peculiarly privileged situation – we have the whole range of our theatrical history actually living with us, from ancient folk rituals to postmodern theatres. In England, Elizabethan Shakespeare, that is, the form of Shakespeare that was performed in his own time, has not been preserved intact. Each generation of English directors has endeavored to destroy the previous style and to create their own new, innovative approach. That is the way the tradition has been handed down in the west. In Japan, on the other hand, we can see Noh, Kabuki, and Bunraku in a form preserved virtually unchanged since the times when they were originally performed centuries ago, in spite of many minor changes they have undergone in the course of time. What is more, these traditional theatres are still very much alive and active, drawing a great number of spectators. Thus, modern directors have to compete with them not simply in artistic terms but in terms of box-office as well. Zeami and Chikamatsu are not only figuratively but literally our contemporaries; they form an important part of our contemporary theatre experiences.

Such being the case, our awareness of tradition cannot but be acute; when we see a play or produce a play, we cannot help almost instinctively mapping it in the historical context in the sense explained above. That is to say, the Japanese directors of Shakespeare cannot but be keenly conscious of Shakespeare as a classic, as the western counterpart of Noh and Kabuki. Not that they have applied the specific style or techniques of Noh and Kabuki directly to their productions of Shakespeare; instead, they have tried to create something new that can rival the traditional Japanese theatres in intensity, depth, and universal appeal. In short, Shakespeare is to them a theatrical touchstone to prove their artistic identities, or a mirror held up to nature on which they have to project their own ideas of theatre. The apparent Japanesque features of their productions are nothing more than an incidental outcome, and not the goal, of their own creative activities.

2

Japan as "half-civilized": an early Japanese adaptation of Shakespeare's *The Merchant of Venice* and Japan's construction of its national image in the late nineteenth century

YOSHIHARA YUKARI

Sakuradoki Zeni-no yononaka (Life is as fragile as cherry blossoms in a world of money; henceforth *Zeni*)[1] is the second Japanese adaptation of Shakespeare's *The Merchant of Venice*. It is based on Inoue Tsutomu's *Jin-niku shichire saiban* (The flesh-pawning trial, 1883), the first translation of *The Merchant of Venice* chapter of Charles Lamb's *Tales from Shakespeare*.[2] Udagawa Bunkai, an eminent journalist, rewrote Inoue's translation for serialization in the *Osaka Asahi Shimbun* newspaper, where it appeared in April and May, 1885. The story was immediately adapted for an experiment in the theatre-improvement campaign (*Engeki kairyô undô*) by Katsu Genzô, a disciple of the great Kawatake Mokuami, the leading playwright of the day.[3] The early Meiji period saw numerous kinds of improvement (*kairyô*) campaigns, and in most cases "improvement" was a euphemism for westernization.

In the prologue to the adaptation, a fictional college student says, "*Eigaku* (English education) is the best way to civilize and enlighten Japan," and also refers to Shakespeare as the supreme icon of the west's superiority. If it is correct to say that Shakespeare is a poet who is discovered and invented as the national poet, an embodiment of "Englishness" in the age of British colonial expansion, then what are we to make of this student's Japanized Bardolatry? What I am trying to do in analyzing this adaptation, a "Japanized" or nationalized *Merchant of Venice*, is to historicize and contextualize the ideological significance of English literature as introduced to, consumed and appropriated by Japan in the age of the construction of its "national" culture. The reception of Shakespeare's works contributed, in its small way, to the construction of the modern Japanese nation-state, for it offered opportunities to invent an imaginary Japaneseness through partial and often mutually contradictory identification with and differentiation from the west, as represented by Shakespeare. In other words, I am interested in the ways the global, or universal, or English Shakespearean work, was appropriated and abducted to invent and construct the local or national culture of Japan. What kind of mission does Shakespeare's work have in Japan in the late nineteenth century?

The most remarkable achievement so far in postcolonial readings of English literature in Japan is Masaki Tsuneo's *Shokuminchi gensô – Igirisu bungaku to hi yôroppa* (a colonial fantasy – English literature and non-Europe, 1995). In the last chapter he writes:

> We must never forget that what is called "modernization" is actually the westernization or homogenization of the world based on Eurocentric value standards. Eurocentrism disguises even colonial exploitation as a sacred mission for "civilization." . . . Our criticism of Eurocentrism must lead us to reflect on our own past as a colonizer. Lagging 400 years after Europe, Japan tried to make a "world" of Asia under Japanese hegemony, called *Dai tô-a kyôeiken* (Asian co-prosperity). This was the direct political and economic result of Japan's "modernization." This process involved the formation of a hierarchized racism, the Japanese at the top and the "natives" in South-East Asia at the bottom . . . Japan's invasion of Asia was not a result of its failed modernization, not of its clinging to traditional culture, but of its exceptionally rapid and thorough modernization (when compared with other Asian countries), for modernization is the Europeanization of the world, and at the heart of Western modernity is the ethos of colonization.[4] [English translation mine.]

In what follows, I shall present a reading of the second Japanese adaptation of Shakespeare's *The Merchant of Venice*, following Professor Masaki's formulation of Japan's modernization as westernization.

Saô's (Shakespeare's) spirit, the traditional Japanese fictive style

Bibliographically, *Zeni* is an adaptation of a translation of an adaptation of Shakespeare's *The Merchant of Venice*. What was thereby appropriated was not the Renaissance Shakespeare, but the National Bard in the age of the British colonization of India. (It is worth remembering that Charles Lamb was a metropolitan officer of the East Indian Company.)

According to the author's foreword, *Zeni* was a great hit both in the newspaper and on stage, and the author claims it was written in "Saô's spirit, in the traditional Japanese fictive style." The phrase is a version of the *Wakon-yôsai* catchphrase ("civilize Japan with western technologies, but retain the genuine Japanese spirit") popular in the early Meiji period. In *Zeni*'s foreword, the phrase is playfully reversed.

The main text is set in Osaka at the end of the feudal Edo era, presumably around 1854, when Japan opened its doors to foreign intercourse. Shôtarô

(Bassanio) has spent his inheritance because of his youthful follies. But he is now an industrious, though poor, young scholar versed in Chinese, western, and Japanese scholarship. Tamae (Portia) is the sole daughter of Nakagawa, Shôtarô's mentor – Tamae's father is wrongly supposed dead. Shôtarô has a close friend, Denjirô (Antonio), a prosperous merchant. Oume (a hybrid of Nerissa and Jessica) has lost her father and is now under the guardianship of her uncle Gohei (Shylock). Gohei, a usurer, treats her harshly, confiscates her inheritance, and even conspires to sell her as a prostitute. Tamae saves Oume, and Oume then becomes her handmaid. Faithful to her father's will, Tamae announces that the man who rightly guesses which of the three caskets, gold, silver, and iron, contains his testament will marry her. In order to join the guessing game, the candidates must pay a fee of 300 ryô. Shôtarô is appointed as one of the candidates, but he has no money, so he asks Denjirô to provide the amount. As Denjirô does not have the amount in ready cash, he pawns one pound of his flesh to Gohei for the amount. Between Denjirô and Gohei, there has been a long-standing antagonism. Shôtarô wins the hand of Tamae, but Denjirô is arrested. At the court, Gohei insists on the exact execution of the bond, and tries to kill Denjirô lawfully. Tamae, disguised as a young male judge, urges Gohei to cut one pound of Denjirô's flesh without shedding a drop of his blood. Gohei acknowledges his defeat, and his fortune is confiscated and given to Oume, his niece. In the last scene, Tamae's father miraculously revives; Gohei heartily repents his past and willingly joins the circle of "good" characters. Finally, the double weddings of Tamae and Shôtarô, Oume and Denjirô are celebrated.

In 1854, Japan opened its doors to foreign intercourse, under pressure from the United States navy. In an earlier phase, westerners were represented as barbarians to be driven away from Japan, to keep its domestic purity intact. However, Japan could not withstand the pressure of the hegemonic west, and the image of westerners as barbarians suddenly changed into that of the west as the epitome of civilization. In 1868, the emperor was restored to political authority at the Meiji Restoration, the new Meiji administration continuing the Tokugawa administration's policy of nationalization through westernization.

In the early Meiji Period, numerous western writings were introduced through translation and adaptation. The most influential translation was Nakamura Masanao's translation of Samuel Smiles' *Self-Help*, titled *Saigoku risshi hen* (Tales of successful men in the west, 1871).[5] Nakamura's translation created a vogue of the ideal *Risshin shusse seinen* or self-made man, who succeeds in the world not owing to his birth but to his personal talent and industry. As we shall see later, *Zeni* deeply reflects the Meiji ideal of the bourgeois industrious youth.

As for Shakespeare's works, the early translations and adaptations were based mainly on Lamb's adaptation. An exception is Tsubouchi Shôyô's *Jiyû-no tachi nagorino kireaji* (All for democracy, 1884), a translation of Shakespeare's *Julius Caesar*.[6] The title of this translation reflects the emerging democracy movement, but, as Takada Yasunari has shown, Tsubouchi adds a translator's afterword to show his own reservations concerning democracy and his support of the Japanese imperial system.[7] Tsubouchi also set standards for modern Japanese writing in his 1885 publication *Shôsetsu shinzui* (The spirit of the western novel) in which the realistic depiction of characters in western novels was valued highly in contrast to the didacticism of Japanese traditional novels.[8] Most importantly, Tsubouchi was to be the first to translate Shakespeare's complete works.

"Improvement" or "civilization" (*Bunmei kaika*) was a governmental policy pursued to maintain Japan's political independence. Westernization was felt to be an antidote to colonization by the west. Fukuzawa Yukichi, a prominent ideologue of westernization, published *Datsu-a ron* (Japan must transcend Asianness) in 1885, just after British marines had occupied an island in Korean territory.[9] Fukuzawa supports the occupation on the basis that only "civilized" countries are qualified to keep political independence. His tone is both arrogant and nervous when he states that if Japan is slow to civilize itself, it will be colonized like China and Korea. In most instances, he does not add any epithet to the term "civilization," suggesting that for him civilization is to be equated with westernization.

Even while the governing elite pursued westernization, at the popular level antipathy towards governmental policy was becoming predominant around 1885: the government-led official nationalism had a tendency to support westernization, while popular nationalism tended to be against westernization. The anti-western type of nationalism tended to be seen as a reactionary movement for getting back to "national tradition." But, in fact, the "tradition" itself was a modern invention after the fact of westernization in the case of *Zeni*. The strategy of the adaptation's author – to "nationalize" *The Merchant of Venice* by presenting it as a play in the feudal Edo style – can be categorized as contributing to the process of nationalization through westernization.

English education as the best way to "civilize" Japan

Zeni has a prologue in which three fictional students discuss western and Asian literature. The first student is an advocate of westernization, the second a traditionalist, and the third compromises between westernization and tradition. The prologue is a highly self-conscious commentary on the ongoing process of Japan's nation-state building through westernization. In the prologue, the advocate of westernization describes Japan as half-civilized:

WADA *Jin-niku shichire saiban* is a translation of *A Pound of Human Flesh* by a famous English dramatist, Saô. The original *shôsetsu* [novel] tells us how morality and the law are intertwined, and it is entertaining too.

NAKAMURA Western novels are surely superior to Chinese or Japanese novels in their high spiritual and moral standards. Yet, it seems to me, Chinese and Japanese novels are better in that they are much more entertaining than western ones.

WADA I disagree. Western novels might seem less entertaining, but it is because our taste is not totally civilized. In the west, because people's minds are civilized, they do not want savage, superstitious and barbaric entertainment from their novels. On the other hand, Asians seek only savage and superstitious entertainment from their novels. So for us Japanese, who are *han-kai* [half-civilized], Western novels seem to be less entertaining.[10]

The contemporary European taxonomy of races and cultures provides a useful analogue to Wada's formulation of Japan as half-civilized. For example, in Mitchell's *New School Geography*, which was employed as an English textbook in Japan, races and cultures are divided into five categories: savage, barbarous, half-civilized, civilized, and enlightened. Europeans are described as a race with the highest achievement in civilization and progress; the Americans, the English, the French, and Germans are categorized as civilized and enlightened. The Mongolians are said to be patient and industrious, but slow in progress. The Japanese are categorized as half-civilized.

Mitchell's mapping of the world is typical, in that it reflects Eurocentric racial ideology disguised as a scientific discourse. The minute itemization of five types might look at first sight like an acknowledgment of cultural singularities and differences, but it actually homogenizes and reduces them into steps in a single and monolithic scale of progression.

Mitchell's was employed as an English textbook in Japan in the early days of westernization (1872).[11] As such, Wada's saying that "*Eigaku* is the shortest way to civilize Japan" can be paraphrased as "English education in Japan was an institutionalized means to make the Japanese elite internalize Eurocentrism."

Wada's representation of Japan as half-civilized is of interest particularly because literature, especially Shakespeare, is said to have a civilizing mission. If Nakamura finds western novels less entertaining than Asian ones, it is a sign of his less-civilized artistic tastes. For someone like Wada, to show that the Japanese can appreciate the Bard's works is one way to prove that the Japanese are a civilized nation with civilized artistic tastes. The political circumstances that gave the Bard's works "universal" currency –

England's domination in the global markets of economy, language, and literature – are absent from Wada's consciousness. I diagnose Wada as a typical case of Japanese Bardolatry, in which the universal appeal of Shakespeare is uncritically celebrated, with a disregard for the political situation that made him the universal poet.

The third fictional student, Torida, an author figure, offers a compromise in order to settle Wada and Nakamura's controversy. He promises to compose an eclectic novel, blending Inoue Tsutomu's *Jin-niku shichire saiban*, with a record of a trial in the final phase of the feudal Edo era, and another novel written in a traditionally Japanese style. Torida claims, though jokingly, that his novel would surpass western ones in combining the merits of western novels and of Asian novels: a spiritually high standard and an entertaining quality, respectively. His eclectic strategy is one solution to the problem of the contradictions in Japanese nationalism, in which, while westernization is a must for the maintenance of Japan's political independence, national cultural identity must be imagined and national tradition re-invented.

In caricaturing Wada, the author of the adaptation criticizes the Japanese internalization of Eurocentric logic. The theatre-improvement campaign to which *Zeni* contributed was intended to "improve," that is, westernize Japanese theatre performances – and it is quite interesting that the author seems to intend to improve not only Japanese theatre but also Shakespeare's original work. The adaptation's strategy can be regarded as an instance of resistance to Eurocentric logic. If the theatre-improvement campaign can be termed a submission to the cultural colonization of literary and stage works and to cultural Eurocentrism, the author seems to be trying to colonize, abduct and appropriate Shakespeare's original work by Japanizing and nationalizing it. However, his claim (voiced by Torida) that the main plot of *Zeni* would dialectically solve the oppositions between western literature and Asian literature is disconcerting because of its ominous resemblance to Japan's colonial claim that it can transcend the limitations of western civilization and of modernity, owing to its unique combination of modernization and Asianness.

The three caskets: gold, silver, and iron

The central narrative is situated in the final phase of the Edo era, rather than 1885 when the prologue is set. Curiously, however, the characters' modes of thought and behavior are basically those of people living around 1885. Why did the author make the main plot such a monstrous patch-up of the Meiji

spirit in the period costume of the Edo era? I would argue that the retrospective projection of the Meiji spirit onto the feudal Edo spirit gives the illusion
that the modern, westernized Meiji spirit was already existent in the Edo era.
This manipulation of time scheme enables the invention of "national tradition" as if it were existent anterior to westernization. It in turn enables the
imaginative invention of a tradition somehow combining western virtues
such as industriousness with domestic purity. Among the constituents of the
Meiji spirit retrospectively projected onto the Edo period, I shall focus on the
idea of industriousness and industrialization.

In various places in the text, Shôtarô (Bassanio) is praised for being *kimben*
and *benkyô*. Here I translate *kimben* and *benkyô* as "industrious," and later I
shall modify the definition. Symbolic of his bourgeois industriousness is his
choice of the iron casket in the three caskets scene. In *The Merchant of Venice*,
the three caskets are gold, silver, and lead; in the adaptation, they are gold,
silver, and iron. Shôtarô's rival, Kawashima, chooses the golden one because
he believes gold is essentially valuable. Shôtarô chooses the iron one because
iron is more useful in industrializing Japan, for instance, in the construction
of the railroads. In the original work, the lead casket is symbolic of an accep-
tance of mortality; in the adaptation, the iron casket is symbolic of the bourgeois idealization of utility.

It seems rather anachronistic to endow Shôtarô, an Edo youth, with a
knowledge of things western such as the railroad. More significantly, it is
anachronistic to characterize Shôtarô as a youth with a modern sense of
industriousness and industrialization. Though I translated *kimben* and *benkyô*
as industriousness, the translation is rather misleading, for there was almost
no verbal and conceptual connection between the idea of industriousness
(*kimben, benkyô*) and that of industrialization (*kôgyô*) in Japan in the Edo
period. In English usage, the verbal and conceptual connection between
industriousness and industrialization is evident, but in Japanese, it is not. In
Japan, the connection between industriousness and industrialization is a
modern, Meiji invention, devised under the influence of western notions of
industry expressed in, for example, Samuel Smiles' *Self-Help*. The feudal
usage of terms such as *risshin-shusse, kimben,* and *benkyô* seems to have been
radically different from the Meiji usage. In the feudal Edo era, the ideal of
success seems to have meant contentment in promotion within the social
class one was born to, while the modern ideal of success involves the destruction of the feudal class structure.

It was the west's overwhelming industrial superiority that forced Japan to
acknowledge its cultural inferiority. The western notion of industrious-
ness/industry must have been quite alien to the Japanese in the earliest days of

the encounter with the industrialized west. The industrialization of Japan was an urgent necessity, but the notion of national industrialization was simply non-existent. So it was convenient to invent a connection between the traditional notion of personal industriousness, *kimben*, and the western notion of national industrialization. Representing Shôtarô as a young man with the modern bourgeois virtue of industry (in its double sense) effectively creates the illusion that the imported virtue of modern industrious-ness/industrialization is actually a Japanese native virtue. The fearful alien quality of the western notion of national industrialization was exorcised and domesticated, by making it look connected to the traditional notion of *kimben*.

The Japanese ideology of the self-made man differs slightly from Smiles' idea of the self-made man, in that the Japanese term has an explicitly nation-alistic purpose. Denjirô (Antonio) encourages Shôtarô to seek worldly success, saying "your wide-ranging learning should be used to seek personal fame, more importantly to help your family prosper, and most importantly to serve the best interests of *hinomoto* [Japan, 'the land of the rising sun']." The promotion of individual industriousness is intended to contribute directly to nation-state building.

Women must not be men's slaves

Tamae (Portia) is also represented as an industrious young woman. Influenced by her father, she believes that industrious scholarship makes women spiritually independent of men. Criticizing the traditional, feudal relationships between the sexes, she declares that women must not be men's slaves and that industrious study of utilitarian knowledge is the best way to liberate Japanese women. She criticizes not only Japanese men's treatment of women as mere household slaves, but also women's subservient attitudes. She maintains that women must not feel content only with domestic house-hold chores such as cooking, sewing, and washing like women in the feudal age, but that they must acquire a broad range of higher knowledge and tech-nical skills in order to liberate themselves. She declares to her unwanted suitor Kawashima that she is going to keep her spiritual independence even when she gets married.

However, Tamae is not really subversive of domestic ideology, for she holds that the ultimate aim of a woman's education is to become a good wife and a wise mother (*ryôsai-Kembo*): "Women must be wise, for mothers have the greatest influence on their children, and it is up to mothers whether chil-dren become wise or foolish." She does not really intend to endanger the gender hierarchy between men and women, even though her argument that men and women are equal under heaven and her disguise as a male judge could have the potential to endanger it. Like her original, Portia, Tamae's actions hardly dismantle the gender system.[12]

In the figures of Shôtarô and Tamae, we witness the process of the construction of domestic ideology in late-nineteenth-century Japan, "domestic" in its double sense of "the home" and of "one's own country." Shôtarô's formation of industry/industriousness as a domestic, native Japanese virtue corresponds to Tamae's formation of domestic, good wives and wise mothers. *Zeni* is a text that appropriates Shakespeare's work to naturalize the national, domestic ideology of Japaneseness and of femininity and masculinity.

Money changes everything

The title of the adaptation, *Zeni-no yononaka*, is suggestive of the situation Japan was facing with its incorporation into the world economy. *Zeni* means "money," *yononaka* means "the world." The title as a whole suggests a world in which money changes everything, but the world of the text would better be described as a world in which money is not everything, or as a world in which industriousness, industrialization, and faith bring victory.

In 1885, Fukuzawa Yukichi published a series of articles urging the necessity of Japan's industrialization and the cultivation of its subjects' industriousness as a source of industrialization. The titles of the articles are "Western civilization is a civilization of zeni (money)," "Japan is not yet a nation of zeni," and "How to make Japan a nation of zeni."[13] One of them begins with a line saying "the Western countries are *zeni-no-yononaka*." Though there is no direct proof that the author of *Zeni* read Fukuzawa's articles, the verbal correspondences look significant. Fukuzawa argues that in the west, as money is worshipped so much, one is judged on the basis of how much money one has. Motivated by this, westerners work industriously, and this leads to the west's industrialization. He argues that because of the traditional Japanese contempt for money, Japan cannot industrialize itself and must remain a poor country. He sarcastically claims that the shortest way to make Japan a rich country is to make its subjects money-worshippers like westerners.

The title *Zeni-no yononaka* can be taken as a sidelong reference to the west imagined as the place where money changes everything. By creating a fictional world where money is not everything, the author of *Zeni* (despite his title) invents a fictional Japanese world where industriousness does not necessarily mean money-worshipping.

I Pray to the gods to make my money beget more money

Tamae, disguised as a male judge, says to Gohei, "Gohei, you are a subject of the gods' country, *hinomoto*. You must surely worship the gods." Gohei replies, "Of course. I pray to the gods night and day to make my money beget more money." Gohei is ridiculed as a sot who confuses worship of the gods with worship of Mammon.

Around 1885, the Japanese imperial system became established. Essentially, the institutionalized worship of the emperor, *tenshi* (son of the gods), is not a revival of an ancient religion, but a modern invention made in order to reorganize the Japanese as subjects of the state embodied by the emperor. Shintô became a national religion only in the Meiji period. Just like "industriousness," the idea of Japan as "the gods' country" is retrospectively projected onto the Edo era, and thereby made to assume the false grandeur of age-old tradition.

Furthermore, by making Gohei a caricature of a money-worshipper, the author concocts the illusion that Japanese industrialization and modernization are different from money-worshipping. The Japanese form of industrialization is imaginatively connected not to money-worship but to emperor worship.

As David Goodman and Masanori Miyazawa show, *The Merchant of Venice* has had a far-reaching impact on Japanese thinking about Jews.[14] Whether the Jews are imagined negatively or positively in Japanese thinking, the real issue is how the Japanese imagine and invent their own auto-image through identification with and/or differentiation from imagined Jewishness. The popularity of early translations and adaptations of *The Merchant of Venice* was due to the preoccupations, anxieties, and insecurities of Japanese culture in the process of constructing its national identity and its national culture, and not to the fact that Shylock was a Jew.

The absence of racial conflict in *Zeni* can be understood as a sublimation of the frustration felt by the Japanese that they would never be fully accepted by the west because of their race. The initial period of Japan's modernization coincided with the heyday of what is known as "scientific racism" in Europe and the United States. To represent Gohei as a person discriminated against because of his racial difference must have been too reminiscent of the fact that Japanese racial inferiority was held to be, by the lights of western science, empirically verifiable. Put differently, as the anxieties about Japanese racial inferiority are projected onto Shylock, through the Japanization of Shylock into Gohei, the cultural anxiety about race is silenced. The negative aspects of the modern capitalist world are projected onto the miser usurer Gohei based on the archetypal miser character in the Kabuki repertory, while the entrepreneurial spirits, which it was hoped would make Japan an international economic power, are projected onto Denjirô.

Iron is useful just like paper bills

Shôtarô curiously compares the usefulness of iron to the usefulness of paper currency in the three caskets scene. He prefers paper currency to gold currency because paper currency is more useful in accelerated economic exchanges.

In 1885, Japan was barely recovering from the destructive shock brought about by its incorporation into the world economy. Mainly because of the differences in the exchange rates of gold and silver in the domestic and in the world economies, Japan was suffering from an outflow of gold. And this, together with heavy civil war expenditure, led to hyper-inflation in the 1860s and 1870s. To put a lid on hyperinflation, Matsutaka Masayoshi, the first Minister of Finance, introduced a strict deflationary policy from the late 1870s through to the early 1880s. The first convertible bank notes were issued by The Bank of Japan in 1885. They were the first national bank notes. Shôtarô's argument that iron is useful just like paper bills is symbolic of the birth of the Japanese national economy.

NOTES

1   Katsu Genzô, *Sakuradoki Zeni-no yononaka* (Tokyo: Bumpô-dô, 1885).
2   Inoue Tsutomu, *Jin-niku shichire saiban* (Tokyo: Nagashima Eihô, 1883).
3   Kawatake adapted Lytton's *Money* in 1879. The adaptation was titled *Ningen banji kane-no yononaka* (A world of money), and Katsu Genzô, in giving a similar title to his adaptation of *The Merchant of Venice* as *Zeni-no yononaka* (*kane* and *zeni* mean money), pays homage to his mentor.
4   Masaki Tsuneo, *Shokuminchi gensô* (Tokyo: Misuzu, 1995), 239–47.
5   Nakamura Masanao, *Saigoku risshi hen* (Shizuoka: Kihira Yuzuru, 1871).
6   Tsubouchi Shôyô, *Jiyû-no tachi nagorino kireaji* (Tokyo: Tôyôkan, 1884).
7   Takada Yasunari, "Shîzaru kidan nagorino kireaji," in Aoyama Seiko and Kawachi Yoshiko, eds., *Sheikusupia hihyô-no genzai* (Contemporary Shakespearean criticism), (Tokyo: Kenkyûsya, 1993), 55–58.
8   *Shôyô senshû* (Selected works of Shôyô), Supplements vol. 3 (Tokyo: Daiichi syobô, 1977), 1–160.
9   *Fukuzawa Yukichi zenshû* (Complete works of Fukuzawa Yukichi), vol. 10 (Tokyo: Iwanami, 1970), 238–40.
10 Elsewhere in the prologue, Wada mentions that English is taught even in primary schools – this is based on a historical fact: Mori Arinori, the first

Minister of Education, proposed making English a required subject in primary schools in 1885. The first English department in Tokyo Imperial University was established in 1887. Mori was assassinated by an anti-western ultra-nationalist in 1889.

11 Erikawa Haruo, "Eigo teikokushugi-no zuzôgaku" (Iconography of English linguistic imperialism), in *Gendai Eigo Kyôiku* (Modern English Education), May 1995 (Tokyo: Kenkyûsya), 16–19.

12 Jean E. Howard, *The Stage and Social Struggle in Early Modern England* (London: Routledge, 1994), 269–78.

13 *Fukuzawa Yukichi zenshû*, vol. 10, 269–78.

14 David G. Goodman and Masanori Miyazawa, *Jews in the Japanese Mind* (New York: The Free Press, 1995), 29–36.

3

Shakespeare in Kabuki

JAMES R. BRANDON

During most of Kabuki's history, performance can be characterized by what I will call here a "balance of yin and yang." We find fluctuating change and stability, the unknown and the known side-by-side, and the new and the old coexisting: that is, a balance of unstable yin and stable yang. Kabuki is an art that originated and flourished during the Tokugawa period (1603–1868). In early winter, in anticipation of the new Kabuki season, the main members of the troupe gathered to select the worlds (sekai) for each of the company's five or six productions. A world was a known constellation of actual or legendary figures acting out the crucial events in their lives. These dramatic worlds were completely familiar to the spectators, giving stability to the play. Iizuka Tomoichirô has identified 275 worlds that Kabuki playwrights used during the Tokugawa period.[1] In the course of the annual theatre season, house playwrights crafted new plays based on these worlds through the device of fabricating unusual or unexpected plots (shukô). In principle, every play was "new" and received its own unique title. Hence, the present-day researcher faces the mind-numbing circumstance that upwards of 10,000 Kabuki play titles lie in indexes and bibliographies. Shukô and sekai provided a yin–yang balance in play creation. I believe that much in Kabuki can be viewed this way.

Most Japanese and western observers privilege the traditional, the stable, the positive, the yang side of Kabuki, emphasizing family acting traditions and established conventions of performance. Some major acting families go back twelve and fifteen generations. Distinctive plays and acting styles in these families have been passed on from father to son for centuries. A system of hereditary theatre managers, especially in the city of Edo (Tokyo), contributed stability and continuity to the production system. We who translate Kabuki plays choose favorite pieces that are part of the traditional or "classic" repertory. In this paper, I would like to redress this imbalance in a small way. I will focus on the unstable, the uncertain, the indeterminate, and the new, the yin of Kabuki, taking as a point of departure the case of Kabuki's engagement with the plays of Shakespeare. As Kawatake Toshio has pointed out, Kabuki and Shakespeare share a similar "baroque" spirit and the two would seem to be natural partners.[2] Indeed, the idea that Shakespeare and Kabuki naturally go together is something of a cliche. I will suggest here that the meeting between Kabuki and Shakespeare in Japan has not been natural or simple, or, for that matter, particularly successful. In my opinion, Kabuki artists have responded to Shakespeare in three radically different ways, none of which have satisfactorily fused the unique strengths of Shakespeare (the new, desta-bilizing, outside yin element) with their own theatrical art (the familiar, stable, inside yang element).

When, in the nineteenth century, Shakespeare became known to Kabuki artists, they faced this newly imported drama and theatre of Europe with long experience in facing and assimilating the new. Although we commonly speak of Kabuki as a "classic" or a "traditional" theatre, these terms are descriptive only of Kabuki as we know it today. However, Kabuki was a theatre that flour-ished by growing and changing throughout most of its three-hundred-year history, from the time it was created by the singer-dancer-actress Okuni in 1600, until western cultural influences began flooding into Japan, roughly beginning with the reign of the Meiji emperor in 1868. Numerous factors contributed to instability and change in Kabuki during its long history. Theatre buildings burned every few years and, when they were reconstructed, new design ideas were incorporated, so that, after almost three centuries, the Kabuki theatre was quite a different architectural form from the early Kabuki stage. The incessant fires wreaked financial havoc on theatre managers, often causing bankruptcy and forcing abandonment of productions. Actors were in continual competition with each other, moving from troupe to troupe and from theatre to theatre in the constant attempt to advance their careers. As many as 3,000 actors jostled for audience attention at any one time, perform-ing in a hundred theatres or more spread across the country (most theatres were in the great cities of Edo, Osaka, and Kyoto; others were set up in provin-cial cities and at major shrines, temples, and pilgrimage sites).[3] Acting was a precarious occupation, as we can see from the sad fact that scarcely 5 percent of the approximately 600 acting family names (myôji) found in the eighteenth century have continued down to the present time.[4]

The practical need to court a popular audience on a daily basis put a premium on the actor's ability to create new styles of acting. Much like docudramas on television or gossip items in supermarket tabloids today, sensational current events – lovers' suicides, public vendettas, and scandal-ous murders – attracted large audiences into the theatres. Each resident acting company needed five or six *new* play scripts every year to fill its season; hence playwrights were judged on their ability to conceive fresh characters and depict exceptional events for the Kabuki stage.

Therefore, when the Meiji period (1868–1912) burst upon the Japanese people and brought Shakespeare into their midst literally overnight, Kabuki had had two-and-a-half centuries of experience in adapting to new circumstances. It wasn't strange for actors and managers to keep Kabuki up-to-date; they had always done so. During the first decade of the Meiji period, owners and managers built large new Kabuki theatres in the up-scale Ginza and Azabu districts in the center of Tokyo, quickly reaching the legal limit of ten. In the first two decades of the Meiji era, that is, the 1870s and 1880s, new types of Kabuki plays were created that responded to the influx of European customs, technology, and ideas. Ichikawa Danjûrô IX (1839–1903), known as the greatest Kabuki actor of his generation, publicly declared his disgust with traditional Kabuki plays and acting styles in 1878, vowing to "reform" – that is, to westernize – his art.[5] He adopted several strategies to accomplish this aim. He developed a plain, realistic acting style he called *hara gei*, literally "stomach art," that is, instinctual or "gut" acting. He eschewed Kabuki's conventional *mie* poses and the old musicalized style of elocution (*yakuharai*) that was used for dialogue written in the traditional meter of seven-and-five syllables (*shichigochô*). He also chose to act in a new style of serious drama called living history plays (*katsureki geki*) written for him by Kabuki's preeminent playwright, Kawatake Mokuami (1816–93). The plays purported to return to historical truth and, when performing in them, Danjûrô gave up traditional white face makeup and wore real armor to be true to life.[6] These efforts, his intellectual adviser Fukuchi Ôchi assured him, would improve the artistic level of Kabuki and help bring social respectability to the previously despised theatre form. During four overseas missions on behalf of the Meiji government, Ôchi had seen that in Europe, ballet and opera were patronized by the elite, and he wanted Kabuki to hold a similarly favored position in Japan's modernized culture.

Danjûrô's contemporary and rival, Onoe Kikugorô V (1844–1903), enthusiastically supported the writing of new plays set in the Meiji present. They were popularly called cropped-hair plays (*zangiri mono*) because men were required by the new Meiji government to cut their hair short, in western style, in order to be part of the contemporary world. All of the physical trivia of modern, that is European and American, life was put on display for the amazement and edification of audiences. We can see something of the adventuresome, offbeat spirit of the cropped-hair plays in the following example. In 1891, an Englishman named Spencer was making spectacular balloon ascents in Ueno Park in Tokyo. Within months the cropped-hair play, *Riding the Famous Hot-Air Balloon (Fûsen Nori Uwasa Takadono)*, was written by Mokuami and staged at the Kabuki-za in Tokyo starring Kikugorô V as Spencer. The play was extremely popular and had a run of thirty-three performances. Suspended from a balloon high in the theatre's rigging, Kikugorô made a speech in English, "Ladies and gentlemen. I have been up three thousand feet. Looking down, I was pleased to see you in this Kabuki-za. Thanks [sic] you. Ladies and gentlemen, with all my heart, I thank you."[7]

Throughout Kabuki's history, new types of plays and performing techniques had been devised to express the concerns of each new era – bravura history plays (*aragoto-jidaimono*) and gentle domestic love stories (*wagoto-sewamono*) during the Genroku period (1688–1704), adaptations of puppet theatre plays and performing style (*maruhonmono* or *dendenmono*) in the 1740s and 1750s, long dramatic dance plays (*buyô geki*) after the 1780s, and plays about gangsters and crime (*kizewamono*) in the mid-1800s. Therefore, when playwrights and actors of the Meiji period created living history and cropped-hair plays, they were continuing the usual process in Kabuki of molding play forms to suit contemporary audiences.

Kabuki actors and managers examined western theatrical practice to see what they might adopt. When it was discovered that European societies allowed actresses on the stage, the possibility that women might play female roles in Kabuki arose (as is well known, in 1629 actresses were banned from all professional performances in Japan). Indeed, Kabuki reformers sought to do away with the male actor of female roles, the *onnagata*. In 1879, Morita Kan'ya XII placed English actresses on stage at the Shintomi-za. The play, *A Strange Tale of Castaways: a Western Kabuki* (*Hyôryû Kidan Seiyô Kabuki*), was newly written by the Shintomi-za house playwright, Kawatake Mokuami, and starred Danjûrô IX, Ichikawa Kodanji V (1850–1922), and Iwai Hanshirô VIII (1829–82), all top actors. Stage settings were constructed to show the hero in San Francisco, London, and Paris. Kan'ya imported a troupe of ten English and American actors and musicians from Hong Kong, led by a Mr. Wilson, to play in a scene set in a Parisian theatre. The play was a huge disaster: audiences did not understand the English dialogue and, by some reports, the foreign actors were inept. Because of his staggering losses, Kan'ya was forced to relinquish control of the theatre.[8] It is probable that the person most responsible for women appearing in Kabuki was the talented actress Ichikawa Kumehachi (1846–1913). She trained in Kabuki dance as a child, apprenticed with actor Iwai Hanshirô VIII, and then became a favored pupil of Danjûrô IX. Soon after 1868, she began performing Kabuki in public and in time gained a reputation starring in classics such as *The Subscription List* (*Kanjinchô*), *The Maid of Dôjô Temple* (*Musume Dôjôji*), and *The Heron Maiden* (*Sagi Musume*). In 1887, she performed with male Kabuki actors at the newly built Azuma-za in Asakusa. A police regulation in 1890 noted that "mixed casts of actors and actresses have been appearing at the Azuma-za," and went on to say that because "foreigners will ridicule the extremely licentious custom of men dressing as women," henceforth "when performances by actresses and actors occur in the future, this will be allowed."[9] We can say that when Kumehachi brought her all-female troupe to the Misaki-za in Kanda in 1891, she was the first woman to appear legally on the professional stage in two centuries.[10] Kabuki seemed to have moved far in the direction of modernization (and westernization) in these first twenty-five years of the Meiji period.

But these cases proved to be exceptions; other actors did not follow Danjûrô's or Kikugorô's, or, for that matter Kumehachi's, examples. Men continued to play female roles in Kabuki, as they do today. Danjûrô was cruelly satirized for the nit-picking historical research he carried out for living history plays: one famous cartoon shows Danjûrô surrounded by long-nosed demons (tengu) shouting jeeringly, "Go look at the scrolls in Hôryû Temple! Go look at the treasures in Tôdai Temple!"[11] By all accounts, audiences found Danjûrô's new acting style simply dull. By the end of the 1880s, even Kikugorô had abandoned his experiments and no longer did cropped-hair plays.

Playwrights turned to European drama for ideas, situations, and characters, and even to scenes and whole plays that they thought could be adapted to the Kabuki stage. They used western locales as exotic settings for some plays, just as the James Bond films use foreign locations for exotic appeal. In 1872, at Kyoto's Kitagawa Theatre, A Tale of Western Success (Saikoku Risshi Hen) was set in Paris, and the Kabuki cast played the roles of Frenchmen dressed in chic Western frock coats and trousers.[12] At the Shintomi-za in Tokyo, in 1879, Kan'ya staged Mokuami's adaptation of Bulwer-Lytton's Money (titled Ningen Banji Kane no yononaka, Humankind: the world of money). The play had an excellent run of sixty days; still Kan'ya went deeply into debt because of the expense of paying thirty-three Dutchmen to come up from Yokohama every night to fill the stage. The typical Kabuki program of the time was made up of several independent plays (midori) and Money was one of four items on the bill.[13] Among important western plays that were adapted for Kabuki performance were Robinson Crusoe, preceded by an explanatory lecture, at the Sakai-za in Kyoto in 1887; Sardou's La Tosca at the Kabuki-za in 1891; Hugo's Hernani, moved into the world of novelist Kyokutei Bakin's mammoth The Story of Eight Virtuous Warriors (Hakkaden) at the Meiji-za in 1905; Schiller's William Tell, placed in the world of The Virtuous Commoner of Sakura (Sakura Giminden), set in seventeenth-century Japan, also at the Meiji-za in 1905; and Osanai Kaoru's adaptation of The Bells, at the Meiji-za in 1911.[14]

During the first two decades of the twentieth century, Kabuki management and leading actors tried to use the wondrous new performance technology imported from Europe and America called "action pictures" (*katsudô shashin*) to hold their audience, starting in 1898.[15] A film was used as a backdrop for a Kabuki production as early as 1901 at the Ichimura-za. Some twenty Kabuki plays were recorded on film in the first decade of the century, beginning with *The Maple Viewing* (*Momijigari*) starring Danjûrô IX and Kikugorô V and *Two Maids of Dôjô Temple* (*Futari Dôjôji*) with Ichimura Uzaemon XV (1874–1945) and Onoe Baikô VI (1870–1934), both filmed on stage in 1899. Audiences were so enthralled with the new Kabuki films that in 1911 the Association of Tokyo Theatres (Tokyo Gekijô Kumiai) attempted to ban Kabuki actors from appearing in them.[16] Of course, the cinema would grow into an entertainment industry that soon surpassed Kabuki in size and ability to interpret current life.

In the early decades of the twentieth century, Kabuki found itself in competition not only with film, but with two new forms of live theatre as well. Shimpa, literally "new style" drama, staged contemporary events set in Meiji-period Japan, while Shingeki, "new drama," was European modern theatre transplanted to Japan, based on the dramas of Chekhov, Strindberg, Maeterlinck, and Ibsen. Some young Kabuki actors were fascinated by the realism of Shingeki and hoped to bring its style of acting into Kabuki. New theatres were built to accommodate the needs of the new genres: in Tokyo the Masagoya-za, Hongô-za, and Meiji-za for Shimpa, the Yûraku-za and the Tsukiji Shôgekijô (Tsukiji Little Theatre) for intimate Shingeki productions, the Teikoku Gekijô (Imperial Theatre) for large-scale modern drama, as well as for opera and ballet, and scores of movie theatres. The managers of the staid Kabuki-za, the premier Kabuki theatre in Tokyo, recognized the appeal of European theatre and booked light western entertainment in the intervals between monthly Kabuki programs: the Charlie Taylor Company from Europe playing *Rip Van Winkle* and *Cross Purposes* in repertory (January 1901), the W. E. Davies variety show from England, matinee and evening performances (February 1902), and the Carmansuela Troupe, an all-girl singing and dancing show from the United States (November 1903).[17] In order to draw an up-market, educated audience, the Kabuki-za even lent its stage to scholar Tsubouchi Shôyô's Literary Arts Society (Bungei Kyôkai) for its first production in November 1906. One item on its program was the trial scene from *The Merchant of Venice*, directed by Shôyô, and acted by the Society's amateur actors.[18]

Against this background, let us see how Kabuki initially encountered the plays of Shakespeare. Shakespeare was known in Japanese in the early Meiji period as Shahikiô, in shortened form Saô or Shaô, the latter being the *ateji* or phonetic reading of the characters for *sha*, "sand," and *ô*, a respectful form of address for one's elder, hence the name "Old Master Sha(kespeare)."[19] Dramatic sequences suggestive of Shakespeare have been identified in a handful of Tokugawa-period Kabuki plays. Kawatake Toshio calls attention to the offer of human flesh, to be taken in compensation, in Chikamatsu Monzaemon's 1695 puppet drama *Birthday Picture of Buddha* (*Shaka Nyôrai Tanjôe*), a situation that somewhat parallels *The Merchant of Venice*. The 1771 puppet play, *Mount Imo and Mount Se: An Exemplary Tale of Womanly Virtue* (*Imoseyama Onna Teikin*), by Chikamatsu Hanji and others, shows two young lovers who are kept apart by their feuding families, a situation similar to *Romeo and Juliet*.[20] It is not yet understood how knowledge of Shakespeare might have reached Japanese playwrights in the seventeenth and eighteenth centuries.

In 1875, the writer Kanagaki Robun published *Hamlet: A Western Kabuki* (*Seiyô Kabuki Hamuretto*) in three installments in the *Illustrated Syllabary Newspaper* (*Hiragana Eiri Shinbun*), and in 1879 playwright Kawatake Mokuami began a retelling of *Hamlet* for Kabuki which he did not complete.[21] Neither of these adaptations was staged. The first Kabuki production of Shakespeare of which we have certain knowledge was an adaptation of *The Merchant of Venice* performed as a domestic play (*sewamono*) at the Ebisu-za in Osaka in 1885. It was given a fanciful title, *A Time of Cherry Blossoms: A World of Money* (*Sakura Doki Zeni no Yo no Naka*), and proved to be a tremendous success. Katsu Genzô's adaptation proved successful with Kabuki actors and with audiences alike: it was the basis of at least twelve separate productions in Osaka and Tokyo between 1885 and 1908, usually under the title *The World of Money* (*Kane no Yo no Naka*).[22] In one revival, Shylock was called Yokubari Gampachi (Stubborn Tightfist), in that way identifying the character's nature while hiding his western origin.[23]

The next two Kabuki productions of Shakespeare, in 1907 and 1908, of *Hamlet*, were also adaptations set in Japan. We need to see them in the context of Kabuki's difficulties in the first decade of the twentieth century. In 1903, the two greatest stars of Meiji-period Kabuki, Danjûrô IX and Kikugorô V, died leaving no mature successors.[24] That same year, 1903, the Shimpa troupe, led by the husband and wife team of Kawakami Otojirô and Kawakami Sadayakko, returned home from a year-and-a-half tour of Europe and America where they performed successfully and studied western theatre. Before the year was over, they mounted ambitious Shimpa-style adaptations of *Othello*, *Hamlet*, and the Trial Scene in *The Merchant of Venice*, all set in Japan. As the first productions to be staged by Japanese actors who had seen theatre in the west, they excited intense public interest. Shimpa drama was then in its so-called "Golden Age" and troupes were quick to bring Shakespeare's plays into their repertories via adaptations. Not counting the Otojirô-Sadayakko offerings, Minami identifies forty other professional Shimpa productions between 1901 and 1915 of *Julius Caesar*, *King Lear*, *The Merchant of Venice*, *Hamlet*, *Othello*, *Romeo and Juliet*, *Macbeth*, *Henry IV*, *Twelfth Night*, *Merry Wives of Windsor*, and, most popular of all, *Timon of Athens*, staged twenty times.[25] Shimpa represented an undeniable threat to Kabuki at this time. Not only that, in 1908 the newly formed Actress' Theatre (Joyû-za) staged *New Hamlet* (*Shin Hamuretto*) at the Misaki-za, suggesting a new direction for Japanese theatre.[26]

Given these circumstances, it is not strange that several adventuresome Kabuki producers and actors looked to Shakespeare for play material. In 1907, Ichikawa Kodanji V starred in Yamagishi Kayô's adaptation of *Hamlet* and, the following year, the rising star of Kabuki in Osaka, Nakamura Ganjirô I (1860–1935), revived the script to considerable success. Kawatake Toshio refers to the production as an example of "new Kabuki" (*shin Kabuki*).[27] The adaptation was titled *Hamuretto*. The hero's pseudo-Japanese name slightly suggested the exotic; otherwise, the story was wholly localized. The action was placed in Ashikaga period Japan (fourteenth to sixteenth centuries) and the script was written in traditional, old-fashioned Kabuki style with sections of *jôruri* chanted narrative.[28] Shakespeare's melancholy Dane was not used to promote a new style of drama or performance in Kabuki. Photographs of *Hamuretto* show all the physical attributes of a standard Kabuki history play – settings, costumes, wigs, makeup, and stage positioning[29] (see photo 1).

In these productions, Shakespeare's stories were adapted to fit Japanese culture and Kabuki theatrical form. Shakespeare's foreign dramatic material was assimilated into Kabuki dramatic worlds (*sekai*) and characters were presented through Kabuki acting techniques. Further, the productions were staged in Kabuki theatres as part of a regular Kabuki season: their "otherness" was not emphasized by placing them outside the Kabuki production system. In brief, managers and actors presented audiences with a more or less normal Kabuki performance and, in order to do this, Shakespeare's presence was completely or largely erased. (It is extremely interesting to note that Shakespeare's stories were localized and absorbed into popular performing styles in India, China, and Korea in a similar fashion.)

Direct translations of Shakespeare's plays into Japanese were not used for these early Kabuki productions. Rather, playable scripts were worked out from second- and third-hand sources. In the 1880s, adaptations of Shakespeare's stories began appearing in serial form in illustrated newspapers (*eiri shinbun*). We are indebted to Kawatake Toshio for publishing a

1 *Hamlet* localized as Kabuki. A localized adaptation of *Hamlet* placed in 14c. Japan. Hamlet, costumed and performed in pure Kabuki style, played by Nakamura Ganjirô I at the Naka-za, Osaka, 1908.

number of fascinating illustrations of the serial of *Hamuretto* that appeared in the *Tokyo Illustrated Newspaper* (*Tokyo Eiri Shinbun*), in October–November, 1886.[30] The drawings and etchings show conventional images of Kabuki actors; some posed with the crossed eye (*nirami*) that is familiar from *ukiyoe* prints of Kabuki. The adaptation included sections of *jôruri* narrative, which was typical of Kabuki scripts of that time[31] (see photo 2). The characters have Japanese names: some readers or spectators might hear Hamlet in the name Hamura Maro, or Ophelia in Orie Hime, but the sound of Shuzen does not suggest Polonius.

Kabuki's relationship to Shakespeare was significantly altered when directors and actors in the Shingeki movement introduced modern European dramaturgy and realistic staging to Japan. After the second World War, Shingeki would become a direct competitor for Kabuki and Shimpa audiences. But earlier, its importance lay in the radically new ideas and attitudes it introduced into the Japanese theatre world. Here, let me suggest two aspects of the new theatre movement that I believe have had profound and lasting effects on Kabuki interpretations of Shakespeare.

First, attendant on the development of modern theatre in Japan, the vast corpus of western drama was translated into Japanese language for Shingeki performance. Ten of Shakespeare's plays were translated into Japanese

2 An illustration of the serial novel *Hamuretto* (*Hamlet*) published in *Tokyo Eiri Shimbun*
(*Tokyo Illustrated Newspaper*), 1886 shows the Kabuki visualization of the story. Claudius,
flanked by Miyauchi Shuzen (Polonius) and Mikariya Hime (Ophelia) are dressed in
Kabuki costumes and wigs. All three are portrayed with powerful Kabuki facial
expressions.

between 1905 and 1910 by Tozawa Masayasu and Asano Wasaburô.[32] Between 1907 and 1928, Tsubouchi Shôyô (1859–1935), professor of English literature at Waseda University, finished his monumental translations of Shakespeare's complete works.[33] Shôyô's translations especially have been acclaimed and widely performed. As the new translations (*hon'yaku*) became available, the older adaptations (*hon'an*) came to be seen as inferior and Kabuki actors stopped using them.[34] For example, Matsumoto Kôshirô VII (1870–1949) used an adaptation when he first played Othello in 1917, but when he played the role a second time in 1925 at the Kabuki-za, with Ichikawa Sadanji as Iago, he used Shôyô's direct translation.[35] A translation was valorized as "following the original text," conferring on it the authority of Old Master Shakespeare himself. So when Kôshirô and others learned a scholar's translation, they gave up, largely unnoticed it seems, their extremely important power to act spontaneously in the moment.

Improvisation during performance contributed life and vitality to Tokugawa-period Kabuki. The stage directions contain many places where the actor is told to do the sequence as he wishes. To take one play as an illustration, I looked through the script of the classic drama *The Forty-Seven Samurai* (*Kanadehon Chûshingura*), and found 182 stage directions that call for actor improvisation or choice.[36] The open-ended direction "as the actor wishes" (*yoroshiku* or *yoroshiku atte*) occurs fifty-one times. It was easy for actors to continue their old habits of improvising when they were playing Shakespeare in adaptation, because the script was in no way sacrosanct. But a translation *was* Shakespeare and was inviolate. In this new relationship between text and actor, text held the dominant position and the actor served it (rather than the text serving the actor as was the case in Tokugawa-period Kabuki). We can only imagine how inhibiting it must have been to the creative actor.[37]

Second, faithful translations stamped the word "foreign" on every page of Shakespeare's plays. In performance, "authentic" settings and costumes cried out England, Italy, Scotland, Denmark, and Greece – never Japan. Japanese audiences read the translations as irrevocably "other"; characters moved and spoke as if they were Europeans motivated by Judeo-Christian beliefs, not as Japanese motivated by Buddhist-Shintô beliefs. The task of the Kabuki actor doing Shakespeare in translation, then, was to portray a foreigner convincingly, a Hamlet, a Lady Macbeth. When an English observer wrote that Kôshirô VII acted Othello so excellently in 1925 "it was in no way different from seeing the play in London and New York,"[38] this was taken, quite naturally, to be the supreme compliment.

A small number of Kabuki actors chose to perform Shakespeare in translation in the period 1905–25. They did so because Shakespeare was a part of the "modern," that is western, world they wished to enter. They were attracted by exotic European culture and hoped familiarity with it would advance their careers, another case of keeping up-to-date within Kabuki. So when Kabuki actor Sawamura Sônosuke I (1886–1924) became interested in modern drama, he joined the Western Drama Study Group (Yôgeki Kenkyûkai), composed mostly of amateur Shingeki actors and English teachers. Sônosuke and a handful of other Kabuki actors dared perform Shakespeare in English: *Juriasu Shiizaa* (*Julius Caesar*) at the new Tokyo Gekijô (Tokyo Theatre) in 1907,[39] and the trial scene from *The Merchant of Venice* at the Teikoku Gekijô (Imperial Theatre) in 1915.[40] These were exceptional events, for knowledge of a foreign language by "beggars of the riverbed" was a great rarity. And of course, playing in English was also playing at being English, a modern, stylish thing to do.

The Kabuki actor most enamored of western theatre was Ichikawa Sadanji II (1880–1940). Sadanji set off for Europe in 1906, a young man of twenty-seven, to see theatre and to attend acting school in London. His eight-month trip to Europe was the first by a Kabuki actor.[41] A year after he returned home, he played Shylock in *The Merchant of Venice* and, in 1909, he co-founded the famous Free Theatre (Jiyû Gekijô) with Osanai Kaoru. His aim was to retrain Kabuki actors to perform modern drama, or, as the slogan went, "turn professionals into amateurs."[42] For fifteen years, Sadanji and the Free Theatre focused on contemporary western drama, but, in 1925, the group staged *Julius Caesar* and *Othello* in February and October of that year using new translations by Osanai. Sadanji played Antony and Iago opposite the great Kabuki star Matsumoto Kôshirô VII as Caesar and Othello. Other roles were taken by Kabuki actors Ichikawa En'nosuke II (1888–1963), who later studied theatre in Europe, Nakamura Matagorô I (1885–1920), and Sawamura Sônosuke, among them. A photograph of Sadanji as Iago shows him dressed in lace collar, velvet jacket, and tights.[43]

Morita Kan'ya XIII (1885–1932), whose father had built the Shintomi-za, was eager to bring Kabuki into the twentieth century. Among his activities, he organized the Literary Arts Theatre (Bungei-za) which became active in 1915. He gathered around him young reform-minded Kabuki actors, such as Otani Tomoemon VI (1886–1923) and Ichikawa En'nosuke II. They joined together with actresses trained at the Imperial Theatre's acting school to study the new modern drama of the west. Kan'ya's troupe of Kabuki actors and modern actresses mounted ten productions of new plays and of translated western drama through 1925. Kan'ya acted in *Romeo and Juliet*, the group's second production in 1918 and played a highly acclaimed Hamlet in the group's fourth production in 1919, both using Shôyô's direct translations.[44] Typical of

Kan'ya's troupe, he, a thirteenth-generation Kabuki actor, acted opposite a newly trained Shingeki actress, Otowa Kaneko, who played Ophelia.[45] The Literary Arts Theatre had use of the large, new Teikoku Gekijô (Imperial Theatre), which had been built in western renaissance style. When we look at photographs of these productions, they do not just deny Japan; they deny Kabuki, too. Kan'ya is gaunt and dressed in black tights, indistinguishable in appearance from a canonical English Hamlet.[46] Kabuki actors in the 1880s and 1890s had tried to subsume their adapted Shakespeare into Japanese patterns of Kabuki performance; now, two decades later, Sônosuke, Sadanji, and Kan'ya tried to submerge Kabuki into the European world of Shakespearean drama and theatre. Simply put, when translations were performed, Japanese bodies were put to the service of a foreign, English Shakespeare (see photo 3).

In candor, we must admit that neither of the two meetings between Kabuki and Shakespeare that I have discussed here have produced long-lasting results. The early "localized" Shakespeare productions done in Kabuki style were immediately ridiculed for being vulgar distortions of the works of a foreign dramatic genius. Tsubouchi Shôyô's comment that Kawakami Otojirô's *Othello* in 1903, "unnecessarily changed tragedy into rough domestic comedy, thereby killing the original's magnificent nature,"[47] expressed a typical scholarly attitude toward adaptations in general. The later "authentic" productions that presented Shakespeare in English fashion were so far removed from Kabuki that most actors were not attracted. It seems to me highly significant that for a period of thirty-five years, from 1925 until 1960, no Kabuki actor appeared in any play by Shakespeare. We can understand that Shakespeare's plays could not be performed in Japan during the war years when England was a national enemy. But the separation (divorce?) continued for a decade and a half after the war was over. It was as if, in spite of honest efforts, the Bard and Kabuki had been judged incurably incompatible.

Then Shakespeare and Kabuki were brought together in a new kind of relationship. High-profile theatre organizations invited Kabuki stars to take leading roles in commercial, large-scale productions. The first such production starred Matsumoto Kôshirô VIII as Othello at Sankei Hall in Tokyo in 1960. Following this, his son, Matsumoto Kôshirô IX, played Hamlet (1972, 1987, and 1991), Romeo (1974), Lear (1975), and Othello (1994); Bandô Tamasaburô V played Lady Macbeth (1976) and Desdemona (1977 and 1978); Nakamura Kanzaburô XVII played Richard III (1964); Onoe Shôroku II played Othello with his son Onoe Tatsunosuke I as Iago (1969 and 1977); Tatsunosuke played Richard III (1980); and Kataoka Takao I played Hamlet (1984 and 1990). These are important productions, widely covered in the press, treated respectfully by critics, and sure of sold-out houses.[48]

3 Morita Kan'ya XIII in Tsubouchi Shôyô's direct translation of *Hamlet*. Kan'ya played Hamlet wearing black velvet tunic and tights in the canonical English tradition at the Teikoku Gekijô (Imperial Theatre), 1919.

Whatever else one may say about these post-war productions of Old Master Shakespeare, they are not "Kabuki." The Kabuki actor in these cases is not hired "to play Kabuki," but because he has box-office appeal and a powerful stage presence that might carry a big production. At the same time, the play's publicity emphasizes the star's special status as a Kabuki professional. And so we are enmeshed in an ambivalent world of pretense and denial. We can't be surprised that Ninagawa Yukio, who directed Matsumoto Kôshirô as Othello in 1994, makes ingratiating remarks about his star: "I am thankful that Kôshirô is a cultured man. Raised in the world of Kabuki, he is able to give life to traditional skills."[49] Yet how are we to take this "praise of Kabuki"? Is it really expected that a Kabuki actor will maintain his traditions when he is surrounded by Shingeki, musical theatre, film, and television actors in other roles and when his director, designer, and choreographer are all from outside Kabuki? A review in the journal *New Trends in Art* (*Geijutsu Shinchô*) of the 1977 *Othello*, that starred Shôroku, Tatsunosuke, and Tamasaburô, claimed to find Kabuki acting and did not like it: "The heavy and slow tempo and intonation of Kabuki overpowered the meaning of the speeches, hindering the natural development of the play."[50] Reviewing some of the performances of the 1970s mentioned above, Hasebe Kazuko struck a more cautious note: "Their sophisticated classic and perfectly trained voices and acting as Kabuki players evoke a unique ambience to Shakespeare's plays."[51]

"Unique ambience" is not the same as "Kabuki," of course. Fortunately, we can examine still photos, films, and videotapes, as well as live performances, today, and we can make our own evaluation of the way postwar Kabuki actors have performed Shakespeare. In my opinion, most of the overall style of Kabuki acting has been suppressed and all of Kabuki's artistic techniques have been banished in productions based on translations.[52] Ninagawa and others may have lauded Kabuki acting, but neither Shôroku nor Kôshirô used any specific Kabuki acting skills when they played Othello in 1969 and in 1994. Their directors, despite flattering words, did not want them to. The prime movers of current productions are commercial sponsors and theatre organizations – Sunshine Theatre, Nissei Theatre, Sankei Hall, Globe Theatre, Shiki and Kumo Theatre Companies, Tôhô Theatrical Corporation, and Shôchiku Theatrical Corporation. Among them, only Shôchiku now has ties with Kabuki. Shôroku, who was a famously blunt and forthright person, understood very well his position in *Othello*, saying, "I will work to avoid playing in a Kabuki manner."[53]

What are these performances then? At heart, they are realistic Shingeki productions that happen to have a Kabuki star in a leading role. That actor brings poise, physical control, and a powerful voice to his acting, but he is placed within the context of a "doublet and hose" production designed to replicate an English model. Kôshirô's 1972 Hamlet, for example, was directed by John David from England. As if to demonstrate Kôshirô's authentic Englishness, his photo as Hamlet appears in the program alongside pictures of great English Hamlets – Gielgud, Olivier, Scofield, Helpmann, Redgrave, Guinness, Burton, O'Toole, and Williamson.[54]

There is one interesting exception to this record of missed chances. I am thinking of the brilliant onnagata actor, Bandô Tamasaburô V (b. 1950), whose portrayals of Lady Macbeth and Desdemona, noted above,[55] were extravagantly, and I think rightly, praised. Surrounded by the usual cast of modern drama actors, he projected an intense, even dangerous, presence in these roles that was quite exceptional. I was fortunate to see Tamasaburô as Lady Macbeth in 1976, and I still retain a clear memory of his majestic, yet delicate, carriage and his steely, insinuating onnagata voice. I suppose he was not "playing Kabuki," but he brought his Kabuki sense and technique to bear on the role much more directly than other Kabuki actors have done. He stood out against the bland, lifeless, and powerless Shingeki performers surrounding him (see colour photo 1).

Could it be otherwise? I think it could. I will mention two suggestive examples of what Kabuki actors might achieve, were they to bring their talents and training unabashedly to Shakespeare. The Kabuki actor Ichikawa En'nosuke III (b.1939) has built a new audience with his so-called "Super Kabuki," unorthodox productions of new scripts written specifically for En'nosuke's company of Kabuki actors. The first "Super Kabuki" was the extravagantly grand Yamato Takeru that premiered in 1986 and has been revived several times since then. En'nosuke has developed a spectacular, imaginative, rapid-paced performing style in "Super Kabuki" that is in the spirit of Edo-period popular Kabuki even while it doesn't necessarily follow traditional acting forms.[56] In a 1995 television interview conducted by Donald Keene, En'nosuke said one of his fondest desires is to stage a story of contemporary life in Kabuki, perhaps a nonsensical spy story dressed in a modern suit and tie, bright kumadori makeup on his face, posing in mie and doing a hopping roppô exit down the hanamichi. "I don't know if others would call it Kabuki," he said, "but if an actor can bring his sense of Kabuki to it, then that's what I would call it." En'nosuke has never staged Shakespeare, but I don't doubt that a King Lear or The Tempest in "Super Kabuki" style would be intensely dynamic and more true to Kabuki than the very ordinary productions starring Kabuki actors that have been staged during the past three decades.

En'nosuke leads his own group of full-time professional Kabuki actors. The Flower Group Theatre (Hanagumi Shibai) is a neo-Kabuki troupe that exists apart from the traditional Kabuki world. It was formed in 1987 by young male actors who were not from Kabuki families but who were enam-ored of Kabuki's high theatricality, including *onnagata* cross-dressing. Flower Group Theatre devotes itself to doing Kabuki-derived and Kabuki-related plays. The troupe did its first Shakespeare, *Hanagumi's Shakespeare Drama: The Tempest* (*Hanagumi Saô-geki Tempest*) in 1993 adapted from a 1992 Bunraku puppet version of the play and directed by troupe leader Kanô Yukikazu. The company put aside its usual campy style of parody (*onnagata* wearing horn rim glasses and high heels) and played *The Tempest* straight. They utilized Kabuki costuming and makeup, *mie*, *tsuke*, off-stage *shamisen* music, and other traditional staging devices. The play was further revised for performances in Seattle and Los Angeles in 1995.[57]

To recapitulate, certainly the circumstances are more complex than I am able to suggest here, but I believe that people within the theatrical institution of Kabuki responded to Shakespeare's plays first strongly and optimistically and then with less and less effectiveness as the decades passed. In the earliest approach, in the 1880s and 1890s, the new "tales from Shakespeare" were adapted, re-adapted, revised, re-revised, and enfolded into well-known Japanese dramatic worlds (*sekai*). The resulting adaptations were staged as tra-ditional Kabuki theatre. Shakespeare was Japanized and localized, erasing his foreignness in the process. Then, in the 1900s and 1910s, the most modern-minded Kabuki actors tried to play Shakespeare in western realistic mode. They were inspired by the *difference* they perceived between modern Shingeki and Kabuki. In this second approach lie several paradoxes, hardly recognized at the time. Surely, it is a profound paradox that Shôyô and other Meiji scholars used Shakespeare to speak for Japan's modern present, when in fact the Old Master represented a European past that was already several centuries dead. Another paradox, and one with dire practical consequences for Kabuki, was that even though Sadanji, Kan'ya, and Kôshirô did not use Kabuki performing techniques, they nonetheless were imbued with the basic Kabuki attitude that new material could be incorporated into their art. They were using the social institution of Kabuki to "try on" western patterns of life, to stay up-to-date, all within the Kabuki system. Because Kabuki actors had always acted in new material, it was not immediately understood that Shakespeare contained no links to the Japanese past. Could the new material be integrated into Kabuki if there were no known *sekai* into which Shakespeare's stories could fit? An important link in the chain was missing. And a final paradox was that the Kabuki actor of the 1920s, a master of highly developed music, dance, and acting codes (*kata*), was expected to replicate the behavior and customs of Europeans realistically. Could he do this and still function as a Kabuki actor? It seems to me these were all insurmountable dilemmas.

I believe that in the end neither the early efforts to assimilate nor the later efforts to replicate were successful. By the 1920s, the production system of Kabuki could not provide a viable milieu for Shakespeare productions. And it can be said that when Kabuki gave up on Shakespeare and other western drama, it also withdrew from modern Japan. After this, contemporary events in Japanese life would be excluded from the Kabuki stage. Japan's present, including Shakespeare who was a part of Japan's modernity, would be abandoned, first to Shimpa, and then to Shingeki and the movies. As Kawatake Shigetoshi writes, by the 1920s, "Kabuki had surrendered" modernity to Shingeki and "changed from its original status as a modern drama to become a traditional theatre."[58]

Were Shôyô's mutual passions for Shakespeare and for Kabuki a personal idiosyncrasy? I don't think so. I believe Shôyô was remarkably prescient when he remarked that Shakespeare was "western Kabuki," thereby suggesting a potential for the two arts to meld in the future. That this did not occur can be credited to a crucial failure of nerve within the Kabuki world after the 1900s. It is usually said that the Meiji-period "movement to reform Kabuki" (engeki kairyô undô) failed. It is true that the feudal evils of Kabuki – the geza music, the hanamichi, the onnagata – that reformers wanted to abolish in the name of modernity, were not exorcised. These unique characteristics of performance constitute the core of "Grand Kabuki" today. But in another sense, the reform movement succeeded all too well. In retaining these traditional features, Kabuki paid the steep price of breaking its ties to contemporary Japanese society. The experiments with living history and cropped-hair plays ended. Kabuki actors who have performed Shakespeare through most of the twentieth century have done so only by denying Kabuki. If it is true, as Shôyô believed, that Shakespeare is the western drama most akin to Kabuki and the most likely to be performed successfully within the Kabuki artistic system, it is also true that the strengths of each have never been genuinely fused in past productions by Kabuki actors.

One attempt has been made in this decade to maintain Kabuki form within Shakespeare's *Hamlet*. Titled *Kabuki Version "Hamlet"* in English and, in Japanese, *Hamuretto Yamato Nishikie* (Colored print of a Japanese *Hamlet*), the text was acted in pure Kabuki style by a company of Kabuki actors in 1992 and again in 1997. Following the Kabuki tradition of the star enacting several roles, the leading actor, Ichikawa Somegorô VII (b. 1973), played Hamlet (Hamura Maro) and Ophelia (Mikariya Hime) by using quick-change costume techniques (*hayagawari*). Director Kawatake Toshio followed Kanagaki Robun's 1886 adaptation, which set the play in fourteenth-century Japan, thus reviving the pattern of localized Kabuki adaptations of a century ago. This "sensational" production traveled to England and Ireland in 1992 and was restaged in September 1997 at the Sunshine Theatre (Sanshain Gekijô) in Tokyo.[59]

I applaud this approach, yet note with disappointment that Kabuki did not directly confront Shakespeare's text. As someone who passionately admires the power and beauty of Kabuki performance, I would like to see contemporary Kabuki actors bring their superb art to bear on Shakespeare's own text, something that has not happened in our lifetime.

NOTES

1 Iizuka Tomoichirô, *Kabuki Saiken* (Survey of Kabuki drama), (Tokyo: Daiichi Shobô, 1926), 5–55.

2 Kawatake Toshio, *Hikaku Engekigaku* (Study of comparative drama), (Tokyo: Nansôsha, 1967), 201–02.

3 See Moriya Takeshi, *Mura Shibai* (Village theatres), (Tokyo: Heibonsha, 1988), 250–57.

4 See Kabuki Hyôbanki Kenkyûkai, ed., *Kabuki Hyôbanki Shûsei* (Compilation of Kabuki actor critiques), 10 vols., (Tokyo: Iwanami Shoten, 1972–77), 158–278.

5 See Ihara Toshirô, ed., *Kabuki Nempyô* (Kabuki chronology), 8 vols., (Tokyo: Iwanami Shoten, 1956–63), VII: 233–36.

6 See Karatani Kôjin, *Origins of Modern Japanese Literature* (Durham and London: Duke University Press, 1993), 55, quoting comments by the scholar Itô Sei.

7 Ihara, *Kabuki Nempyô*, VII: 375.

8 See Kawatake Shigetoshi, *Nihon Engeki Zenshi* (History of Japanese Theatre), (Tokyo: Iwanami Shoten, 1959), 780–81; Ihara, *Kabuki Nempyô*, VII: 248–49; Ihara Toshirô, *Meiji Engekishi* (History of Meiji Theatre), (Tokyo: Hô Shuppan, 1933 (1975)), 246.

9 Ihara, *Kabuki Nempyô*, VII: 369.

10 Kumehachi's career is fascinating and deserves further attention. She performed with Shimpa actors and in Shingeki, as well as Kabuki. See Nojima Jûsaburô, ed., *Kabuki Jinmei Jiten* (Biographical dictionary of Kabuki), (Tokyo: Nichigai Associates, 1988), 77.

11 See Faith Bach, "The contributions of the Omodakaya to Kabuki," diss., Oxford University, 1990, 17, quoting Toita Yasuji, *Kabuki Kono Hyakunen* (This hundred years of Kabuki), (Tokyo: Mainichi Shimbun, 1974), 16.

12 Ihara, *Meiji Engekishi*, 769.

13 Kawatake, *Nihon Engeki Zenshi*, 779; Ihara, *Kabuki Nempyô*, VII: 243.

14 Kawatake, *Nihon Engeki Zenshi*, 852, 872–74; Ihara, *Kabuki Nempyô*, VII: 320, 331–32, 380–81, and VIII: 182, 184.

15 In 1907, the Kabuki-za advertised a special showing of "great colored motion pictures" (*dai chakushoku no katsudô shashin*) by the British M. Pathé Company. See Ihara, *Kabuki Nempyô*, VIII: 241.

16 Nojima, *Kabuki Jinmei Jiten*, App: 31–32.

17 Ihara, *Kabuki Nempyô*, VIII: 64, 118, 156.

18 *Ibid.*, VIII: 223; see also *Engei Gahô* (January 1907).

19 Kawatake, *Engeki Hyakka Daijiten*, II: 552.

20 For an English translation of the play, see C. Andrew Gerstle, Kiyoshi Inobe, and William P. Malm, *Theatre as Music: The Bunraku Play "Mt. Imo and Mt. Se: An Exemplary Tale of Womanly Virtue,"* Center for Asian Studies (Ann Arbor: University of Michigan Press, 1990).

21 Kawatake Toshio, *Kindai Engeki no Tenkai* (Development of modern theatre), in *Shin NHK Shimin Daigaku Sôsho* (Japan Broadcasting Company Public University New Writings), 11 (Tokyo: Nihon Hôsô Kyôkai Shuppan, 1982, 1997), 149.

22 I want to thank Minami Ryuta for allowing me to consult his excellent "A chronological table of Shakespearean productions in Japan," (1996) 2–6; Ihara, *Kabuki Nempyô*, VII: 441, 531.

23 Toyoda Minoru, *Shakespeare in Japan: an Historical Survey*, Shakespeare Association of Japan (Tokyo: Iwanami Shoten, 1940) 8.

24 Kawatake lists the top eighteen actors in 1919: half were in their teens and twenties; only four were over forty. See Kawatake, *Nihon Engeki Zenshi*, 866–67.

25 Minami, "A chronological table of Shakespearean productions," 4–13.

26 Kawatake, *Hikaku Engekigaku*, 406.

27 *Ibid.*, 416–18.

28 Kawatake Toshio, *Zoku Hikaku Engekigaku* (Study of comparative drama continued), (Tokyo: Nansôsha, 1974), 216–25.

29 Kawatake, *Hikaku Engekigaku*, before 1.

30 *Ibid.*

31 *Ibid.*, 188–89; Kawatake, *Kindai Engeki no Tenkai*, 151.

32 Toyoda, *Shakespeare in Japan*, 45–47.

33 See Peter Milward, "Shakespeare in Japanese," in *Studies in Japanese Culture: Tradition and Experience*, ed. Joseph Roggendorf (Tokyo: Sophia University Press, 1963), 187–207: 190–91.

34 In his study of eighteen *Hamlet* productions, Kawatake Toshio concludes that the transition from adaptation to translation occurred over an eight-year period, 1903–11. After 1911, only translations were performed. See Kawatake, *Hikaku Engekigaku*, 405–06.

35 See Kawatake Toshio, "Nihon no 'Oserô'" (Japan's "Othello"), in *Nissei Gekijô Program* 62 (Tokyo: Nissei Gekijô, 1969), 20–21: 21.

36 For an English translation of most acts of the Kabuki text, see James R. Brandon, ed., *Chûshingura: Studies in Kabuki and the Puppet Theater* (Honolulu: University of Hawai'i Press, 1982). See also Toita Yusuji, ed., *Kabuki Meisakusen* (Selection of Kabuki masterpieces) vol. 1 (Tokyo: Sôgensha, 1955), 1–116.

37 Article Ten of the "Theatre Control Regulations" (*gekijô torishimari kisoku*) of 1890, aimed at new plays, says, "actions outside the written play script may not be performed." See Matsumoto Shinko, *Meiji Engeki Ronshi*, (History of Meiji theatre criticism), (Tokyo: Engeki Shuppansha, 1980), 612.

38 Kawatake, "Nihon no 'Oserô,'" 21.

39 Ihara, *Kabuki Nempyô*, VIII: 236; Kawatake, *Nihon Engeki Zenshi*, 1040.

40 See Arai Yoshio, *Sheikusupea-geki Jôenron* (Performance of Shakespeare's plays), (Tokyo: Shinjusha, 1972), 388.

41 Sadanji was also the first Kabuki actor to act abroad. He performed in Moscow and Saint Petersburg at the head of his own troupe in 1928. See Shôchiku Kabushiki Kaisha, *Kabuki Kaigai Kôen no Kiroku* (Records of foreign tours of Kabuki), Tokyo: Shôchiku Kabushiki Kaisha, 1992, 45–48.

42 Komiya Toyotaka, comp. and ed., *Japanese Music and Drama in the Meiji Era*, Edward G. Seidensticker and Donald Keene, eds. (Tokyo: Ôbunsha, 1956), 292.

43 Kawatake, "Nihon no 'Oserô,'" 20.

44 Kawatake, *Engeki Hyakka Daijiten*, 4: photo facing 475 and v: 134).

45 See Sanshain Gekijô, *Sanshain Gekijô News: Rongu Ran* (Sunshine theatre news: long run), December 10, 1993, 4.

46 Kawatake, *Engeki Hyakka Daijiten*, IV: facing 475.

47 Tsubouchi Shôyô, "'Oserô' Dan" (Conversation on *Othello*), *Kabuki* 34 (March 1903), 1–7: 1.

48 The number of productions is small compared to the fifty-to-sixty productions of Shakespeare that are staged in Tokyo each year at present; see Minami, "A chronological table of Shakespearean productions."

49 Ninagawa Yukio, Interview in the television documentary, *Othello*, September 1994.

50 Quoted by Hasebe Kazuko, "Recent Shakespeare translations and stage productions in Japan," *Shakespeare Translation* 5 (1978), 61–78: 65.

51 *Ibid.*, 63.

52 For example, a television documentary (1944), sic, described how three generations of Matsumoto Kôshirô played Othello. The program contained still photos of Kôshirô VII in 1925, film clips of his son Kôshirô VIII in 1960, and a video record of the complete stage production of his grandson Kôshirô IX in 1994. None of the actors deployed identifiable Kabuki acting techniques.

53 Onoe Shôroku and Asari Keita, "'Oserô' de no kokoromi" ("Othello," an experiment), in, *Nissei Gekijô Program* 62 (Tokyo: Nissei Gekijô, March 1969), 4–6: 6.

54 Nissei Gekijô, *Nissei Gekijô Program* 6 (Tokyo: 1972), 45.

55 See Tamasaburô Bandô and Shunji Ohkura, *Onnagata* (Tokyo: Heibonsha, 1983).

56 Bach discusses "Super Kabuki" productions in detail; see Bach, "The contributions of the Omodakaya to Kabuki," 166–72.

57 Lawrence Kominz kindly called my attention to Hanagumi Shibai.

58 Kawatake, *Nihon Engeki Zenshi*, 1064.

59 See Sanshain Gekijô production flyer, 1997, 1–2.

4

Osanai Kaoru's version of *Romeo and Juliet*, 1904

MATSUMOTO SHINKO

In November 1904, the monthly magazine *Kabuki* published a version of Shakespeare's *Romeo and Juliet* written by Suzuki Shumpo as dictated by Osanai Nadeshiko, a pseudonym for Osanai Kaoru, a student at Tokyo Imperial University (now Tokyo University). How Osanai's script came to be published in *Kabuki* is a bit complicated. In the brief preface to the play, Osanai did not mention the fact that he undertook this task at the request of Ii Yôhô,[1] the leading actor of the Masago-za Theatre, who wished to produce a Shakespearean play for his company's upcoming season.

Then regarded as one of the most gifted actors of his generation, Ii Yôhô felt compelled to update the repertory of the Masago-za Theatre, partially in response to debates regarding theatre practices at the time. In 1903, the death of two prominent Kabuki actors, Onoe Kikugorô V and Ichikawa Danjûrô IX, signaled the fact that the Kabuki profession was at a turning point. Even reputable critics prophesied the demise of Kabuki due to the scarcity of talented actors. By contrast, upstart theatre companies with so-called *shin haiyû*[2] or "new actors," heretofore marginalized by the Kabuki establishment, became energized by the unexpected turn of events. Beginning with the great success of a series of war-dramas in 1894, attendance at new theatres had been steadily increasing during the course of the decade. Despite severe criticism of the skills of the actors and the aesthetic value of such populist-minded entertainment, these upstart companies appealed to a new generation of theatregoers unfamiliar with the codes and traditions of Kabuki.

In 1902, Ii Yôhô's company presented eight plays of Chikamatsu Monzaemon at the Masago-za Theatre. Despite the fact that the Masago-za Theatre was rather inconveniently located, the prospect of seeing Chikamatsu's plays presented in a style that departed from the Kabuki tradition attracted the attention of both intelligentsia and ordinary theatregoers, and it is safe to say that Ii Yôhô's fame was established through these innovative productions. Nevertheless, Ii could not rest on his success, since he was also aware of the broadening interest in western-style cultural forms. In the Meiji Era, international pressures had heightened Japanese attention towards the various affairs of foreign countries not only in the fields of politics and economics, but in cultural matters as well.

4 *Othello*, directed by Kawakami Otojirô for the Kawakami Ichi-za, at Meiji-za Tokyo, 1903. Kawakami Otojirô played the title role as the Japanese general, Muro Washirô, in a localised adaptation, performed in Shimpa style.

In the early years of the twentieth century, Shakespeare caught the attention of Japanese men of theatre, particularly those associated with the new theatres producing hybrid genres not bound to any particular tradition or style. For instance, Kawakami Otojirô's company, upon returning from their second European tour in August 1902, staged three adaptations of Shakespeare's plays: *Othello* (February 1903), *The Merchant of Venice* (June 1903) and *Hamlet* (November 1903). Kawakami was generally recognized as the most outstanding "new-actor" at the time, despite his rather coarse acting style, mostly owing to his great success in a series of war-plays in 1894. Since his debut in Tokyo in 1890, he had tried hard to find ways to distinguish his company from other troupes of new-actors.

In 1893, he had a chance to visit Paris by himself. On his return to Tokyo, he reproduced the plays he had witnessed in Paris at Le Théâtre du Chatelet, shifting the context to contemporary Japan. *Nisshin-Sensô (Sino-Japanese War)*, which was presented at Asakusaza Theatre in August 1894 and established his nation-wide fame, was a synthesis of two French dramas: *Michel Strogoff* by Jules Verne and Adolphe D'Ennery, and *La Prise de Pekin* by Adolphe D'Ennery. He hoped his adaptations of European drama would be a reliable recipe for box-office success and he improvised several war-dramas on the same lines, which brought good results.

5 Poster for *Romeo endo Jurietto (Romeo and Juliet)* directed by Osanai Kaoru, at the Masago-za, 1904. As in the production, western elements mingle with indigenous elements in the poster design.

In March 1900, while his company was visiting Boston, he had a chance to witness Sir Henry Irving's production of *The Merchant of Venice*. This was probably Kawakami's first encounter with Shakespeare's play. In February 1903, he produced a Japanese version of *Othello* at Meiji-za Theatre that was written by Emi Suiin, a popular novelist. Though well received by the Meiji-za customers, this production did not impress the well educated as having any vestige of authenticity. In fact, evidence suggests that Kawakami himself was less concerned with mounting an authentic production of this world renowned tragedy than he was with using Shakespeare's name to elevate his own status in Japanese theatrical circles. In June of the same year, Kawakami performed Shylock in Doi Shunsho's translation of *The Merchant of Venice* at the Meiji-za Theatre. This was a short-term production for charity. Since the text was a translation by Doi, who had some knowledge of English literature and had accompanied Kawakami's second European tour, it should have been a bit more authentic than *Othello*; however none of the drama critics commented on this.

Then, in November, Kawakami staged *Hamlet* at Hongô-za Theatre, which focused theatregoers' attention on his own drastic reformation of theatre management rather than on the production itself. *Hamlet* was a mixture of translation and adaptation: Doi Shunsho taking responsibility for the translation and Yamagishi Kayô for the adaptation. Fujisawa Asajiro took the title role of "Hamura Toshimaru," and Kawakami the roles of "Count Hamura" (the ghost) and "Kurando" (Claudius). In a later production of *Hamlet* in Kyoto, Kawakami took the role of "Hamura Toshimaru" and appeared on a bicycle in western attire in the scene of the fourth soliloquy. I should mention that the important female roles in those Shakespeare productions were all taken by Sadayakko, Kawakami's wife, who became sensationally famous in Europe during their first tour.

Despite the skepticism of such intellectuals as Tsubouchi Shôyô and Mori Ôgai, who questioned Kawakami's understanding of these Shakespearean dramas, Kawakami became recognized as the leading actor in the European style. For his part, Ii Yôhô must have felt disquieted by Kawakami's swift appropriation of Shakespeare. He had known Kawakami from his early days as an actor, and while he knew that Kawakami's acting skills were inferior to his own, he also knew that Kawakami could be a shrewd and formidable rival. In addition, there was the popularity of Sadayakko, Kawakami's wife, who had been hailed by the Europeans as Japan's "first-actress."[3]

Although Osanai Kaoru's *Romeo and Juliet* was one-tenth the length of Shakespeare's play, all of the dramatis personae appeared, except very minor ones. In addition, the setting was changed from feudalistic Verona to contemporary Tokyo. One unusual feature was that Friar Lawrence was transformed into a tutor employed by the Motoda family, though Osanai retained "Lawrence," a foreign name. It is possible that since Osanai feared that the word "friar" might be translated as "Buddhist mendicant," he made Lawrence a westerner appointed to teach foreign languages and "western science" to Motoda Kumeo (Romeo). It should also be noted that since marriage was not at that time considered a religious ritual, Lawrence was not needed to lead Kumeo and Yurie (Juliet) to the altar; as a progressive westerner, he merely had to give advice to the young couple and provide the potion for Yurie.

Notices for the play written by two female critics, Shin'nyo-joshi and Kin'ei-joshi,[4] appeared in the December 1904 issue of *Kabuki*, giving us some idea of what the production was like. The prologue is omitted, and Act 1 starts with a part of Gregory's speech, "here comes two of the house of Montague," actually spoken by Sampson (Sankichi). The puns scattered among the lines spoken by the servants of both families must have proven far too difficult for Osanai, and so he but sketched the verbal play that accompanies Shakespeare's fight scene. Osanai, like all translators of Shakespeare, had to contend with not only the richness of Shakespeare's language, but also the high esteem he was accorded in Japan at that time. Although Osanai majored in English literature at the Tokyo Imperial University, his facility with English had not yet reached the level where he could either comfortably appreciate Shakespearean English, or render in translation the nuances of Shakespeare's verse. Moreover, as this was his first theatrical venture, he was inexperienced in regard to the complex interaction between playwright and actors. This, combined with the fact that the Masago-za company was comprised of both not very-high ranking Kabuki actors and so-called "new actors," must have made the situation more than a little complex. It seems, therefore, that Osanai was requested to accommodate two styles in his adaptation, prose and *shichigochô* (verse in seven and five syllables); and that furthermore, he was asked to give priority to casting requirements over regard to the overall harmony of the play. Osanai's translation, then, can best be described as an extract of Shakespeare's play, although he cleverly selected lines which advanced the plot and incorporated the main features of each character.

Returning to Osanai's dramaturgical maneuvers, after the initial fight scene, Kumeo appears. Here, Shakespeare's "grove of sycamore" is reset in a maple forest, and Kumeo enters in what was then considered fashionable, but which today would strike us as an incredible combination of western and Japanese attire: a grey-colored kimono with a light-grey undershirt, a black *haori* coat with five family crests (signifying very formal attire), and brown shoes with black socks. According to Shin'nyo-joshi's description, upon his first entrance Kumeo carried a maple twig with tinted leaves. Whereas in traditional forms such as Kabuki and Noh, carrying a weeping willow branch suggests the bearer's mental disorder, Kumeo's sprig of maple, which may or may not be derived from tradition, holds none of the sinister associations of the weeping willow, and merely suggests a state of glorious impermanence.

Interestingly, Osanai eliminated Act 1, scene 3 of the original version, thereby postponing the introduction of Yurie and her Nurse. This results in the entire first act being played as a street scene. Act 2 of Osanai's version (Shakespeare's Act 1.5) begins in the domestic setting of the Kanô family banquet room with the exchange of the servants prior to Yurie's birthday celebration. Here, Ii Yôhô or the management of the Masago-za Theatre could not afford to ignore the success of Kawakami Otojirô's production of *Othello*, in which the banquet scene was well received by the public owing to its sumptuous deployment of Kabuki elements. In fact, *Tsuru-Kame* (Crane and Tortoise), a dance performed by Ichikawa Kumehachi[5] in the banquet scene, was the centerpiece of Kawakami's production. In Ii Yôhô's *Romeo and Juliet*, while Kumeo wore a very simple farmer's blue costume, the other guests (particularly those played by the better-known actors), were arrayed in the colorful Kabuki costumes of such well-recognized roles as Benkei, Ushiwakamaru, Sambasô, etc. Naturally, they could perform nothing but the traditional Japanese dances in such attire, but the average audience member would have been well entertained. In the party scene, Kumeo and Yurie do not exchange words at all, but rather "fall in love" in dumb show. The role of Yurie was played by Seki Kiyomi, a skillful female impersonator in Ii's company whose acting and elocution were praised by the critics, although both Shin'nyo-joshi and Kin'ei-joshi felt that the style of Seki's wig was a bit too decorative for a young lady of a respected family. The next scene (Act 2.1) was performed in front of a light-blue *asagi-maku* curtain, which was then pulled off to reveal the next scene in Motoda's orchard, in which a spiral staircase and a small balcony were installed.

The dialogue in this, one of Shakespeare's most famous scenes, must have been particularly difficult for Osanai to translate. Wisely, Osanai structured the couple's lines so as to capture the general atmosphere of the scene, while avoiding the poetic allusions in Shakespeare's text. "It is nor hand, nor foot . . . ," for example, could have been quite unintentionally hilarious had he attempted a literal translation into Japanese. Osanai's innovation here was to interpolate the scene between Friar Lawrence and Romeo, which in the original transpires at Lawrence's cell (Act 2.2), as the conclusion to the balcony scene. In Osanai's version, therefore, Lawrence appears in the orchard just after Yurie retires, and Kumeo immediately asks for his assistance in arranging their marriage. Other modifications of Shakespeare's text by Osanai appear to be based on cultural considerations as well as difficulties in language. Since in Osanai's version Lawrence has no chance to meet Yurie prior to the lovers' fatal moment, he neither tells them "you shall not stay alone till holy church incorporate two in one," nor does he unite them in matrimony before God. Even if Osanai had attempted a literal translation of Lawrence's line, they would have made little sense to a majority of the audience in Meiji Tokyo.

The brawl that opens Osanai's Act 3, which in the original is set in a public place in Verona, was re-contextualized by Osanai in the precinct of a shrine. The young men of the two rival families were all dressed in the navy blue jackets with stand-up braided collars that were emblematic of students of the Gakushûin School.[6] Seeing young men in such uniforms fighting and scuffling must have been quite compelling to the audience, since Gakushûin students always maintained an air of self-possession and aloofness in real life.

This was followed by the scene in which Yurie hears news of the death of her cousin Taizô at the hands of Kumeo, although the banter between the Nurse and Juliet in the original text is largely jettisoned. Furthermore, Yurie refers to Kumeo as her husband.[7] In the scene in Lawrence's cell which follows, Osanai eliminated much of the interchange between Romeo/Kumeo and the Nurse, who appears only to convey Yurie's message and the ring. Osanai eliminates Shakespeare's next scene (3.4) between Capulet and Paris, jumping instead to Yurie's room (3.5, set in Capulet's orchard in Shakespeare), in which the lovers, after having spent a joyful night, bid their farewells, confident of their future encounter. Although this scene is shortened considerably, Osanai is quite faithful in his interpretation of Shakespeare's text.

As for the next scene in Lawrence's cell (Shakespeare 4.1), Osanai seems busy enough just following the plot, and nothing very interesting dramatically occurs other than the explanation of the remedy which may free Yurie from marrying Haruo. In the next scene of Osanai's version, the wedding banquet for Yurie and Haruo, Osanai seems to have been at pains to encapsulate every incident depicted in scenes 2, 3 and 4 of Shakespeare's Act 4, perhaps as a cost-cutting device. A single setting, therefore, functions variously as Yurie's bedroom, a banquet hall, and a gallery. It is also possible that Ii Yôhô and the Masago-za management may have felt compelled to make the wedding banquet as lively and cheerful a scene as possible, thereby making the rather monotonous scenes which preceded it, and Yurie's "death" at the scene's end, more palatable to an audience whose tastes they had judiciously to consider. In making their production choices, however, Ii's company certainly seemed more conscientious and innovative than Kawakami Otojirô with his *Othello* banquet, despite the fact that his *Othello* set the precedent. For their musical selections, for instance, they chose *Kanjinchô*[8] accompanied by piano and violin. Some western musical instruments were also employed in the early birthday party scene, but the types of musical instruments were not as clearly discernible as those in the wedding banquet scene, which thus took on a distinctively western tone. Every drama critic must have been taken aback by this extraordinary idea, even though the ordinary Masago-za theatregoer would have been delighted to hear such familiar Kabuki music; Shin'nyo-joshi, however, simply commented that the *Kanjinchô* should have been sung more clearly and loudly since it was accompanied by piano and violin, although she did not criticize or praise the idea itself.

As in the original, Osanai's Act 5 is divided into three scenes. In the first scene, Kumeo hears of Yurie's death, unaware of Lawrence's scheme, and in the next scene he obtains poison from an apothecary, leaving before Lawrence's servant has the chance to advise him of Lawrence's "plot." The final scene of the tragedy is almost identical structurally to the original, though here again, all lyrical speeches are transformed into simple, if flat, Japanese prose.

As a whole, Osanai Kaoru's version of *Romeo and Juliet* must be considered an abridgement of Shakespeare's play. In the December 1904 issue of *Kabuki*, he himself writes that he omitted Act 1 scene 4, Act 3 scene 4, Act 4 scene 2, and Act 5 scene 2, as well as many of the speeches of the Nurse and Kusuo (Mercutio). A detailed analysis shows, however, that considerable portions of many other scenes and a considerable number of lines from most characters are also omitted. However, Osanai's obviously sincere efforts in attempting to interpret Shakespeare in Japanese theatrical terms can be best discerned by the careful and delicate choice of words spoken by each of the characters in his version. In this respect, Osanai's attitude was entirely different from Emi Suiin, who nonchalantly reformulated *Othello* into a melodrama to suit the tastes of Kawakami Otojirô.

Unfortunately, most of the drama critics of the time did not appreciate Osanai's sensitivity to Shakespeare's language and dramaturgy. The reviews of *Romeo endo Jurietto* appeared in six daily newspapers, indicating the formidable reputations of both Shakespeare and his play. Furthermore, more sophisticated theatregoers were likely to have recognized the attempt of Ii Yôhô's company as the first serious Japanese production of Shakespeare, particularly with the endorsement of Miki Takeji, the editor of *Kabuki*. Still the majority of critics found Osanai's language a bit crude and unmelodious by Japanese standards, even if some admitted a certain freshness to the dialogue. Masamune Hakuchô of the *Yomiuri Shimbun* wrote that Osanai's

version did not sound like contemporary speech, while Hassen-koji of the
Tokyo Nichinichi Shimbun pointed out that a literal translation of Lawrence's
line, "Wisely and slow: they stumble that run fast," was admirably delivered.
A common complaint of the critics was Osanai's re-contextualizing of both
time and place in drama. Some wrote that the brawl at the shrine could not
have occurred in a public place since Japan was a civilized country; while
others pointed out that Yurie's drug-induced slumber for forty-two hours
was unscientific and hence implausible in the enlightened Meiji Era. One
critic in particular, Kisen, complained that a story of this sort must have the
medieval era as its historical background and that Kumeo should have been
dressed in samurai costume. The criticism of Osanai's translation mostly
centered on the dialogue between Kumeo and Yurie. For instance, in those
days in Japan, lovers would never say "I love you" to each other. In traditional
dramas, girls are often more forward than boys in the love scenes; however,
they do not reveal their thoughts so directly. Furthermore, Osanai's use of the
word *kekkon* (marriage), which at that time was merely a legal term, contributed to the foreign and unnatural feeling to the words spoken by the actors of
the Masago-za production.

Osanai dismissed such critical commentary as trivial in the December 1904
issue of *Kabuki* by cross-referencing his version to the original text and
stressing the significance of his choices in adapting the tragedy. In making
his claims, Osanai referred to part of a speech delivered by Lord Lytton at the
one-hundredth production of *Romeo and Juliet* at the Lyceum Theatre in
London, in which he said that "[the play's] true dramatis personae are not
mere mortal Montagues and Capulets, they are those beautiful immortals,
love and youth, in an ideal land of youth and love." Osanai sensed that the
critics' disapproval of the historical backdrop of his adaptation was due to a
misconception about European theatre prevalent in the Japanese theatre
world, namely the expectation that any historical play must be faithful to the
historical epoch in which it is set. If the tragedy of *Romeo and Juliet* was set in
the early fourteenth century, why couldn't Kumeo and Yurie also "live" in
fourteenth-century Japan? Such feuds as that between the Montagues and
Capulets were nothing unusual in those tumultuous years due to a long-
standing civil war. This criticism reflected the opinion of the Japanese intelligentsia at the time that the theatre of the western world authentically
replicated the real life of people, if not the historical facts. This notion was
reinforced by critical interest in the emergence of theories of Naturalism in
literature and art, and the "problem play" in drama.

Another complicating factor was that five years after the Imperial
Restoration in 1868, the new government – believing that the theatre of

civilized nations served to educate the masses – issued an edict to theatre practitioners that historical subjects be presented accurately and without anachronisms. While over thirty years had passed between then and the production of Osanai's *Romeo and Juliet*, such misconceptions were still prevalent for both the Imperial Government and the critical establishment. The conflation of issues demanded by public policy and new currents in dramatic theory generated a profound conflict, which preoccupied the intelligentsia and theatre practitioners alike. The question was whether the trends in Realism and Naturalism could be substituted for the exact replica of history that the Meiji Imperial Government asked of the theatre.

One can only guess at the shock of Ii Yôhô and the Masago-za Theatre managers, who in their efforts to replicate a "realistic" *mise-en-scène*, had been made aware of Elizabethan theatre and performance conditions. The Masago-za Theatre not only had exceptionally advanced lighting capabilities,[9] but the scenery was created by the young artists Tamaki Terunobu and Kitamura Kintarô, who had returned from France, instead of by the traditional craftsmen. According to newspaper accounts, each scene looked like a genuine oil painting, with the balcony scene and the interior settings being particularly impressive to the audience. While I have no evidence as to whether Osanai had collaborated in the *mise-en-scène* or even how he felt about the results, it seems that the majority of theatregoers and critics admired the production values of *Romeo and Juliet*, if they did not always agree with Osanai's literary choices.

As a whole, this production of *Romeo and Juliet* seems to have been successful. I myself feel that the efforts of the translator and the actors were rewarded with the approbation of the intellectuals in the audience, despite the fact that it proved to be a box-office disappointment. Moreover, most theatre historians refer to it as Japan's first conscientious Shakespearean production, even if the adaptation and acting style have not been highly regarded. What is surprising, however, is that none of the critics censured the Kabuki actors participating in this production. The roles of Montague, Capulet, and the Nurse were all taken by Kabuki actors (though not high-ranking ones), and they must somehow have managed to present the characters envisioned by Osanai in his version.

In November 1909, Osanai Kaoru premiered his new theatre company Jiyû-Gekijô, named after André Antoine's Théâtre Libre, with a presentation of *John Gabriel Borkman* at the Yûraku-za Theatre. Defying the expectations of the literati and the new actors that Ii Yôhô would co-operate in this venture, Osanai's partner was in fact the young Kabuki actor Ichikawa Sadanji II.[10] Some researchers have suggested that Ii Yôhô was not progressive enough to involve himself with such a new enterprise. I feel, however, that Ii Yôhô was just as anxious to improve his acting techniques and achieve a higher level of skill in his own style as Osanai was to realize his own vision of a theatre free from box office pressures. The genre to which the so-called "new actors" belonged became known as Shimpa (new sect) in 1906, and it was to gain rapidly in popularity in the Japanese theatre. It would be understandable for Ii Yôhô to curry public favor in such circumstances, rather than attempt to win the approval of the highbrow minority. But, while it seems that he lost interest in western theatre, Sadanji II, who had recently inspected European theatres, felt the need to distinguish himself outside the Kabuki world where he was expected to be heir to his father's fame. From his experience with the *Romeo and Juliet* production, Osanai knew that talented Kabuki actors had the capacity to adapt to modern drama techniques when given proper direction. In the early years of the Jiyû Gekijô, Osanai stressed two points to his actors: not to sing but to speak, not to dance but to walk. Since the "director" of western theatre had not yet been incorporated into Japanese theatre practice, Osanai was not in a position to perform such functions in the Masago-za production of *Romeo and Juliet*. At the Jiyû Gekijô, however, he was to establish the position and function of the director for the first time in Japan. Perhaps if he had directed the Masago-za production, there would have been remarkable differences in both the acting style and elocution of Ii Yôhô's company.

Osanai Kaoru again attempted to translate Shakespeare in 1926, and his version of *The Merchant of Venice* became the fourteenth production of The Tsukiji Shôgekijô,[11] which he founded in June 1924 with Hijikata Yoshi. He also directed Shôyô's translation of *Julius Caesar* in January 1925 for the company's nineteenth production. In his work with the young actors at the Tsukiji Shôgekijô, however, Osanai encountered certain obstacles to his goals. While he was aiming at an aesthetic theatre, the majority of the younger company members were inclined to view theatre as a tool for spreading ideology, favoring Expressionist plays which often called for an exaggerated, even grotesque acting style.

It is perhaps no coincidence that his first experiences in the theatre had been with Ii Yôhô, one of the most refined actors in Shimpa theatre, and that his first attempt at European drama was adapting the most delicate of romantic tragedies. Additionally, he had visited Russia twice, in 1912 and 1927, and was greatly impressed by the theatrical subtlety advocated by the Moscow Art Theatre. However, on December 25, 1928 Osanai died of a sudden heart attack at the young age of forty-eight and his company was disbanded.

NOTES

1 Working in Kobe as a bank clerk, Ii Yôhô (1871–1932) was so impressed by a performance of the so-called new theatre, that he joined the Saibikan Theatre Group led by Yoda Gakkai, an enthusiast for theatre reform. Although productions of the Saibikan group in 1890 were not successful, the company made its mark in modern Japanese theatre history as it took advantage of the government's official permission allowing women to appear on stage with men. Ii Yôhô went on to form his own company in 1896. Closely associated with the Shimpa theatre, Ii Yôhô came to be recognized as an outstanding actor of his day, a reputation held to this day.

2 In December 1887, the Japanese government issued an edict exiling approximately 600 people as dissidents from Tokyo for openly repudiating the government's policy of suppressing their pro-democratic movement. Some of these exiles gathered in Osaka, Japan's second largest city, where the police were not as strict, and where they sought the support of farmers and workers in nearby provincial towns. These political-minded people were referred to as *sôshi* (high-spirited men), although many of them were simply idealistic youngsters. Because they were banned from making public speeches, a group of *sôshi* led by Sudô Sadanori got the idea of performing at a small theatre in Osaka as a way of conveying their political messages. The *sôshi* involved in theatrical activity were called *shin-haiyû* (new actor) or *sôshi haiyû*.

3 A very popular and talented geisha, favored by prominent politicians, Sadayakko married Kawakami Otojirô, but never dreamed of being an actress until she accompanied his troupe to America and Europe. Sadayakko was asked by her husband to appear on stage because western spectators did not accept the idea of female impersonators. In Europe, she became very popular, and was favorably compared to Eleonora Duse and Sarah Bernhardt. Many items such as perfumes, robes, sandals, and even a distinctive hairstyle were named "Yacco" after her. (See 'Introduction', note 10.) See also Chiba Yoko, "Sada Yakko and Kawakami: Performers of Japonisme," *Modern Drama* 35:1 (1992), 35–53.

4 Mori Hisako (Shin'nyo-joshi), wife of Miki Takeji, editor of *Kabuki*. Okada Yachiyo (Kin'ei-joshi), younger sister of Osanai Kaoru, author, drama critic, and playwright. "Joshi" is a sort of title for ladies with respectable professions.

5 A magnificent female dancer, Ichikawa Kumehachi (1846–1913) often performed with Kabuki troupes.

6 Established in 1877 in Tokyo under the patronage of the Imperial Household Agency. Opened to the public after World War II.

7 In the samurai class, a betrothed couple called each other husband and wife, whether or not they had the approval of their families.

8 The title of a famous Kabuki drama, as well as the title of a *nagauta* musical piece accompanying the play.

9   Inoue Masao notes in his memoirs, *Bakesokoneta Tanuki* (A badger that failed to transform itself), published in 1947, that the Masago-za Theatre had a set of footlights on the stage.

10   After working with the Jiyû Gekijô, Sadanji II (1880–1940) created a new genre called shin-Kabuki with Okamoto Kidô, an outstanding dramatist.

11   Built in 1924 with a seating capacity of 497, the Tsukiji Shôgekijô became the Mecca of Shingeki (modern, western-style Japanese theatre), until it was destroyed by an air raid in March 1945.

5

Some Noh adaptations of Shakespeare in English and Japanese

UEDA MUNAKATA KUNIYOSHI

I

Anyone who is deeply moved by the poetry and music of Shakespearean English might balk at the idea of translating Shakespeare into another language. When Tsubouchi Shôyô translated *Hamlet* into Japanese and presented it on stage in Tokyo in 1911, Natsume Sôseki (1867–1916) wrote a review for the *Asahi Shimbun*, saying that Shakespearean poetry would not permit translation into Japanese.[1] He criticized Tsubouchi's Kabuki style and contemporary adaptations of Shakespeare. Furthermore, Natsume, former professor of English at Tokyo University who succeeded to the chair vacated by Lafcadio Hearn, suggested in his newspaper review that if Shakespeare had to be translated into Japanese, it might be interesting in the unique poetic style of Noh.

Tsubouchi Shôyô (1859–1935) was respected not only as the first Japanese translator of the complete works of Shakespeare, but as professor of English at Waseda University and a popular writer of novels and plays. He admired Chikamatsu Monzaemon (1653–1724), the Edo period playwright of Jôruri and Kabuki drama, and had translated Shakespeare for Jôruri and Kabuki productions. Because he compared Chikamatsu to Shakespeare, it did not occur to him to adapt Shakespeare into a Noh play. Having as a child practiced Noh singing under his strict brother, he hated Noh training. Although, as a professor of drama, he recognized Noh as a traditional theatre, he believed it should be preserved as one of Japan's national treasures, but not as a living theatre art. He advised his students of Shakespeare first to study Chikamatsu, for the two bore a close resemblance.[2] Thus Kabuki actors took up Tsubouchi's translations for their productions and have been performing them ever since in various styles. Bandô Tamasaburô (b. 1950), for example, the most popular Kabuki actor for the last quarter century or so, has already performed several Shakespearean roles including a highly acclaimed Lady Macbeth in 1976.

Natsume's proposal, on the other hand, was neglected. Nobody attempted to take up Shakespeare in Noh style, although Natsume, who became a famous modern novelist, had many distinguished disciples as scholars, writers, and critics. Nogami Toyoichirô, for example. who specialized in English and became a Noh scholar and later the President of Hôsei University, founded the now well-known Hôsei University Noh Institute. And still Natsume's idea was not realized. The reason was, I suspect, apart from the Japanese psychological reluctance to run counter to received opinion, the great influence of Tsubouchi over the academic, literary, and theatre worlds, which lasted even after his long life. Natsume died in 1916 at the age of forty-nine, while Tsubouchi was up and doing until he was seventy-seven, founding Waseda University Theatre Museum in 1928 and The Shakespeare Society of Japan in 1930. This, I suspect, is the main reason why no Shakespearean Noh play was seen until the 1980s.

What qualifications, then, are needed for a Noh performance or play to be considered Noh? Zeami (1363–1443), one of the two founders of Noh, says repeatedly that the two essential elements of Noh are song and dance, establishing them as "the two basic arts."[3] A play or a script without Noh chant and dance choreography may not be called a Noh play. Yeats saw Itô Michio's Noh dancing, but Itô had not practiced Noh dance or singing in Japan. Hence, his was probably not an orthodox Noh dance, even though it may have impressed Yeats and T. S. Eliot. Conversely, we may say that any performance that combines *shimai* (Noh dance) and *utai* (Noh chant) may be called Noh. All other factors such as instrumental music, masks, costumes, the stage, and so on are of secondary importance.

Kurosawa Akira has used some Noh techniques: slow movements, some small properties and some Noh music in *Kumonosujô*, *Ran*, and *The Bad Sleep Well*, which are based on *Macbeth*, *King Lear*, and *Hamlet* respectively. But all these effects are not sufficient to make a Noh play, even if they could create a Noh-like atmosphere. The actors' movements and standing postures, and their speaking or singing styles, are completely different from Noh. Certainly, sometimes Noh and Kyogen actors and actresses appear in modern plays, but they are not usually acting in Noh or Kyogen styles. Mishima Yukio's *Modern Noh Plays* are written without Noh chants or movements and they are basically modern prose plays. The same can be said of Ninagawa Yukio's *Macbeth* and other productions, as well as Suzuki Tadashi's *Macbeth* and *Lear*. Noh is in a sense pure art. Noh lovers can tell immediately whether or not a performance is Noh, if they have had some training in Noh dance and chant.

In what follows, I would like to outline my own experience in adapting Shakespeare to Noh performance, and to Noh literary and dramatic conventions. The main reason I took up *Hamlet* as my first English Noh play was that, apart from my own love of the play and the urging of some Bostonian friends in 1975,[4] Noh is distinctively a theatre of ghosts, or of the subconscious world of dreams. In its world the living and the dead exist together. There are many good Noh plays without ghosts such as *Hagoromo*, *Hanjo*, *Hyakuman*, *Koi-no-Omoni*, *Yuya*, and so on, but the majority of the typical Noh plays are "*mugen* Noh," in which, usually in the second scene, a ghost returns to this world and reflects back on the climactic moments of his or her life. I thought I could transform *Hamlet* into this type of Noh play.

Setting Noh melody to the severely cut Shakespearean lines took me a year. I had no precedent to draw on, and I did not want to sacrifice either the characteristics of English or the Noh singing style. I wished rather to let both of them live more richly in the combination.

In Noh singing, each syllable of every word must be stressed and prolonged. Most Japanese words end with a vowel, while English words end mostly with consonants that cannot be prolonged. There are many unstressed syllables in English, and the very slow tempo and microtonality of Noh singing sound foreign to English ears. But still I wanted to sing my favorite Noh melodies in English. When I had almost finished the work, I met several enthusiastic people interested in both Noh and Shakespeare and founded "The Noh Shakespeare Group" in Shizuoka in 1981.

Training actors to sing Noh style in English was not easy when we premiered *Noh Hamlet* in English the next year in Shizuoka. But we were fortunate to have the help of Japan's leading Noh instrumentalists as well as some Kanze school actors including Nanjô Hideo, director of The Japan Noh Troupe which toured Britain in 1983 and 1984. The same musicians staged the Tokyo production with us: they were Isso Yukimasa, a flautist; Ôkura Genjirô, a *kotsuzumi* drummer; Ôkura Shônosuke, an *ôtsuzumi* drummer; and Mishima Gentarô, a *taiko* drummer. Though they did not understand the English script perfectly, they had no major problems, since for most of the play I had borrowed Noh melodies from familiar classical Noh plays. The dancers, of course, had no problems, but the *ji-utai* chorus had a hard job throughout the rehearsals singing in English, especially in parts where they were to sing rhythmically with the orchestra. In Tokyo, also, I again took the *shite* or main role as well as directing *Noh Hamlet*. For the two performances at Yarai Noh Theatre, about one thousand people came, though the house capacity was only 350 seats. It was televised by NHK on the evening news, so many more people saw it on television all over Japan, and some weeklies included photographs.

One of the highlights of my adaptation was the scene in which, after

Ophelia's death, Hamlet meditates in front of her grave in a posture of *zazen* or Zen sitting. After a long meditation, he understands that he may not have really loved Ophelia, for until now "To be or not to be" has been his most important question. Suddenly, he has an enlightening experience of the sort Buddhists call *satori*. He stands up, and unfolding his fan, sings: "To be or not to be: is no longer the question." Then he dances, expressing his transcendence of death, ending with the words: "To be or not to be, is not the question; the readiness is all." I was accused by some of "blaspheming" against Shakespeare, but there were British actors in the audience who told me they found the meditation scene most impressive. Most Japanese critics and scholars neglected the performance except for a few who understood English.[5]

Concerning structure, I should explain that I first composed *Noh Hamlet* in five scenes, following the traditional one-day program, which consists of five Noh plays in which the *shite* is respectively a god, a warrior, a woman, a mad person, and a devil. While I was considering the structure of *Noh Hamlet* as a classical type of Noh play, I thought the five Acts of *Hamlet* could be made to fit the same five-scene form, having as *shite*: Hamlet's father's ghost (god), Hamlet (warrior), Ophelia (woman), Hamlet in *satori* (madness), and Hamlet's and Laertes's duel (demon).

The performance took over four hours, since each Noh play required twenty to fifty minutes to perform. I believe it was a particularly good introduction to Noh for those who knew *Hamlet* but had not seen a Noh play. We received appreciative letters from non-Japanese, including some Noh connoisseurs. Murakami Upton, Professor of English at Waseda University and the author of the popular *Spectator's Handbook of Noh*, wrote "What was produced was just right, leaving the full essence and sense of *Hamlet*."[6]

After performing this marathon five play/act version of *Noh Hamlet*, I next wrote a two-act version to challenge Japanese Noh specialists' reviews criticizing *Noh Hamlet* for being too long and boring. (Ironically, this is the common reaction to Noh of foreigners who do not speak Japanese.) I decided to rewrite it in two scenes in keeping with the usual Noh format. We showed this version at the National Noh Theatre in Tokyo in 1985. I was afraid, in fact, that the spectators might not appreciate it as they had appreciated the five-scene production, but, in general, the play was favorably reviewed by Japanese critics and scholars.[7] English reviews were generally more favorable and to the point, understanding the meaning of this venture as the unique combination of Noh and Shakespeare.

Donald Richie, the well-known critic of *The Japan Times*, wrote a long appreciative review. He also raised a serious question for the Japanese actors and actresses who performed in this production in English:

I think all these elements – speech, dance, music plus Shakespeare – would have come even closer together if the play had not been given in English. Even though "Hamlet" does happen to be in that language, Noh plays are usually not – and it is the Noh which is naturally the stronger element in this combination. The reasons for my objection are apparent. The Noh is about, as its name suggests, perfection. No one ever saw a Noh play less than "perfect," though there are, of course, degrees of perfection in Japan. Thus, when the level of the music was so high as in this performance and where the motion was at least professional-looking, one was disturbed by pronunciation which could not be perfect since English was not the tongue of any of those performing. And such lines as "incestuous, murderous, damned Dane" call for more than conversation classes can provide.[8]

As a result of this critique, I decided to condense the play into a short Noh dance or a solo version, removing everything non-essential. There is a short dance form called *shimai*, performed in simple kimono, with only a few *ji-utai* chorus members and without orchestra. I thought of cutting even the chorus, so that I could sing the chorus part while I chanted and danced the *shite* main role at the same time. This format made it easier to tour, but perhaps more difficult to appreciate Noh fully for many of those who were seeing it for the first time. In 1990, the production toured to Denmark (Scandinavia Hotel), Sweden (The Puppet Theatre in Stockholm), Britain (Bristol and London), and the United States (Folger Shakespeare Library). So, too, the solo *Hamlet*, presented at the National Noh Theatre during the Shakespeare World Congress in Tokyo in 1992, accompanied by a flautist, but without the chorus and other members, may have been less interesting for those who had expected the ordinary style of Noh play. For such spectators, it stripped away too much of what they think is most distinctive about Noh.[9]

Following *Noh Hamlet*, I wrote *Noh Othello*, *Noh Macbeth*, and *Noh King Lear* in English set to Noh music and premiered them in 1986, 1987, and 1993 respectively. My Noh Shakespeare Group toured through the United States, starting in Macon, Georgia, and going on through South and North Carolina, from Harvard to California with *Noh Othello* and others in 1988.[10]

II

The next phase of my Noh Shakespeare work occurred some years ago, when Horigami Ken, a Noh critic, suggested I take Donald Richie's hint and translate my English Shakespearean Noh plays into Japanese, so that professional Noh actors could perform them. I translated my *Noh Othello* script into Japanese and set the same Noh melodies to it, taking over a year to do so. Needless to say, writing the script in poetic words (Noh is also a highly poetic form) and setting Noh melody to them were both extremely difficult tasks.

When I finished, I met Kanze Hideo (avant-garde Noh actor and brother of Kanze Hisao, who had worked with the Berliner Ensemble and Suzuki Tadashi in the Seventies). After a few months, Kanze answered that the script was already a finished work and thus rather difficult for him to perform. He had expected an unpolished piece which he could adapt in his own way. He even suggested that he would like to use a nude on the Noh stage as Desdemona and he asked for another script having more lines and no set music. I tried to answer his request and wrote another one, spending several hundred hours in the process, but I could not finish it. So I handed Kanze the unsatisfactory script and told him he could use it in any way he liked, but only if I could ask some other actor to perform the original script that he had not liked. He consented to this.

It was in 1992 that Tsumura Reijirô, a Kanze school performer, accepted the job and performed the original version of *Noh Othello*, without any change of words or melody, with his group "Ryokusenkai" at Hôshô Noh Theatre in Tokyo. This was the first Shakespearean Noh performance in Japanese, one such as Natsume Sôseki had suggested in 1911. Fortunately the *Asahi Shimbun*, which had carried Natsume's article eighty-one years before, sponsored it, thanks to efforts by Horigami. I wished that Natsume Sôseki's ghost had been at the theatre to review my play. One of the reasons more people enjoyed my Japanese *Noh Othello* was that they could understand the script, as it was mostly written in modern Japanese. But when this first version of *Noh Othello* was performed in 1992, it was criticized by some scholars and Noh connoisseurs for its mixture of classical and modern Japanese. So, I rewrote the play entirely in modern Japanese with the help of performers to produce a truly modern Japanese version. This 1995 version was also performed by Tsumura Reijirô.

A brief description of the opening scene of *Noh Othello* will give some idea of the play. In silence, a stage assistant carries in a *kosode*-kimono which represents the sleeping Desdemona. (In the 1995 version, we completely changed the opening scene by introducing a live actor, which made the production easier to understand though less symbolic.) The performance starts with flute music, as is the case with many classical Noh plays. Then the *shidai* short thematic song is chanted by the eight chorus members:

> Once put out thy light, where is that Promethean heat
> (Repeated) That can thy light relume? (Repeated)

Then, led by the entrance music, the curtain rises and Othello as *shite* enters slowly. He sings on the *hashigakari* bridgeway:

> It is the cause, it is the cause, my soul –

In the new version, Desdemona as *tsure* enters first, followed by Emilia as the *ai-kyogen*, who narrates for Desdemona. Again, this made the play easier. Then follows the duet between the chorus and *shite*, as the *shite* enters the main stage. He approaches the kimono (Desdemona in the 1995 version) and the chorus continues:

> One more and one more, and this the last.
> So sweet was ne'er so fatal. I must weep.

Hiding his face with a fan suggests a kiss; and holding an open palm in front of his forehead weeping. Desdemona wakes: "Who's there? Othello?" "Ay, Desdemona." (In these productions an actor took the role of Desdemona. In Noh, the gender of the performer is no problem because a mask is commonly used.)

So, the last scene of the original Shakespeare is the first scene of *Noh Othello*. It develops when, realizing he intends to kill her, Desdemona pleads for mercy: "Kill me tomorrow; let me live tonight." "But," the chorus chants: "Othello, whose heart was stone had no more ears/ To hear her last cry . . . he has stifled Desdemona. She does not move any more." Here I added some lines of my own, so as to enhance the intelligibility of the action within the Noh form. (Choral description is not unusual in Noh.) Returning to the murder scene, Othello drops his fan to show that her life has ended. Here, Shakespeare's Othello has some ten lines to express his feeling in poetic language. But, in *Noh Othello* I left him speechless for a few minutes. This is a test for the Noh performer who must draw on his ability to communicate non-verbally with the imagination of the spectator.

Emilia the *ai-kyogen* then enters and reveals the truth after learning what has happened. She also confesses that she knew everything and is really responsible. Why does Iago not appear in *Noh Othello*? I felt that while I could refer to him, he was not needed onstage. Noh works best with an economy of means, leaving more to the imagination, and in Noh, unfolding a plotline is not very important. One of the most popular Kyogen actors today, Nomura Mansai, displayed his excellent performance as the *ai-kyogen* Emilia – an unforgettable experience for the audience.

After Othello has learnt the truth in the second scene, he repents: ". . . being wrought/ Perplex'd in the extreme." And while he is praying: "O Desdemona! Forgive me!" the ghost of Desdemona appears. Most western tragedies end with the death of the hero or heroine. In Noh, death is not the end, but the beginning. The chorus chants for Othello: "O, it gives me wonder great as my content/ To see you here before me!" Othello dances with this phantasm. The climax of the play is approaching, for Noh is a dance opera in which the climax often comes during the performance of dance. "If it were now to die,/ 'Twere now to be most happy! For, I fear/ My soul hath her content so absolute/ That not another comfort like to this/ Succeeds in unknown fate . . ." They feel time cease, for they are blessed with a momentary experience of eternity, or an everlasting experience of the moment.

This could be the ending of *Noh Othello*, but Noh does not usually end this way. In reality, the morning comes, and the ghost of Desdemona disappears, with the chorus chanting:

> And nothing was but the voice of prayers,
> Nothing was left but the voice of prayers.

I wanted to change Shakespeare to be as true to the spirit of Zeami as possible. But here I was more influenced by his son Kanze Motomasa's masterpiece, *Sumidagawa*. In this play, the ghost of a child disappears as morning comes, after meeting its mother on the banks of the Sumida river during a commemorative sutra recitation by villagers on the anniversary of his death. (The play has been adapted by Benjamin Britten as *Curlew River*.)

I changed the last scene again in the 1995 version. I wanted to allow Othello, who repents fully, to be led to heaven by the ghost of Desdemona. I did this because I believe the main purpose of Noh is, as Zeami said, "to serve as a means to pacify people's hearts and to move the high and low alike."[11]

NOTES

1 Natsume Sôseki, "Tsubouchi Hakase to Hamlet" (Dr. Tsubouchi and Hamlet), *Tokyo Asahi Shimbun* June 5 and 6, 1911; *Sôseki Zenshu* (Complete Works of Natsume Sôseki) vol. 11 (Tokyo: Iwanami-shoten, 1965). See also Ueda Munakata Kuniyoshi, "Noh Othello," *Shakespeare Worldwide* 13, 1991.

2 Tsubouchi Shôyô, *Shakespeare Kenkyu Shiori* (Introduction to Shakespeare Studies), (Tokyo: Waseda University Press, 1928).

3 Thomas Rimer and Masakazu Yamazaki, *On the Art of the No Drama: The Major Treatises of Zeami* (Princeton: Princeton University Press, 1984), 64.

4 Ueda Munakata Kuniyoshi, "Noh to Shakespeare" (Noh and Shakespeare), in *The Eigo Bungaku Sekai* (The English Literature World), (Tokyo, August 1975); H. B. Durnell, *Japanese Cultural Influences on American Poetry and Drama* (Tokyo: Hokuseido, 1977).

5 Arai Yoshio, "Noh Hamlet o mite" (Seeing Noh Hamlet), *Noh Hamlet Program*, The Noh Shakespeare Group, 1983.

6 Upton Murakami, "A letter to NSG," *Noh Hamlet Souvenir Programme*, NSG, March 1985.

7 Yamazaki Yuichirô, "Hamlet-Noh saien wo mite" (Seeing revised *Noh Hamlet*), *The Nôgaku Times* 399, May 1, 1985.

8 Donald Richie, "*Hamlet* seen as Noh Drama," *The Japan Times*, March 30, 1985.

9 "Solo-performance" text with Noh musical notes contained together with two other versions in Ueda Munakata Kuniyoshi, *Hamlet in Noh Style: Collected Versions 1982–1990* (Tokyo: Kenkyûsha, 1991).

10 "*Othello* as Noh in the U.S.," *The New York Yomiuri*, September 2, 1988; "The Bard, Noh style" and "To be or not to be? Cover Story," *Telegram Tribune*, San Luis Obispo, Calif., September 3, 1988; Ueda Munakata Kuniyoshi, "*Noh Hamlet* in USA," *The Nihon Keizai Shimbun*, October 24, 1988.

11 Rimer and Yamazaki, *On the Art of the Noh Drama*, 40.

6

The Braggart Samurai: a Kyogen adaptation of Shakespeare's The Merry Wives of Windsor

MICHAEL SHAPIRO

Introduction

In a recent *New York Times* op-ed piece, the novelist Jane Smiley confessed to heresy: "My own feeling about Shakespeare is that all too often the words get in the way. Shakespeare was after all, a playwright, constructing action, theme, character, as well as poetry."[1] As the author of *A Thousand Acres*, a retelling of *King Lear* set in contemporary rural Iowa, Smiley's view is consistent with her own practice, and not much different from Shakespeare's own habit of making plays by adapting prose tales, chronicles, biographies, and other available texts. Subordinating Shakespeare's actual language to his literary and dramaturgical achievements sounds far less heretical outside of the English-speaking world, where Shakespeare has been and still is performed in other languages. Whereas the English-speaking theatre resists any large-scale updating of these early modern texts, elsewhere translation and adaptation are frequently used to bring the plays in alignment with spectators' linguistic and cultural expectations.[2] Recent stagings in Japan by Suzuki, Ninagawa, and others use contemporary, futuristic, timeless, or metaphoric settings, sometimes in concert with stylized performances based on traditional theatre.

There is, however, an important countercurrent toward a more consistent use of traditional Japanese theatrical forms in productions of Shakespeare. One example is Kurosawa's work in film, but there have been live productions of Shakespearean plays done entirely within the mode of Kabuki, Noh, or Bunraku, and which, for the sake of consistency, have relied on translations done with a deliberately archaic verbal palette.[3] When Takahashi Yasunari adapted Shakespeare's *The Merry Wives of Windsor* for performance in Kyogen style, he made no attempt to translate but rather created a new text in language intended to sound somewhat old-fashioned to the modern Japanese ear, as Japanese-speaking informants report. Under the title of *Hora Zamurai* (*The Braggart Samurai*), this version was performed at the Tokyo Globe Theatre in 1991 as part of a series which also included a Kabuki *Hamlet* directed by

Orita Kohji and a modern *King Lear* directed by J. A. Seazer, a disciple of
Terayama Shûji.

Takahashi's adaptation makes no attempt to cover the entire play. It is
limited to six scenes and involves only six characters, but it is still three or
four times the length of the typical Kyogen play. The major emphasis is on
Falstaff, here renamed as Suke-emon Horata, a *rônin*, or masterless samurai.
Just as Shakespeare quarried plays from other sources, often selecting or
rejecting material, remolding or even inventing characters and situations, so
Takahashi extracted from *The Merry Wives* a single line of action – the humiliation of Falstaff for attempting to seduce virtuous wives and cuckold their husbands. Of Shakespeare's three humiliations, Takahashi has dropped the
second – Falstaff's escape from Ford's house disguised as an old woman
whom Ford loathes and so beats – but he has preserved the same two as Boito
did in Verdi's opera, *Falstaff*: (1) his hiding in the basket of dirty laundry and
being dumped in the Thames, and (2) his ritualized punishment by "fairies"
at Herne's Oak. Entirely cut is the romantic subplot, Fenton's successful
wooing of Anne Page, and the comic caricatures of the play – Fenton's two
rivals, Dr. Caius and Slender, the Welsh schoolmaster Evans and his pupil
William, John Rugby, Shallow, the Host, Mistress Quickly and Master Page.
Falstaff's cronies, Pistol and Nym, his letter-bearers who inform Page and
Ford of their master's plan to seduce their wives, are replaced by the generic
Kyogen servants, Tarô Kaja and Jirô Kaja. Takahashi's choice of Kyogen as his
theatrical idiom was both traditional and innovative. While clearly paying
homage to one of Japan's traditional art forms, he chose a form with lower
status than either Noh or Kabuki, and one less well known to western spectators, and perhaps even to many Japanese. Whether performed in Japan or in
the west, one of the intriguing aspects of this production must have been its
integration of the archaic and the novel, as well as the combination of
Shakespearean play with Kyogen style.

History of Kyogen

Although the current repertory of some 260 Kyogen plays dates from the
seventeenth century, the form grew out of older popular entertainments. In
the Muromachi era (1336–1573), Kyogen plays mocked the *kuge*, or members
of the former ruling elite, through caricatures of dimwitted lords and
masters. Under Tokugawa rule (1603–1867), Kyogen and Noh flourished side
by side, with Kyogen providing scenes of comic relief within Noh plays or as
comic interludes between Noh works.[4]

Noh plays draw their material from literary sources, are essentially lyric dramas, stress dance and chant, and use a chorus. Noh actors usually perform in masks, and sometimes depict ghosts or spirits. By contrast, Kyogen plays are short pieces developing simple human situations through spoken monologue and dialogue, as well as through precise and lively movement. Songs, dances and masks are rarely used. Most Kyogen are comically realistic; some expose the frailties of high-ranking characters, while others explore everyday relations between husbands and wives, or masters and servants. Many Kyogen texts show how tricksters, e.g., wily servants and folkloric creatures like crabs, monkeys, and even mushrooms, deflate such powerful authority figures as the mountain priest (*yamabushi*), the arrogant lord (*daimyô*), and in Takahashi's play, the braggart samurai, who is borrowed from the Miles Gloriosus of western theatrical tradition. Kyogen, which is now regarded as one of the traditional arts of Japan, is no longer a purveyor of satire or of symbolic inversion for elite audiences, but must compete for patronage and audiences with other forms of theatre (both traditional and modern) within Japan's secular and commercialized entertainment industry.

Kyogen elements in *The Braggart Samurai*

At the Tokyo Globe-za, a Vitruvian reconstruction of Shakespeare's playhouse, *The Braggart Samurai* was played on a modified thrust stage which faintly echoed traditional Noh/Kyogen stages.[5] Instead of a square platform with a bridge, or *hashigakari*, and its three pines leading to a small off-stage enclosure, one saw at upstage center a large abstract pine tree created by a tall rectangular trunk bifurcating into two jagged branches, suggesting a cubist interpretation of a pine tree or perhaps Herne's Oak. Around the downstage perimeter, long metallic rods sprang gracefully from eight black disks.

In contrast to the postmodernist set (by Isozaki Arata, architect of the Globe), the actors in *The Braggart Samurai* wore traditional Kyogen costumes. The women, played by male actors, wore a length of white cotton cloth twined around the head (*binan boshi*) to signify gender and Horata (Falstaff) wore pantaloons that tapered at the ankle, thereby accentuating his stuffed belly, and sported a tall cylindrical hat of shiny black material (to signify his lordly pretensions) and a black bushy stage beard (highly unusual in Japan).

Kyogen methods of staging are deceptively simple and self-consciously theatrical. The high point of Kyogen technique in *The Braggart Samurai* is the scene with the laundry basket. Tarô Kaja and Jirô Kaja enter miming that they are carrying a large, heavy container from the bottom. After they set it down, several characters mime the rifling of its contents. When Horata needs a place to hide from Yakibei (Ford), he climbs into this virtual basket and of course is unseen by the jealous husband. When Omatsu (Mistress Ford) orders the basket carried away, the two servants grasp opposite ends of a real pole, from which we assume the basket to be suspended, and hoist it off the ground. The servants sing "Fair is foul, white is black . . ." as they circle the stage in a *michiyuki*, a conventional Kyogen travel scene. As they do, Horata sways, jounces, and scuttles as he moves forward in time with them, shifting position as the basket seems to roll from side to side. When the servants reach downstage center, ostensibly the river, they "dump Horata onto the floor . . . with an onomatopoeic sound of a splash, 'BOTCHAAN!'"

Just as Kyogen's parodies of Noh rely on the audience's familiarity with the more serious canon, *The Braggart Samurai* often alludes impiously to other Shakespearean plays. Horata's opening soliloquy, the Kyogen convention of self-identification called *nanori*, quotes Feste's song from the end of *Twelfth Night*. In describing the fallen state of the world and the ingratitude shown to former samurai, he complains that "they shut their gates against knaves and thieves, and as they say, the rain it raineth every day." Similarly, Tarô Kaja recalls an old saying that runs something like "To be or not to be, that is the question," while Yakibei laments "Oh, frailty, thy name is wife!", and Horata repeats part of Falstaff's disquisition on honor from *Henry IV, Part 1*. Horata's letter to Omatsu begins "Shall I compare thee to . . .," and then refers to a famous drama about passionate romantic love, as the flute plays Nino Rota's theme from Zeffirelli's film of *Romeo and Juliet*.

The mix of Kyogen elements and Shakespeare produced reciprocal effects on both traditions. In Takahashi's words, "You cannot kyogenize Shakespeare without at the same time Shakespeareanizing kyogen." Although *The Braggart Samurai* stretched Kyogen beyond its usual range, it also provided a critical lens through which to view *The Merry Wives*.

The Braggart Samurai as a critique of The Merry Wives

Takahashi's radical condensation of *The Merry Wives* stresses the humiliation of the title character and provides an implicit critique of Shakespeare's handling of the same material. At the end of *The Merry Wives*, Falstaff undergoes a kind of ritual punishment. The fairies "Pinch him, and burn him, and turn him about."[6] Shakespeare spends considerable time having Falstaff punished by the fairies, and then scolded and mocked by the householders, before turning to the resolution of the love-plot, and then rounding off the play with movement toward social harmony. In terms of its moral economy, the play poses Falstaff's efforts to seduce the wives as a greater threat to the stability of middle-class marriage than Ford's groundless jealousy, the tragic and near-tragic implications of which Shakespeare explores elsewhere. In short, the original text insists that Falstaff's punishment and recantation precede his readmission to the world of the play.

As Peter Evans has pointed out, in naturalistic productions, Falstaff is pinched by fairies clearly recognizable to him as well as to the audience as local children, sometimes William's schoolmates, with other members of the community participating as if in a masquerade.[7] He is reprimanded rather mildly, and much theatrical stress is placed on his reconciliation with the community by means of final songs and dances, which present the image of Falstaff now symbolically in harmony with the good burghers of Windsor. In Verdi's *Falstaff*, to which Takahashi alludes in a note on onomatopoeic pinching in Italian,[8] the operatic way of representing this social reintegration is to have the entire cast sing the fugue, "*Tutto nel mondo e burla*" (the whole world is a joke), a conclusion similar to that of *The Braggart Samurai*.[9]

But Evans favors another group of productions for creating the impression that "the mortal world has been restored to harmony through the intervention of the world of faery, through a purgation by a punishment."[10] *The Braggart Samurai* avoids any such stress on the genuinely supernatural: the other characters are transparently obvious to us behind their Noh-like masks, even though Horata takes them for the demons who haunt the pine grove. As the final scene begins, Omatsu enters alone and instructs the others, waiting offstage, to enter when she says, "Look there! Those weird Shadows!" She tells them to do whatever they wish to him, "pinch him or scratch him or beat him." When she gives the signal, the other characters enter, "all wearing different masks, accompanied by scary music on the flute." Omatsu pretends to be afraid of these "evil demons" and begs Horata to help her. His response is right out of the battle scene of *Henry IV, Part 1*. Instead of coming to her aid, he lies face down on the ground and pretends to be dead: "Look, everybody, I am dead." The "demons" then torment him physically – pinching, stomping, twisting his arm, kicking, and finally tickling him – accompanied by the Japanese onomatopoeic "*gutsu*." They then make him apologize "for using women disgracefully," for telling "braggart lies," for "drinking far too much sake," for ignoring "the solemn vows of marriage," and for "violating the laws of society." He promises to become a virtuous man, whatever they wish, at which point the demons unmask in turn, taunting him as they do by reminding him of their previous roles in his life – the wives he tried to seduce, the servants who carried him out in the laundry basket, and "the familiar jealous cuckolded husband." United against him for his past behavior, they line up and Yakibei drags him by the hand to face the others, ordering him to "bow down with your head to the ground, and apologize in earnest once more."

Horata's response at this point is totally different from Falstaff's. It is one thing to apologize in order to propitiate a crowd of evil demons, as he takes them to be, and quite another to grovel before angry villagers whom he knows. Instead of capitulating to their communal pressure, Horata stands his ground: "I refuse to apologize," and turning to face the audience he explains why (with an echo of *As You Like It*):

All the world is but a joke, and all the men and women merely jesters. Life is made of laughing at just as much as of being laughed at. The quantity of tears in this world is constant, and so is the quantity of laughter. For everyone who stops laughing, some one starts laughing. I for one will go on laughing until the very end. I will laugh last and best. And I swear by this gigantic belly of mine that my philosophy shall never change.

And he punctuates this defiance, this trumping of morality with the power of laughter, with "a typical Kyogen laugh, a Gargantuan laugh." Unlike *The Merry Wives*, where a penitent Falstaff is generously or patronizingly reintegrated by the Windsorites, Horata forces the others to accept him on his own terms. The finale, in which Yakibei invites them all to "celebrate the festival of our patron god" and "dance the night joyfully away, Sir Suke-emon and all," represents social cohesion as finales of *The Merry Wives* often do, but is here more of a triumph for Horata than for the middle-class townsfolk. It is he who leads the others in a Kyogen dance to the accompaniment of flute and drum, and in singing a song which Takahashi's note tells us incorporates "a very popular traditional dance-song,"

> All the world is a kyogen farce.
> All the men and women are jesters.
>   Hey, hey, nonny nonny, hey, nonny no!
> If it be so, I would rather be
> A dancing jester than a watching one.
>   Hey, hey, nonny nonny, hey, nonny no!

Shakespeare, like many comic dramatists and directors, employs a progression of moves from repentance and forgiveness to social harmony to theatricality. In comedies such as *The Merchant of Venice* and *Twelfth Night*, when a scapegoat figure is driven out of the world of the play, there are usually some gestures toward reintegrating him, but the final image of social harmony is nonetheless imperfect to the degree that he resists such gestures. Nearly all of Shakespeare's comedies make a final move to theatricality, either through a self-referential epilogue or plaudite, and nearly all productions suggest the restoration of social harmony by presenting the entire cast in a concluding trope – a choral song, an ensemble dance, or the curtain call itself.

The Braggart Samurai makes this sequence of moves without the relatively heavy moralizing of The Merry Wives. Instead of an abject, defanged Falstaff, more or less grudgingly admitted to polite society, the Kyogen text makes Horata's refusal to apologize into a celebration, not only of theatre but of a theatrical vision of life as well. His defiance represents a rebellion against the constraints of civilized order, proclaims the superiority of mirth to morality, dissolves ethical issues by invoking the motif of theatrum mundi, and so reminds us that we have come to the theatre to be entertained by professional actors and not to hear a sermon against adultery.

Conclusion

The Braggart Samurai's sharp critique of Shakespeare's moral didacticism should prevent us from viewing it as yet another testimonial to the "Universality of the Bard." From a postcolonialist perspective, such universalizing views are especially troubling, for they usually depend on and at the same time conceal underlying assumptions of a superior imperialistic culture colonizing an indigenous theatrical tradition. Some critics have leveled this charge at a version of King Lear performed in the South Indian style known as Kathakali.[11] But Japan's history is not India's.

From a Japanese point of view, however, and perhaps also from some Indian perspectives, it may not be quite so clear who is appropriating whose cultural property. Although Japan opened itself to western influence, more or less under threat of force, and was occupied by the United States after World War II, it never experienced the lengthy and pervasive colonial domination imposed on many third world countries. A work like The Braggart Samurai might well suggest that (once again) the Japanese have imported something from the west, thoroughly absorbed it, and in so doing transformed it into something quite their own. They have even exported it back to the west, as in the present case, where the play toured in London, as well as in such "colonies" as Wales and Australia. Both in Japan and on tour, part of its appeal was no doubt its blend of old and new.

Whether exported or consumed locally, traditional art forms like Kyogen risk being labeled as quaint and regarded as fetishized commodities, especially when they are cut loose from their historical contexts or proffered as somehow immune to historical change. Historical forces, of course, have shaped the development of Kyogen and all other forms of Japanese theatre, so that while such traditions may be unbroken (unlike those of the English theatre), what has been preserved can be seen as evolved or atrophied – depending on the performers. For that reason, some Japanese question the value of preserving and reviving their classical theatrical forms.

Takahashi's reluctance to engage controversial social or political issues of our own day stands out against many recent English-language productions of *The Merry Wives*, which treat it more explicitly as a vehicle for exploring the vulnerability of women in a patriarchal culture and for celebrating the wit and ingenuity by which they manage to repel a would-be adulterer and cure an insanely jealous husband. It would be interesting to see whether the conventions of Kyogen, especially those governing female impersonation, could be used for comic inquiry into the problematic roles and status of women in modern Japan, where women continue to assume subordinate roles in public life but are said to wield enormous power within their households. Instead of directly confronting such problems, *The Braggart Samurai* focuses on the stylization of Kyogen conventions and on the virtuosity of the leading actor thereby evoking the nostalgic illusion of a timeless artefact.

Although *The Braggart Samurai* does not engage topical issues, it makes some significant cultural and intercultural moves. The use of Kyogen's particular brand of metatheatrical play blurs the boundaries between different levels of illusion and thus achieves a kind of ontological destabilization. Such destabilization reinforces the triumph at the end of the play of theatricality over morality, although this deeply subversive move in turn is safely contained within the social, aesthetic, and commercial frameworks supplied by the theatrical occasion. Takahashi's decision to adapt the play in a Kyogen rather than a contemporary mode is a statement about Japanese cultural politics and intercultural exchange, albeit not a simple one. His radical extension of Kyogen reveals both the richness and the limitations of the traditional form, while his appropriation of *The Merry Wives* indicates both his delight in exploring Shakespeare's play from a fresh point of view as well as his willingness to criticize its homiletic ending.

NOTES

1 Jane Smiley, "Shakespeare in action," *New York Times*, December 2, 1996, sec. A13.
2 Dennis Kennedy, "Shakespeare without his language," in Dennis Kennedy, ed., *Foreign Shakespeare*, (Cambridge: Cambridge University Press, 1993), 5.
3 Kabuki adaptations of *Macbeth* and *Othello* were produced by Satô Shôzô at the University of Illinois at Urbana-Champaign in the 1980s; a Bunraku version of

The Tempest adapted by Fujita Minoru was done in Osaka; and I have seen a videotape of Ueda Munakata Kuniyoshi's Noh adaptation of *Othello* done at Shizuoka University.

4 William LaFleur, *The Karma of Words: Buddhism and the Literary Arts in Medieval Japan* (Berkeley: University of California Press, 1983), 143. For useful background on Kyogen, see chapter 7: "Society upside-down: Kyogen as satire and as ritual."

5 Fujita Minoru and Isozaki Arata, *The Globe: A Shakespearean Scholar Talks with the Architect of the Globe* (Tokyo: The Globe, 1988); for a translation of Takahashi Yasunari's *Hora-zamurai, a Kyogen adaptation of Shakespeare's The Merry Wives of Windsor* (Tokyo: privately printed, 1993) see Mulryne and Sasayama, *Shakespeare on the Japanese Stage* (Cambridge: Cambridge University Press, 1998). Subsequent references to the play refer to this version. I am grateful to Professor Takahashi for sending me a copy of this text and videotape of the Globe production which I had seen during the World Shakespeare Congress in 1991.

6 William Shakespeare, *The Riverside Shakespeare* (Boston: Houghton Mifflin Company, 1974), 5.5.101. All citations of Shakespeare's works refer to this edition.

7 Peter Evans, "'To the oak, to the oak!' The finale of *The Merry Wives of Windsor*," *Theatre Notebook* 40 (1986), 106–14.

8 Takahashi, *The Braggart Samurai*, 22.

9 Arrigo Boito, *Libretto for Verdi's Falstaff*, translated by Walter Ducloux (New York: G. Schirmer, 1962).

10 Evans, "'To the oak!'" 107.

11 Susan Bennett, *Performance Nostalgia: Shifting Shakespeare and the Contemporary Past* (London: Routledge, 1996), 72. Cf. Philip B. Zarrilli, "For whom is the king a king? Intercultural production, perception, and reception in a *Kathakali King Lear*," in *Critical Theory and Performance*, ed. Janelle G. Reinelt and Joseph R. Roach (Ann Arbor: University of Michigan Press, 1992).

PART II

MODERN PRODUCTIONS
(POST WORLD WAR II)

7

Weaving the spider's web: interpretation of character in Kurosawa Akira's *Throne of Blood* (*Kumonosu-jô*)

PAULA VON LOEWENFELDT

It is said that before a Noh actor makes his entrance along the *hashigakari*, or passageway, he sits staring into a mirror at his masked face until his self and the self embodied in the mask are one. It is an apt metaphor for Kurosawa Akira's 1957 film *Throne of Blood* (*Kumonosu-jô*), a film permeated by features of traditional Japanese performance and visual art, but one which is also a unique and compelling personal response to Shakespeare's *Macbeth*. Experiencing Kurosawa's work becomes a contemplation of renaissance drama in a strange yet distinctly similar guise: until the play and the film seem indistinguishable, and this despite differences of culture and genre.

As Anthony Davies observed in 1988, *Throne of Blood* has become "part of our thinking about Shakespeare's *Macbeth*."[1] It continues to be praised as both the finest film treatment of Shakespeare and, as Robert Hapgood noted in 1994, "among the few transpositions of Shakespeare's dramas into other performing arts that have been widely regarded as masterpieces in their own right."[2] And yet, for forty years *Throne of Blood* has been too often categorized – and thus marginalized – by western critics as an essentially "Japanized" version of *Macbeth*, rather than one (albeit Japanese) filmmaker's engagement with *Macbeth*: one which incorporates, but which is not limited by, Japanese traditional forms. The distinction is an important one as it directly shapes both the viewer's response to the film and what the film is allowed to say about the play. Kurosawa's depiction of character, for example, has often been dismissed as a recreation of Japanese theatrical tradition: significant aspects of Kurosawa's film, therefore, have been ignored or misinterpreted. Part of the problem is an assertion – sometimes implied, sometimes quite blatant – that by using Japanese dramatic form Kurosawa denudes *Macbeth* of its complex treatment of human personality.

In 1983, David Desser combined his interpretation of the Noh drama with what he understood to be the Japanese view of nature: "Kurosawa attempts, in *Throne of Blood*, to duplicate the symbology of the Nô theatre through a substitution of nature for humanity . . . There is a constant attempt to let Nature make all the statements here, to let the action occur in Nature . . . Human interaction is eliminated . . . humanity is de-emphasized: form is all."[3] It is certainly true that the highly stylized, symbolically grounded features of Noh are important components of *Throne of Blood*. Kurosawa himself has elaborated on that fact.[4] It is likewise true that man's ineffable interaction with nature has been a recurring theme in Kurosawa's work.[5] But it is hard to reconcile Desser's notions with what actually occurs in the film. From Washizu's and Miki's crazed ride through the rain-swept, lightning-split, demonhaunted forest to Washizu's slow, hypnotic, horrific fall to his death – pierced through with arrows, including one right through his neck – the action may be amplified by nature, but it is most certainly carried out by human beings.

The perception among western critics that the film's characters are dehumanized is by no means confined to those who have focused on Kurosawa's use of Japanese dramatic forms or aesthetic roots. In a 1994 political analysis of *Macbeth* on film, E. Pearlman speaks of the "frigidity of personal relationship" in *Throne of Blood*. Pearlman describes the society as one where communication is "stylized, formal, and stilted," where "relationships between individuals are remarkably sterile," and where the marriage between Washizu and Lady Asaji is one of "understated but unrelieved hostility."[6] This culturally biased critique is an unusually forthright expression of the resistance among many western critics to the notion that Macbeth, his lady, or Banquo can maintain their human identity, complexity, and particularly their warmth, when played in a traditional Japanese – rather than western renaissance – guise.[7]

Perhaps western critics have tried too hard to see *Throne of Blood* through what they think of as Japanese eyes, so that attempts at cultural understanding may result in cultural misunderstanding. In his 1995 essay on globalization and culture, Iyotani Toshio writes: "The idea of Japanese culture evokes *Kabuki*, *Noh*, and *Bunraku*, and these are what shape the image of Japan . . . the forms of such institutions remain the same, however, their meaning changes with the passage of time from one era to another."[8] On the other hand, a Japanese interpretation of a western text may also be artificially constructed. The notion of a "Western culture," according to Iyotani, "was created consciously in Japan as a way to project its own cultural standing in the world." Too often in Japan the tendency is to "assume, implicitly or explicitly, that the polar opposite of the West is Asia."[9]

These cross-cultural pitfalls aside, it is important to recognize that Japan has produced a rich, sophisticated and often experimental Shakespearean tradition of its own: a tradition Kurosawa Akira's *Throne of Blood*, *The Bad Sleep Well*, and *Ran* all draw from and have contributed to.[10] When a western critic asserts, as Davies did in 1988, that *Throne of Blood* "has extended the frontiers of discussion on the play and has made Western scholarship more aware of the universal appeal of Shakespeare's dramatic material,"[11] that critic comes dangerously close to merely reflecting a western bias that persists in ignoring the fact that Shakespeare has been alive and well in Japan for nearly 120 years.

Recognizing that Shakespeare is a familiar commodity in Japan, that his works ceased being an exotic import almost a century ago, lends depth to an appreciation of Kurosawa's personal engagement with *Macbeth*. The challenge is to approach *Throne of Blood* in such a way that Kurosawa's treatment of Shakespeare's *Macbeth* is seen and credited as something particular in and of itself while, simultaneously, acknowledging the inherently Japanese strands – historical, cultural, and aesthetic – that he consciously wove into the construction of this film.

Leah Marcus notes, in a different context, that when directors "localize" Shakespeare they are not just doing something novel. Rather, they are engineering "a set of encounters between disparate cultural situations in order to open up ways for audiences to rediscover the plays at places where remoteness and accessibility meet," and this, in turn, serves to circumvent "the over-familiarity of the traditional Renaissance Shakespeare by showing us the cultural otherness of what we thought we understood."[12] A case in point is Kurosawa's intensification of Banquo's (Miki's) relationship with Macbeth (Washizu) – and, by extension, with Lady Macbeth (Asaji) – a relationship Kurosawa places at the heart of the drama. Foregrounding this triangle, Kurosawa brings a new perspective to the understanding of character in *Macbeth*: in particular, to the comfortable notion of Banquo's inherent, if passive, nobility. Kurosawa localizes these characters, in part, by his use of Noh "masks."

In his 1971 interview with Japanese film critic Satô Tadao, Kurosawa observed that Noh "has a defined style, and in devoting himself to it faithfully, the actor becomes possessed."[13] Kurosawa said that prior to filming he showed each of his principal actors photographs of the Noh mask most reflective of their individual character: to Mifune Toshirô (Washizu) the mask called *Heida*, the warrior; to Yamada Isuzu (Lady Asaji) the mask called *Shakumi*, the "beauty no longer young," which represents "the image of a woman about to go mad"; to Naniwa Chieko (the witch) the mask called *Yamamba*, representing "the witch in the wood"; and to Chiaki Minoru (Miki) the mask named *Chûjô*, the apparition of a nobleman," a more sophisticated, more aristocratic mask than that of *Heida*.[14]

Despite the fact that the amplification and exploration of Banquo's character is surely one of the most significant transformations Kurosawa makes to *Macbeth*, there has been some curious resistance in western criticism to accepting Miki as Kurosawa's Banquo.[15] And yet, when Kurosawa refers to the mask *Chûjô* in the same context with that of *Heida, Shakumi,* and *Yamamba,* and when he specifically speaks of it as representing "the warrior who was murdered by Macbeth and later reappears as an apparition," surely he signals that in *Throne of Blood* Miki is, in fact, Banquo. In the film, Kurosawa moves his Banquo to center stage with all the attendant intricacy and complication of characterization that implies – in the process, radically altering the underlying narrative structure of Shakespeare's play.

Overarching *Macbeth*'s five acts and twenty-eight scenes are the 2,134 lines of poetry. When the text is laid out flat and visualized as a horizontal, Shakespeare's verse narration can be read as a deceptively simple, elegant binary, equally divided in two at the beginning of the banquet scene:

> MACBETH
> Both sides are even. Here I'll sit in the midst.
> Be large in mirth; anon we'll drink a measure
> The table round. (*To First Murderer*) There's blood
> upon thy face.
> MURDERER
> (*aside to Macbeth*) 'Tis Banquo's, then.
> MACBETH
> 'Tis better thee without than he within.
> Is he dispatched? (3.4.9–14)[16]

The physical center of the poetic text becomes the play's dramatic turning point: one side of the narrative divide contains the initial prophecy of the witches and the murder of Duncan; the other sidesteps to the Macduff family subplot before leading, finally, to the inevitable downfall of Macbeth and Lady Macbeth. The assassination of Banquo and his reappearance as a ghost bridge these two sections, marking the moment when all likelihood of redemption ends.

In *Throne of Blood,* Kurosawa eliminates the Macduff family subplot – the Macduff character himself is depicted as the aged retainer, Noriyasu, and relegated to a virtual cameo appearance.[17] With Miki now one facet of a three-part dynamic, Kurosawa uses the mid-point of the film, the scene in the "forbidden room," to highlight the murder of Lord Tsuzuki as the moment when evil is first fully embraced. Kurosawa then divides *Macbeth*'s five acts into three, a construction both reflective of Noh and another way he localizes Shakespeare. As Hapgood notes: "The whole energy system of the film derives from the pattern of extreme containment followed by explosive release that characterizes the rhythm of Noh. Kurosawa's way of describing Noh's pervasive *jo/ha/kyû* structure [in the *Autobiography*] as

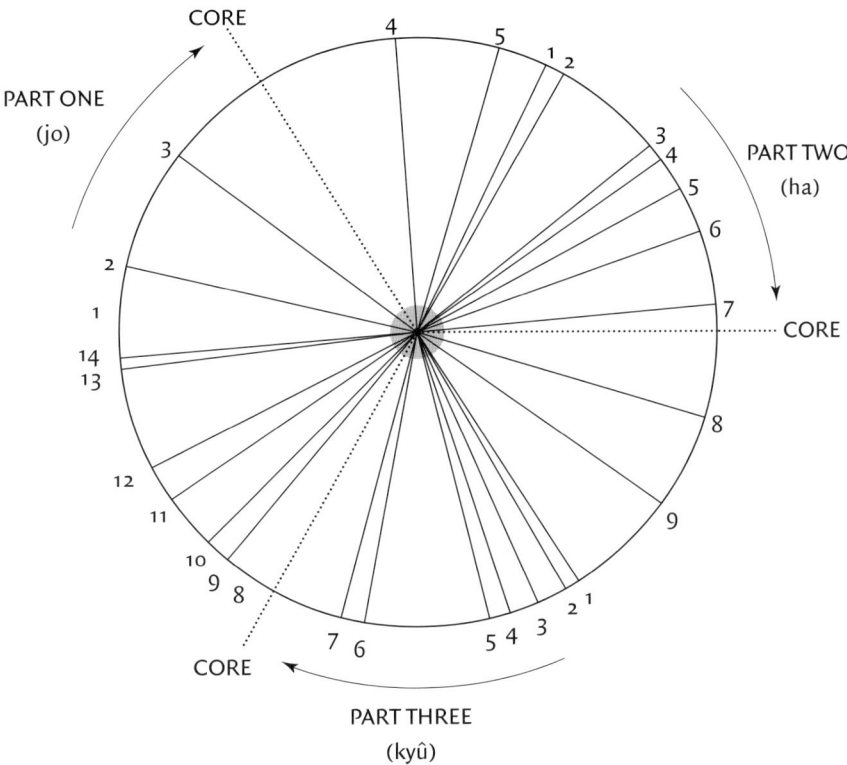

Figure 1 Kurosawa borrows Noh's *jo* (introduction), *ha* (destruction), *kyû* (haste) structure, transforming *Macbeth*'s 5 acts and 28 scenes into three parts of equal duration – each part with an increasing number of scenes (5, 9, and 14) – to produce a continuously heightened speed of narration. Three core scenes are linked visually, thematically, and geometrically, creating a set of references that work recursively across the film.

'introduction/destruction/haste' is full of suggestions when applied to *Throne of Blood*."[18]

While Kurosawa maintains *Macbeth*'s twenty-eight scene count, the three parts are of equal duration with each part containing an increasing number of scenes: the first part has five, the second nine, and the third fourteen.[19] This produces the effect (see figure 1) of a continuously heightened speed of narration. Part one ("jo, introduction")[20] lingers over the witch's initial prediction and Washizu's and Miki's approach to Cobweb Castle; part two ("ha, destruction") vividly details the events surrounding Lord Tsuzuki's murder and the reactions of the main characters; finally, part three ("kyû, haste"), in rapid-fire succession, depicts Miki's murder, the banquet scene, Asaji's miscarriage,[21] the witch's second prediction, Asaji's madness, the assault on Cobweb Castle and, finally, Washizu's bizarre execution at the hands of his own men.[22]

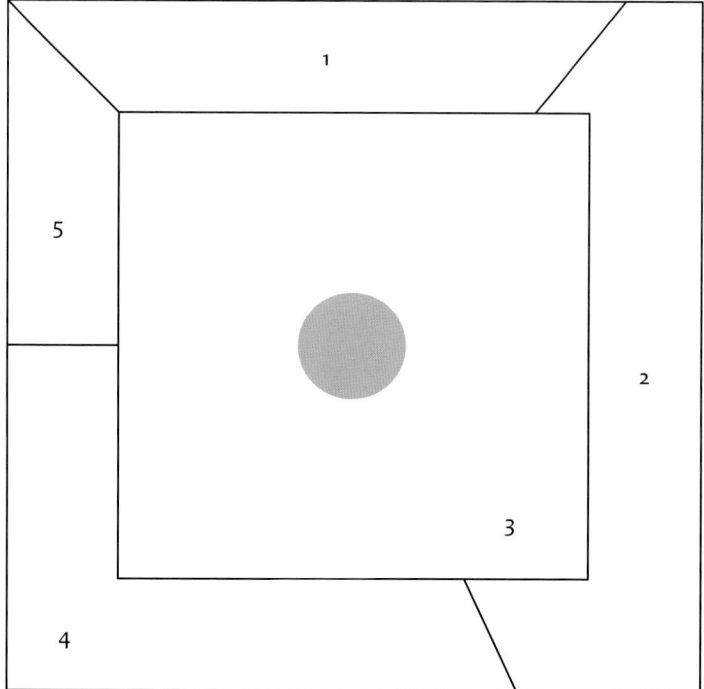

Figure 2 Part I, *jo* (introduction), 5 scenes: (1) foreshadowing, the fog-drenched plain and the ruin of Cobweb Castle; (2) inside the Castle, Lord Tsuzuki gets word of the fighting; (3) in this first core scene, Miki and Washizu stand deep in the Cobweb Forest at the hut of the demon woman, Yamamba, listening to her prediction; (4) Washizu and Miki criss-cross the fog-bound plain and, resting at the outskirts of the Castle, laugh at the predic-tion; (5) the prediction begins to come true when Lord Tsuzuki honors the two men.

Each of the three parts then has a core sequence, which is linked visually, thematically, and geometrically – their relative positions form 120-degree angles in figure 1 – with the cores of the other two parts, creating a set of references that work recursively across the film. By sketching the confluence of these core sequences, we can see Shakespeare's elegant, linear narrative, whose surface forms a pentahedron, but which operates at a deeper, binary level, become the circular, intricately interlaced, three-dimensional construction that gave the film its Japanese name, a name which clearly evokes evil: *Kumonosu-jô* (The Castle of the Spider's Web).[23]

At the heart of part 1 (see figure 2), Miki and Washizu stand deep in the Cobweb Forest at the hut of the demon woman, Yamamba, listening to her prediction. They are contained within the globe of the darkened woods and starkly lit enclosure, but they are not yet part of that evil. The demon at first

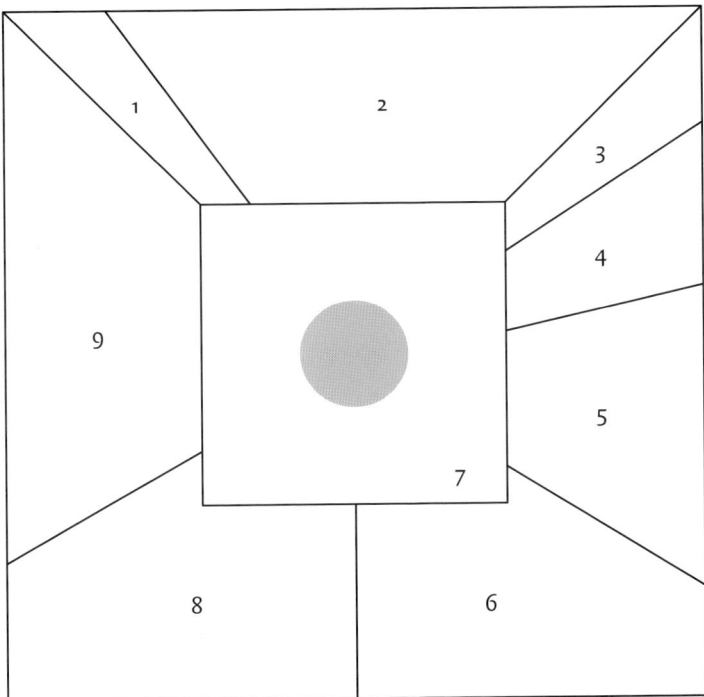

Figure 3 Part II, *ha* (destruction), 9 scenes: (1) idyllic shots of North Castle; (2) Lady Asaji warns Washizu of Tsuzuki's intentions and Miki's duplicity; (3) Tsuzuki arrives at Castle, gives Washizu command of forces; (4) Asaji again warns Washizu to act; (5) Washizu's retainers see the blood-stained wall in the Forbidden Room; (6) Asaji says this is the moment, then drugs the guards; (7) core scene of Washizu going to murder Lord Tsuzuki and Asaji's "dance" before the blood-stained wall; (8) Noriyasu flees with Tsuzuki's son, and Miki refuses them entrance to Cobweb Castle; (9) Miki meets Washizu at the head of Tsuzuki funeral cortege and escorts him into Cobweb Castle.

appears to symbolize the forces of a benevolent universe – she sits profiled, dressed all in white, spinning and chanting. She actually embodies a malevolent, capricious fate, a force that has the power to consume: having completed her prophecy, she stands and, along with her hut, vanishes into the air, leaving behind a mound of human skulls.[24]

The core sequence of part 2 (see figure 3) takes place in the "forbidden room" at North Castle from which Washizu goes out to murder Lord Tsuzuki. Washizu and Lady Asaji are foregrounded before a wall stained with another traitor's blood. Regarded closely, that blood stain takes on the appearance of a pine tree – the symbol of spiritual presence that backdrops Noh's traditional performance space.[25] Like the Cobweb Forest, whose wood harbors the witch's hut with its background of mounded skulls, the sacred pine is now evil, made of human blood. When the scene's imagery is read this way,

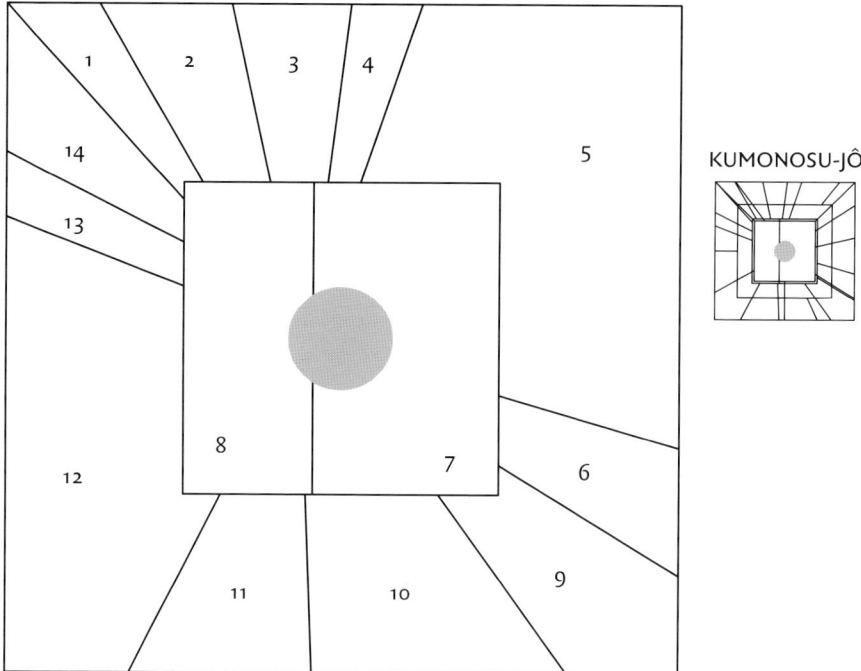

KUMONOSU-JÔ

Figure 4 Part III, kyû (haste), 14 scenes: (1) Washizu's men on turrets of Cobweb Castle;
(2) Washizu to make Miki's son his heir, but Asaji says she's pregnant; (3) Miki scorns his
son's disbelief in the prediction; (4) Miki's horse returns riderless; (5) banquet scene and
Miki's ghost; (6) servants talk of trouble; (7) Asaji miscarries, rebellion starts, and, in the
third core shot, Washizu rides through the gates of Cobweb Castle towards (8) the witch
and three apparitions in the wood; (9) attacking forces mass; (10) Washizu rallies men
with the second prediction; (11) birds overwhelm the Castle; (12) Asaji goes mad and the
"forest" approaches; (13) Washizu killed by his own men as Noriyasu leads the attack on
the Castle; (14) the Cobweb Castle fades into fog.
    Insert: the confluence of the three core scenes forms a three-dimensional spider's web.

Lady Asaji's weird spinning movements before the blood-stained wall look
less like frenzied dancing[26] and more like the stomping Noh step called *ashi-
byôshi*. According to Japanese director Suzuki Tadashi, this step is "not necessarily to tread down or suppress evil enemies, but to arouse their energy."[27]
Asaji's spinning doubles that of Yamamba even as it attempts ultimately to
harness and control the witch's power.[28]

    The central image of part 3 (see figure 4) mirrors, overlays, and subsumes
those of parts 1 and 2. Washizu rides out of the gates of the Cobweb Castle,
heading toward the demon in the woods. He leaves the familiarity of the
human fortress to demand a second prophecy from Yamamba. Seen poised at
a gallop within the gates of the Cobweb Castle, Washizu is still an

embodiment of the soul caught within the space between two worlds.[29] In the next scene, after he blindly accepts Yamamba's final prediction, the demon will vanish to be replaced by three apparitions whose words signal that Washizu is now one of them. They counsel an unbridled, savage violence: "If you walk the way of the demons, walk it in the most cruel, hideous manner"; "If you build a mountain of dead bodies, build it so it reaches the sky"; and, "If you want to shed blood, let it run like a river."[30]

Judging from their costumes, the apparitions ultimately derive from *The Tale of the Heike*, the twelfth-century saga about the historic, bloody rivalry between the Taira and Minamoto clans. Along with *The Tale of Genji*, the *Heike* is both a traditional and a consistent influence on all forms of Japanese art and drama; it is a historical backdrop for Kurosawa's *jidai-geki*, or period pieces.[31] In the *Heike*, the most heinous crime is perpetrated at the end of the long civil war by the victorious Yoritomo, the head of the Minamoto clan. Pathologically insecure – even about his own relations, whom he eventually hunts down and kills at the insistence of his wife Masako[32] – Yoritomo orders the round-up and slaughter of all the Taira children. It is his retainer, Tokimasu, who is charged with carrying out the massacre; the *Heike* says of him, "Many times a father and a grandfather himself, Tokimasu did not like what he was doing, but there seemed no alternative; men must accommodate themselves to the times."[33] If Yoritomo's violent megalomania is a plausible referent for Washizu, the philosophical acquiescence of Tokimasu serves the same function for Miki.

Miki plays a pivotal role across the film's three-part structure. In part 1, he appears in every one of Washizu's scenes, in virtually every shot: forcing their way through the Cobweb Forest; encountering the witch; crisscrossing the fog-drenched plain to come to rest at the approach to Cobweb Castle. Miki says to Washizu: "We dream of what we want. What samurai does not want to become lord of a castle." After the first part of the prediction has come true, they walk grim-faced, shoulder to shoulder, back toward the camera. In a very real sense, part 1 belongs to both these men.

In part 2, Miki appears less frequently, but he is under constant suspicion, first by Lady Asaji and later by Washizu when Miki is made protector of the Cobweb Castle itself. After Lord Tsuzuki's murder, Miki refuses sanctuary to Tsuzuki's son and Noriyasu, even driving them from the gates. However, when Washizu appears at the head of Tsuzuki's funeral cortege, Miki rides out to meet him. There is a moment's silent confrontation, they turn and together escort the coffin into the courtyard, and Miki remarks, "The evil spirit in the forest did see the future very clearly." The last shots in this sequence mirror those of part 1: only this time, as Miki and Washizu move toward the camera, they no longer walk side by side. Miki goes ahead and, looking back over his shoulder, says, "We will talk some other time."

In the banquet scene in part 3, Miki's ghost appears in close-up: white, profiled, the apparition is visually reminiscent of the witch in the wood at the moment when her malevolence has not yet been revealed. This is a key to Miki's character. Shortly before he is murdered, Miki upbraids his son for not believing in the prophecy. They are the last words he speaks. "I do not care what you think," he tells the boy. "It is no dream that Washizu has offered to make you his heir. Think, you can make a whole castle your own without shedding a drop of blood."

It is relatively safe to assume that one of Kurosawa's models was his life-long friendship with Uekusa Keinosuke, whom he describes in *An Autobiography* as a "novelist, scriptwriter, playwright, friend from grammar school days."[34] Kurosawa writes of a temporary estrangement from Uekusa that occurred following their collaboration on the screenplay for the 1948 gangster film, *Drunken Angel* – it stemmed from an ideological dispute over the individual's responsibility in the face of evil:

Our separation at this point was not caused by that terrible gap, that unbridgeable gulf that Uekusa claims he found between our fundamental natures. Nothing so serious as that. That's only his excuse . . . our fundamental differences are not differences at all. Uekusa and I are just very good friends from our days of battling on stilts: we are fighting friends.[35]

The passage suggests an intellectual, emotional, even physical rivalry. There is a tone of one-upmanship here, a hint of smugness, even disgust. Nonetheless, there is also evident a profound understanding of the other person, the kind of understanding that is deeply rooted in long, mutual experience. It consists of knowing just how far the other will go, perhaps even just how far he can be trusted. The danger – as both Banquo and Miki find out – is that the loyalty produced by this kind of friendship may be based on an illusion of security founded on nothing more substantial than one's own needs.

Perhaps because Banquo is murdered early on, and we cannot fully engage his character, the nature and extent of his complicity with Macbeth remain somewhat ambiguous.[36] Kurosawa's Miki is a different story. His is an overt complicity; his loyalties are clearly drawn. *Throne of Blood* is set in pre-Tokugawa Japan, a society marked by opportunism and one in which samurai like Washizu and Miki were often power brokers. Miki sides with Lord Tsuzuki's murderer, doubtless because Washizu is an old friend, but also because Yamamba's predictions have come true. Washizu has won the castle, and Miki's own family fortunes have benefited as a result.

Working from *Throne of Blood*'s geometric design is not simply an exercise in form-for-form's sake (Japanese or otherwise). Rather, it offers a way of seeing the film's many components as separate and essential strands in a complex and extraordinary transposition of *Macbeth*. It provides specific reference points for the features of Japanese culture and history, as well as the reflections of Kurosawa's own life experience, that may be read in the film. It even makes possible a discussion of the culturally loaded question of Kurosawa's depiction of human relationships from a less culturally grounded point of view. Perhaps most important, by presenting an immediately accessible comparison of the structures of the play and the film, it helps pinpoint those aspects of *Macbeth* that Kurosawa found compelling.[37]

In *Macbeth*, Banquo has only a minor role. He is an active presence for little more than 50 percent of the drama – on stage, alive but in the wings, or manifest as a ghost – and he speaks less than 120 lines. Nevertheless, Kurosawa is clearly drawn to the possibilities inherent in the Banquo/Macbeth relationship, a relationship whose significance is suggested by the transitional positions held by the Banquo murder and the banquet scenes. Miki's participation in more than 78 percent of *Throne of Blood* is ample evidence of the depth of Kurosawa's personal engagement with the questions of friendship, loyalty and betrayal he found in Shakespeare.

Each of the three main characters in *Throne of Blood* is destroyed by an illusion: Washizu that he is protected by Yamamba's prediction; Lady Asaji that she can harness the spirit world and create her own fate; Miki that he can survive by bowing to the inevitable and, like Tokimasu, accommodating the times. Miki's illusion is the most chilling precisely because, compared to Washizu and Asaji, he seems so ordinary, so practical, so sane.

NOTES

1 Anthony Davies, *Filming Shakespeare's Plays: the adaptations of Laurence Olivier, Orson Welles, Peter Brook and Akira Kurosawa* (Cambridge: Cambridge University Press, 1988), 154.

2 Robert Hapgood, "Kurosawa's Shakespeare films: *Throne of Blood, The Bad Sleep Well*, and *Ran*," in Anthony Davies and Stanley Wells, eds., *Shakespeare and the Moving Image: The Plays on Film and Television* (Cambridge: Cambridge University Press, 1994), 234–49: 234.

3 David Desser, *The Samurai Films of Akira Kurosawa*, Studies in Cinema 23 (Ann Arbor: UMI Research, 1983), 73.

4 Roger Manvell's "Kurosawa interview" in *Shakespeare and the Film* (New York: Praeger, 1971), 103ff.

5   Stephen Prince discusses Kurosawa's use of nature to signify psychological states in *The Cinema of Akira Kurosawa: The Warrior's Camera* (Princeton: Princeton University Press, 1991).

6   E. Pearlman, "*Macbeth* on film: Politics," in Davies and Wells, *Shakespeare and the Moving Image*, 250–60: 256–57.

7   Takeo Doi, *The Anatomy of Self: The Individual Versus Society*, trans. Mark A. Harbison (Tokyo: Kodansha International, 1986).

8   Iyotani Toshio, "Globalization and Culture," *Japan Foundation Newsletter* 23.3 (December 1995), 4–5.

9   *Ibid.*, 3.

10 Takamiya Toshiyuki summarizes the history of English literary studies in Japan in "Chaucer studies: a personal view," in Martin Stevens and Daniel Woodward, eds., *The Ellesmere Chaucer: Essays in Interpretation* (San Marino, Calif.: Huntington, 1995), 327–35.

11 Davies, *Filming Shakespeare's Plays* 154.

12 Leah S. Marcus, *Puzzling Shakespeare: Local Reading and Its Discontents* (Berkeley: University of California Press, 1988), 39–40.

13 Quoted in Manvell, "Kurosawa interview," 103.

14 Keiko McDonald, "The Noh Convention in *The Throne of Blood* and *Ran*," in Kevin K. W. Chang, ed., *Kurosawa: Perceptions on Life, An Anthology of Essays* (Honolulu: Honolulu Academy of Arts, 1991), 24–32. I thank Ian Carruthers for noting class distinctions between *Heida* and *Chûjô*.

15 Davies, *Filming Shakespeare's Plays* (155) asserts that one cannot "assume that the expressions on the faces of Washizu and Miki . . . articulate the very feelings and emotional complexities of Banquo and Macbeth" and that Kurosawa has not "created dramatic equivalents in the film's characterizations."

16 Stanley Wells and Gary Taylor, *The Oxford Shakespeare: The Complete Works* (Clarendon Press: Oxford, 1994).

17 Hapgood (235) notes the film's "chief omission, the MacDuff family subplot, makes even tighter a progression that is already tight; and very little else is left out." See J. Blumenthal, "*Macbeth* into *Throne of Blood*," *Sight and Sound* 34.4 (1965), 190–95. This early appraisal mistakes the Macduff character, having Noriyasu disappear after telling Miki of Lord Tsuzuki's murder. Noriyasu actually leads the final attack on Cobweb Castle.

18 Hapgood (239) fails to examine *Throne of Blood* as a three-part construction, reading it, instead, in four acts. See James Goodwin, *Akira Kurosawa and Intertextual Cinema* (Baltimore: Johns Hopkins University Press, 1994), 184–87, for an alternative application of jo/ha/kyû structure to *Throne of Blood*.

19 Division of the film into these particular segments is my reading.

20 Kurosawa's reference to Noh structure in *Throne of Blood* is extrapolated from his *Something Like An Autobiography*, Audie E. Bock, trans. (New York: Knopf, 1982), 193. I use quotes here to designate my reading.

21 As often noted, Lady Asaji's pregnancy is unique to Kurosawa's version of *Macbeth*. By means of this, she is able to force her husband's hand. Hapgood (236) calls it "one of the most striking of Kurosawa's departures from Shakespeare."

22 Pearlman (257), while criticizing the film's personal relationships, praises Kurosawa's political message as "uplifting . . . for its confidence in human capabilities."

23 Hapgood (240) refers to the opening titles as "seen through a web of branches," and says *The Castle of the Spider's Web* "is much apter than is *Throne of Blood*."

24 The Noh play, *Yamamba* (The mountain hag), is a classic Japanese allusion. See *On the Art of the No Drama: The Major Treatises of Zeami*, J. Thomas Rimer and Yamazaki Masakazu, trans., (Princeton: Princeton University Press, 1984), 285. Kurosawa revisited this demon hag thirty years later in the episode from *Dreams* titled "The blizzard."

25 See Kawatake Toshio, "Traditional Japanese performing arts on the world stage," *Japan Foundation Newsletter* 22.6 (1995), 1–4.

26 For Kurosawa's use of dance, mime, and cinematic patterning, see Marsha Kinder, "*Throne of Blood*: a morality dance," *Literature/Film Quarterly* 5.4 (1977), 339–45.

27 Suzuki Tadashi, "Culture is the body," trans. Matsuoka Kazuko, in *Interculturalism and Performance: Writing from PAJ*, Bonnie Marranca and Gautam Dasgupta, eds., (New York: PAJ, 1991), 241–48: 246–47.

28 Reading Lady Asaji as a double for Yamamba has a long tenancy in Kurosawa criticism. See, for example, John Gerlach, "Shakespeare, Kurosawa, and *Macbeth*: a response to J. Blumenthal," *Literature/Film Quarterly* 1.4 (1973), 352–59: 355 or Ana Laura Zambrano, "*Throne of Blood*: Kurosawa's *Macbeth*," *Literature/Film Quarterly* 2.3 (1974), 262–74: 273. I believe Kurosawa's Lady Macbeth is much more complex than this too-facile "doubling" allows.

29 Davies, *Filming Shakespeare's Plays* (156–66), says conflict in *Throne of Blood* is presented through the opposition between castle and forest, a polarity emphasized through camera angles.

30 The dialogue is transcribed from *Throne of Blood*'s English subtitles. The apparitions are based on Japanese medieval battle scrolls. See Zambrano for a discussion of Kurosawa's use of this art form.

31 See Goodwin, *Akira Kurosawa*, 5.

32 Ian Carruthers notes that Masako, who kills her own sons, is a Hôjô vassal: like Lady Kaede in *Ran*, she favors the other side. Hapgood "Kurosawa's Shakespeare films," (235–8) treats Kurosawa's use of actual historical figures for his female characters in *Throne of Blood* and *Ran*.

33 *The Tale of the Heike*, Helen Craig McCullough trans., (Stanford: Stanford University Press, 1988), 409.

34 Kurosawa, *Something Like an Autobiography*, xii.

35 *Ibid.*, 158–59.

36 Banquo's complicity may be purposely ambiguous on Shakespeare's part. See Alan Sinfield, *Faultlines: Cultural Materialism and the Politics of Dissident Reading* (Berkeley: University of California Press, 1992), for an analysis of state-sponsored violence in the renaissance and its application to *Macbeth*.

37 Cf. Kristin Thompson, *Breaking the Glass Armor: Neoformalist Film Analysis* (Princeton: Princeton University Press, 1988).

8

Innovation and continuity: two decades of Deguchi Norio's Shakespeare Theatre Company

SUEMATSU MICHIKO

The Shakespeare Theatre was the first Japanese professional theatre company formed with the sole purpose of staging Shakespeare. Its young artistic director, Deguchi Norio, started a drama school in 1974 after a few experiences of directing Shakespeare productions in major Shingeki companies.[1] In that same year, he was appointed to take charge of the monthly Shakespearean productions at the JeanJean, a small underground theatre in Shibuya, a fashionable downtown area in Tokyo. With the initial twenty-two members of his drama school, Deguchi founded The Shakespeare Theatre in January 1975, and straightaway launched an enterprise to stage the entire canon. It was a venture that only a young and untried company would have dared to tackle. To their surprise, however, no sooner had their monthly productions started than they began to gain a popular following among the young, and within six years had successfully completed their initial project.

During those six years, the company never wavered in their choice of translator and theatre venue. The new translation of Odashima Yûshi as well as the small underground theatre JeanJean became the lynch pins of their productions throughout the first run of the entire canon.

Though the choice of Odashima's translation was at first coincidental, it proved both advantageous and influential to their acting style.[2] Odashima's translation of the Complete Works, which subsequently furnished the standard text of Shakespearean productions on the Japanese stage, had made its unofficial debut in the late 1960s. Unlike his predecessors, Odashima translated Shakespeare neither as propaganda against the established theatre tradition nor as text for literary appreciation. His new translation specifically aimed to exploit the possibility of Shakespeare's text as a script for performance.[3] Because he himself was a keen theatregoer and thoroughly acquainted with the significance of audience involvement, his translation aimed to offer a lively theatrical experience both for actors and spectators.[4] Moreover, Odashima's translation achieved an unprecedented degree of clarity and contemporaneity. Colloquial and rhythmical in style and abounding in puns and modish expressions, his lines required speedy and colloquial delivery. This coincided with the standard acting style of the new company.

The Shakespeare Theatre also greatly benefited from the charm of their theatre venue, the JeanJean. Above all, the underground theatre in fashionable downtown Shibuya was attractive as a locale. The JeanJean already catered to a young audience with concerts in various genres and now ventured to offer its space as an alternative theatre for Shakespeare – on condition that live popular music be part of the event.[5] Besides its unconventionality, the physical environment of the space itself was also appealing. It was a black L-shaped box with only 110 seats. The stage was small and had only a single entrance at upstage left. Actually, these impediments themselves served to distinguish this venue from the conventional proscenium theatres and made it a thrilling and involving space in which anything might happen.

As Deguchi himself has noted, it was his dissatisfaction with the prevailing trend of Japanese Shakespearean productions in the 1950s and 1960s – gorgeous sets, period costumes, wigs, padded noses, and bombastic delivery – that led him to start his own theatre company.[6] Deguchi wanted to free Shakespeare from all that was supposed to be appropriate for the stage presentation of his plays. This act of defiance obliged Deguchi to compromise with practicality in various respects; fortunately, however, these restrictions out of necessity evolved into a badge of distinction for the company.

On the most mundane level, for example, the company had no financial means. It simply could not afford a set or costumes, and that was why the actors performed in jeans on an empty stage. Deguchi decided to take advantage of their insufficiencies to prove the validity of his belief that a Shakespearean production could capture the intensity of the language and communicate it through the actors' physical presence.[7] A small studio theatre was a perfect place in which to stage such a production concept because an intimate space can disarm an audience out of passive aloofness and encourage them to participate on equal terms with the actors. The development of these communal, ensemble possibilities was a key to the success of Deguchi's production style, which relied heavily on the actors' lines and JeanJean atmosphere.

Lack of acting skills and the absence of stars among the actors actually became an advantage in determining The Shakespeare Theatre acting style. The characteristic emphasis on ensemble acting and the speedy, energetic delivery of lines sprang from a reliance on the physical vitality of the equally inexperienced actors. This energy and emotional drive, accelerated by the abundant use of live rock'n'roll music, were exhilarating to watch and quickly communicated to their young audiences.

At times, the speed and roughness of delivery resulted in poor audibility of lines; however, they did infuse fresh meanings and the feel of the day into Shakespeare's language. By not alluding directly to the cultural or political conditions of society but, rather, living each moment on stage with emotional and physical intensity, they successfully brought contemporaneity within the play's framework.

Besides the physical energy of the acting, the company's productions were noted for their ingenious directorial design, derived from fresh readings of the text. For example, *Romeo and Juliet*, which was first staged in July 1975, focused on the frivolity of modern youth. Because the central issue in this production was the conflict among the young and not the resolution of the conflict between the two houses, youthful rashness – Tybalt's killing of Mercutio, and Romeo's subsequent revenge – was emphasized as a cause of the two lovers' deaths. Naturally, a final union between the houses was unthinkable, for their untimely deaths only intensified the antagonism among the youths on both sides. The poignant sense of futility as well as the absence of lyricism throughout the production shattered any romantic conception of the play and reaffirmed its relevance to the social conditions in 1975. Although the nationwide student movement had subsided by that time, its aftermath, such as the Asama Sansô Siege and lynch laws of the radicals in 1972, still recalled the young generation's susceptibility to violence and bloodshed. Onstage fighting of young men in jeans evoked a threatening reality outside the theatre.[8]

Another unforgettable production, *A Midsummer Night's Dream*, was originally performed in October 1975, and proved the company's success with comedies. The daunting task of staging convincing contemporary fairies led Deguchi to choose an unusual setting for the play. In this production, Oberon was a master of a bar called "The Forest of Arden," while Titania and Puck were respectively its *Mama san* and a student barman. The customers gathered here were transformed into the characters of the play in Puck's drunken dream, and the powerful cocktail, "Love-in-Idleness," invented by Oberon precipitated all of them into the hurly-burly of desire. That the love juice was a real drink made surprising sense as a trigger for the young lovers' uncontrollable instincts. With the help of a drink, the lovers were able to discover an unexpected self spurred on by carnal appetite. This production demonstrated Deguchi's virtuosity in being able to conceive key visual metaphors that could tie the whole play together and release its verbal imagery.

The company also kindled an interest in Shakespeare's history plays, which had been unheeded in the Japanese theatre thus far. One of the most notable examples was *Henry VI*, the three parts of which were performed on

6 *A Midsummer Night's Dream* (The Bar version), directed by Deguchi Norio, Tokyo Globe-za, 1994. One of three parallel productions staged consecutively, this was set in a bar. Proprietors, Theseus/Oberon and Hippolyta/Titania sit downstage of bargirls (the fairies) in the Forest of Arden Bar.

the same day for the first time in Japan. With their typical commitment to physicality, the company highlighted the dynamism of power struggles and the underlying passion for blood in this trilogy, successfully relating the remote history of fifteenth-century England to our society by matching their vital energies to the unflagging drive for power within the play. The production won the Kinokuniya Prize for Drama in 1981.

Although the young welcomed the Shakespeare Theatre with great enthusiasm, it was not necessarily accepted favorably by traditionalist theatre critics and academics.[9] Lack of nuance in delivery, amateurish acting, and bold but naïve interpretations of text became targets of criticism. Despite these reservations, the company's contributions to Japanese Shakespearean performance still remain remarkable.

Above all, the Shakespeare Theatre distinguished itself in the novelty and initiative of its productions. The entire Works of Shakespeare had been staged by a single theatre group for the first time in Japan. Besides, it was a sheer luxury to attend Shakespearean productions monthly and, moreover, to see onstage plays which had hitherto been unperformed.[10] The company's pioneering spirit also resulted in an eight-hour marathon performance of the Histories, which, though not uncommon today, was certainly phenomenal twenty years ago.

According to Deguchi, his rejection of mainstream theatres was partly a product of the Little Theatre Movement prevalent in the 1960s, which was closely related to political activities of student groups and also concurrent with the worldwide trend towards theatrical experimentalism.[11] In staging their avant-garde productions, small experimental theatre groups at the time sought out unconventional spaces such as deserted buildings and tents in defiance of the established theatre. The license of the Little Theatre Movement inspired Deguchi to explore the possibilities of Shakespearean performance unreservedly both in terms of space and acting style. Without this sense of freedom, the 1980s and the 1990s would not have seen such a profusion of Shakespearean plays and their adaptations on the Japanese stage.[12]

Interestingly enough, the triumph of Deguchi's productions was far beyond his expectations. This unexpected success was partly due to the timeliness of the company's activities. For one thing, the Japanese audience had matured enough to welcome unorthodox Shakespeare; for another, Japanese theatre as a whole was undergoing a change in the 1970s. These changes in the Japanese theatre itself were promoted by the booming economy of the 1970s, which encouraged the influx of capital into the arts. The theatre, too, became enmeshed in the new market economy as various business enterprises sought to exploit its commercial possibilities. For example, Seibu and Tôkyû, huge department stores in Shibuya, built theatres and museums to attract customers who sought spiritual as well as material satisfaction in the city.[13] If theatres could offer popular productions continually, they had the opportunity to become the hub of the fashionable downtown, and that was actually what such theatres as JeanJean turned out to be in the 1970s.

Naturally, this change in the theatre was inseparable from changes in audience demography. With the influx of a younger generation into the urban area, city culture consequently had to cater to their interests. Unlike their counterparts in the 1960s, young audiences in the 1970s did not expect theatre directors to take the role of political agitators. For these young consumers of culture, playgoing, too, was a fashion, just another opportunity for entertainment, and their criteria of trendiness – freshness, novelty, and light-heartedness – were also supplied by their choice of Shakespearean production. As a result, the popularity of the Shakespeare Theatre, which could provide all of these elements in its productions, was virtually assured.

Completing the production of the entire canon in 1981, The Shakespeare Theatre moved a step forward in its history. Once it had left its old home ground, the JeanJean, it was impossible to keep on performing in the former

7 Scene from *The Comedy of Errors*, directed by Deguchi Norio at the Aoyama Enkei Theatre, 1987. A masked character confronts a white ball (the world), an important visual symbol in this production.

style. Besides, the departure of a majority of its actors in 1983 soon overshadowed the company's future.[14] It survived this plight by recruiting young actors fresh from drama school; however, The Shakespeare Theatre was now forced to readjust its overall acting policy one way or another.

A pressing concern for Deguchi at the outset was how to cope with the practical problems of space, setting, and costume. He was totally baffled as to how to stage Shakespeare without actors in jeans.[15] Besides, he could no longer rely on the close actor/spectator relationship that the intimate space of the JeanJean had offered in an earlier period. After a few years' quest for a new company identity, the breakthrough came when the company found a new venue, the Aoyama Enkei Theatre. This theatre, opened in 1985, is a medium-sized amphitheatre with 376 seats. Deguchi staged *The Comedy of Errors* here in 1987, and it became one of the most celebrated productions in the second stage of the company's history. Obviously, Deguchi felt at home in this space. Productions on the circular stage of this theatre had to make the most fluid use of the space, while focus had to be on the actors and their words as in the JeanJean. Once again, Deguchi was able to prove Shakespeare's availability to modernity in a new style.

A clue to Deguchi's new directorial principles lay in his renewed interest in props. In the production of *The Comedy of Errors*, Deguchi discovered the potency of props in summoning up the play's resonant images appealingly.[16] On that occasion, props such as a white ball and half-masks became the keys to interpretation. The first was a symbol of peace and order after which every character aspired. In the opening scene, for example, the ball was situated in the center of a bare stage, highlighted with a spotlight. Old Egeon entered and explained his plight before the Duke, staring at the ball. He was not yet allowed to touch it, for it signified what he hoped to attain in the end. At various times during the course of the action, it could also stand for money, or the turning globe itself.[17] A bounce of the ball could intensify as well as clear up the entanglements among characters (see photo 7).

As for the half-masks that every character wore, apart from helping to create the festive atmosphere of commedia dell'arte performance, they helped to convince the audience of the inevitability of the confusion on stage. Deguchi generated a hilarity of confusion in this production, also, with a mixture of slapstick and restrained moments. An apt example is Act 4, scene 1, where Antipholus of Ephesus, a goldsmith, a merchant, and an officer, engaged in a skirmish over a gold chain until interrupted by Dromio of Syracuse's announcement of their ship's imminent departure. Not only were they rendered speechless, but the four became totally motionless in receiving this baffling news. The complete standstill of action was then broken by

8 *A Midsummer Night's Dream* (the Mask version), directed by Deguchi Norio, Tokyo Globe-za, 1994. One of three parallel productions of the play staged consecutively, this was played in the round by actors in masks. In a typically physical routine, the four lovers thrash about in a chain formation.

another burst of commotion, which turned out all the fiercer because of the pause a moment earlier. The quiet entrance of Lady Abbess in Act 5, scene 1 again was strongly contrasted with the preceding boisterous chase before the priory. These contrasting moments effectively created a rhythm with which Deguchi intensified the merry violence of the confusion to the very last. In the final scene of reunion, the full dramatic effect of the masks was felt. Recognizing her long-lost husband, the Abbess gently removed his mask. That is, at the moment when an old, shabby man was identified as Egeon, Emilia's husband, and father of the two Antipholi, the mask had accomplished its purpose. Taking their cue, other characters also unmasked in order to be truly recognized for the first time. This moment of recognition became all the more moving and powerful because of the conventional use of white half-masks to cover their faces until that very instant – strongly emphasizing the play's affinity with romances that end with reunion ensuing from a discovery of the key characters' true identity.

This delightful production was restaged in the Tokyo Globe in 1989, and its success in this new theatre again proved the company's competence in an open space. Built by Isozaki Arata in the previous year, it is a modern version of Shakespeare's Globe. Its thrust stage surrounded by three-story seating is flexible as well as intimate, and it has remained the company's favorite space since then.

The productions that followed *The Comedy of Errors* have similarly been characterized by this imaginative use of props or visual metaphors, which can offer fresh insight into interpretation of text. One of the most memorable was the 1991 production of *The Winter's Tale*. What dominated the stage was a fireplace out of which protruded a steam engine. This unusual item which quoted Rene Magritte's surrealistic painting was an emblem of frozen time.[18] A smoking steam engine, which should have been moving forward, forever remained trapped in that same place, witnessing the unreasonable fury of jealous Leontes and its disastrous consequence for the household. It was a superb visualization of the paradox of time running throughout the play – irreparable and yet remedial, severing and uniting the family.

In commemoration of its twentieth anniversary, the company consecutively staged three versions of *A Midsummer Night's Dream* at the Tokyo Globe in 1994.[19] This was an attempt to reassess their past, which, according to Deguchi, was vital for the company's future, and it showed Deguchi's transition from a young, daring newcomer to an experienced veteran in the course of twenty years.

The latest production, the masked version of *A Midsummer Night's Dream*, was basically similar to the 1987 production of *The Comedy of Errors* in its use of masks except that the three groups of characters were differentiated by specific masks – white masks for the Athenian lords and black masks for the fairies, and the mechanicals playing unmasked. These masks were not removed until Puck's final epilogue (see photo 8).

The second latest, the school version, is one of the most personal Shakespearean productions by Deguchi, for it was a kaleidoscope of haunting memories from his childhood and teenage days. The production opened with the entrance of a dispirited director, apparently Deguchi's substitute onstage. He was doubly troubled by discord with his wife and his inability to conceive a plan for his new production. He fell asleep in despondency and dreamt of his boyhood in a remote country village in the postwar period. In his dream, the production of *A Midsummer Night's Dream* unfolded, with the familiar villagers impersonating the characters of the play. A village boy – himself in childhood – played Puck and his classmates played fairies, while he and his wife played Theseus/Oberon and Titania/Hippolyta. These boyhood memories were overlapped with teenage ones, and his other self also appeared as a young lover engrossed in love entanglements. Thus, the production turned out to be a retrospective voyage of self-discovery through which the worn-out, middle-aged director became rejuvenated. This beautiful production, marked by nostalgia and wry wisdom, clearly contrasted with the bar version, which was chiefly a celebration of youthful physical energy. The retrospective stance in the school version exemplified Deguchi's mellow outlook on life after twenty years in the theatre (see colour photo 2).

Lastly, the restaging of the bar version that had first been performed twenty years earlier provided an opportunity to confirm its enduring fascination. Though the 1970s shock of contemporaneity was certainly lost, the production set in a bar in the 1970s could still appeal to an audience in the 1990s through their nostalgia for a bygone era.

A theatre company that constantly stages Shakespeare is not exceptional today when one can see nearly a hundred Shakespearean productions a year in the greater Tokyo area alone.[20] What makes the Shakespeare Theatre still unique is its distinctive and consistent approach to Shakespeare. For more than two decades, the company has dedicated itself to offering stage interpretations of Shakespeare that have as their hallmark clarity and modern relevance. As the case of Deguchi's *A Midsummer Night's Dream* shows, the Shakespeare Theatre has restaged their past productions with some revision and proved their validity repeatedly. This sense of continuity, along with their commitment to shared experience, nurtures the company style of the Shakespeare Theatre. Deguchi's productions defy being merely consumed as a fashion in the restless contemporary theatre scene.

NOTES

1 At the Bungaku-za, Deguchi directed *Twelfth Night* (1971) and *Hamlet* (1972), and, at the Shiki Company, *Much Ado About Nothing* (1973).

2 In 1968, Deguchi was commissioned to direct a few scenes from *Hamlet* for an in-class production at the Bungaku-za drama school, using a new translation from Odashima, who was a dramaturge at the Bungaku-za at the time.

3 Anzai Tetsuo, ed., *Nihon no Shakespeare Hyakunen* (A century of Shakespeare in Japan), (Tokyo: Aratake Shuppan, 1989), 13.

4 Deguchi Norio, *Shakespeare wa Tomaranai* (There is no way of stopping Shakespeare), (Tokyo: Kodansha, 1988), 111.

5 See "Interview with Deguchi Norio," in this volume, p.184.

6 Deguchi, *Shakespeare wa Tomaranai*, 95–8.

7 Deguchi Norio, "Shakespeare and the Shakespeare Theatre," *Shingeki* 277 (1976), 73.

8 In 1972, fugitive members of Rengô Sekigun (The Japan Red Army), an extremist terrorist group, confined themselves with a hostage in the Asama Sansô, a villa in Gunma. After a ten-day siege, the hostage was released and the fugitives

were arrested. These arrests, however, led to the disclosure of their past lynch law, in which more than ten members of Rengô Sekigun had been killed for the cause of the group and their bodies abandoned on a mountain in Gunma.

9 For examples of harsh criticisms, see Kadono Izumi, "Odashima-yaku to Shakespeare Juyô" (The translation of Odashima and the reception of Shakespeare), in Anzai, *Nihon no Shakespeare Hyakunen*, 159.

10 Out of thirty-seven Shakespearean plays, ten were staged by the Shakespeare Theatre for the first time in Japan.

11 Deguchi Norio, "Shakespeare e Kaeru" (The return to Shakespeare), *Wave* 10 (1986), 175.

12 Particularly in the 1990s, the number of Shakespearean productions, including their adaptations, increased dramatically. In the Tokyo area, approximately ninety productions can be seen yearly, a quarter of which are drastic adaptations by young theatre groups. For the list of productions, see Sasaki Takashi, ed., *Nippon Shakespeare Sôran 2* (Tokyo: Elpis, 1995).

13 Seibu (The Seibu-Saison Group) opened the Seibu Theatre in Shibuya in 1973 (renamed the Parco Theatre in 1985) together with a small gallery. Following this example, in the 1980s, Tôkyû set out to revitalize another area of Shibuya by constructing a huge culture spot, the Bunkamura, which houses the Theatre Cocoon, the Orchard Hall, and the Bunkamura Museum of Art. In the past two decades, more than thirty theatres have been built in the Tokyo area both by private and municipal corporations.

14 Several ex-members of the Shakespeare Theatre founded the theatre group, The Rhyming, in that same year. Since then, the group continually supplied productions of Shakespeare and other British playwrights.

15 See "Interview with Deguchi Norio," in this volume, p. 185–86.

16 Deguchi, *Shakespeare wa Tomaranai*, 42.

17 Ibid., 48.

18 Senda Akihiko, "The Shakespeare Theatre: *The Winter's Tale*," *The Asahi Shimbun*, February 18, 1994.

19 The bar version of *A Midsummer Night's Dream* mentioned earlier in this paper was originally staged at the JeanJean in 1975. The school version (1990) and the mask version (1993) were staged at the Theatre Cocoon and the Tokyo Globe respectively.

20 Other major professional theatre groups that specialize in Shakespeare are the Miki no Kai, led by one of the most celebrated Shakespearean actors, Hira Mikijiro; the Sai no Kuni Shakespeare Company, the artistic director of which is Ninagawa Yukio; and the Tokyo Shakespeare Company led by a female artistic director, Edo Kaoru.

9

Tragedy with laughter: Suzuki Tadashi's *The Tale of Lear*

TAKAHASHI YASUNARI

Suzuki Tadashi reveals in an interview that he regards Shakespeare as one of the four dramatists who really have mattered, and still do matter to him, the other three being Euripides, Chekhov, and Beckett. The first evidence of his fascination with Shakespeare was *Don Hamlet: A Pathetic Play* (1972), "composed" (as is always the case with him) and directed by him. The play, based upon (or at least partially inspired by) *Hamlet*, was produced by the Waseda Little Theatre Company at a tiny theatre upstairs close to Suzuki's alma mater, Waseda University in Tokyo. Then came *Night and the Clock* (1975), a collage, which freely used materials from *Macbeth*.

But we have to wait another ten years for a full manifestation of his concern with the British dramatist. *King Lear* (1984) was his first work that, instead of being a collage, builds itself "single-mindedly" upon a Shakespearean play. (I shall hereafter refer to this work of Suzuki's as *The Tale of Lear*, the title used for English performances.) Together with his Greek works (*The Trojan Women*, 1977; *The Bacchae*, 1978; and *A Tragedy: The Fall of the House of Atreus*, 1983), the work remains an exception up to now in that Suzuki basically has refrained from interpolating extraneous texts, though he does heavily cut the original text. He will later use, to different degrees, Shakespearean materials like *Macbeth* and *Romeo and Juliet*, but without exclusively focusing on single plays. *The Tale of Lear* is indeed so remarkable that its first performance (Toga, 1984) caused certain negative reactions in some of Suzuki's hitherto friendly critics.

One of them thought that the version was "uncharacteristic" of Suzuki because it was too "consistent" in the semantic structure of the drama as a whole. Suzuki framed Shakespeare's *King Lear* within the fantasy of an old man in a hospital (or a nursing home). Obviously an ordinary specimen of present-day society, the old man must have suffered similar (though, of course, much more pedestrian) familial misfortunes in his own life. In all probability, he was put into the nursing home by his daughters. Apparently, he had been reading *King Lear*, and he now identifies with Shakespeare's hero. The story line of *King Lear* was compressed into a 100-minute-long show rather faithfully without serious dislocation of the original play, despite many cuts in the text and the all-male cast. The concomitant implication was that the visual beauty of the dance-like movements and the costume was a little bit too "seamless," as if stylization had become an aesthetic end in itself.[1]

Important changes, however, found their way into a new production (Toga, 1988). This version, first performed in English with an all-American cast, was later to be repeated with a mixed cast as well as an all-Japanese cast both in Japan and abroad. Contrary to the impression of "semantic consistency" referred to above, Suzuki exploited to the full that sharply distancing effect which had always characterized his works. The newest and most telling device responsible for this effect was the introduction of the Nurse (played by a male actor). At the outset of the play, she finds a book on the floor beside the chair on which the Old Man is sitting, probably dropped from his hand as he drowsed. The Nurse picks it up and, squatting by the chair, starts reading it silently but avidly[2] with a box of popcorn beside her. Handel's stately, hypnotic *Largo* announces the beginning of the Old Man's fantasized enacting of the Lear story, but the slow-moving ritualistic entrance of courtiers cannot go undisturbed (for the audience though not for the courtiers) by a raucous cackle from the Nurse.

If the play-within-a-play structure was already clear in the first production, the new version has added another framework. The continual presence of the Nurse leads us to suspect that the dramatic action going on onstage is not only a figment of the Old Man's fantasy but also a representation in "real time" of what she is reading (see colour photo 3). We keep wavering between the two possible perspectives. The double framework, in other words, is far from clear-cut. From time to time, the structure is turned inside out, and parallelism becomes intersection.

For instance, the Nurse, besides being a nurse and thus situating the drama in a contemporary nursing home, plays the role of the Fool in Shakespeare's text as well. In the "riddles" scene, where Lear and the Fool engage in a one-sided combat of wits about the nose standing in the middle of one's face, or the oyster and its shell (*King Lear*, 1.5), the Nurse even manages to carry on a semblance of conversation with the fantasizing Old Man. What she does is to read aloud the lines of the Fool directly from the book she is reading. It may look as if she is improvising, but she is not. Hence a preposterous ambiguity: is this a case of improbable coincidence between the Old Man enacting the story and the Nurse reading it, or should we rather think that the Old Man is enacting just what the Nurse is reading?

Such confounding interactions punctuate and puncture the illusion of the audience, if not of the Old Man. The Nurse's repeated cackles, intruding on the actions taking place on stage, suggest that she probably represents a younger generation for whom Shakespeare's *King Lear*, which she apparently now has come across for the first time in her life, must read like a variety of comic strip. Her cacophonic laughter bursts out in moments that, in usual interpretations of *King Lear*, would be most unlikely to elicit comic reactions, e.g., when Goneril tells the blinded Gloucester to "smell his way to Dover," or when the wounded Cornwall says, "Untimely comes this hurt."

The confusion of levels that undermines the illusion is pushed to the extreme when it is seen to involve the Old Man himself. In the Dover scene, the Old Man as Lear is wheeled in by the Nurse in a hospital garbage cart. Wearing a washbasin on his head instead of a wreath of flowers, he sits up in the cart and delivers the lines on "the great stage of fools," rising to ever more passionate heights of tragic eloquence. But something strange happens in between the savage vision of felt-footed horses and the horrendous cry for murder: suddenly noticing that the Nurse is engrossed in the book, he alters the tone of his speech for a second to say, "Will you stop reading, please?" This is the only instance in the play where Suzuki has ventured to add a "fake line" to the original text. Immediately after this most radically self-destructive turn, the Old Man switches back to his Shakespearean self to cry, "Kill, kill, kill!" and then to implore "Let me have surgeons, I am cut to the brains" (curiously resonant lines, by the way, in the hospital setting), before running away offstage.

It is not just the Old Man who is shocked to see his tragic performance unheeded by the Nurse. It is we, the audience, who are taken aback: could it be that the Old Man has been aware (at least partially aware) of reality all the time? We are faced with an enigma similar to the one we experience when reading *Don Quixote*. Ultimately, such destabilizings of dramatic unity or clashings of the levels of signification force the audience to ask fundamental questions concerning dramatic experience. What is it that makes a theatrical representation feel truly "authentic"? How can a classic text generate a power to move a contemporary audience? Can it do so only if textual purity is preserved intact, or must one necessarily and consciously bring out the fissure between then and now, there and here? Can the actor relate to the classic or foreign text without articulating the gaps yawning between him and it? How is it that the audience can (if it can) be made aware of the fictitious nature of acting and yet be genuinely moved? Can tragic emotion be at the same time punctured and kept deepening?

Or it might even be arguable at this point that, for Suzuki, Shakespeare's text is merely a pretext in order to pose these questions as pithily as possible to himself, to his actors, and to the audience. But what a formidable task it is! Suzuki has to wrestle with the overwhelming richness of the original text in

1 *Macbeth*, directed by Masumi Toshikiyo for Shôchiku Company Ltd., Nissei Theatre, 1976. Accompanying Shingeki actor Hira Mikijirô in the title role, Kabuki star Bandô Tamasaburô V played Lady Macbeth with a strong aura of traditional *onnagata* acting.

2 *A Midsummer Night's Dream* (*The School version*), directed by Deguchi Norio, Tokyo Globe-za, 1994. One of three parallel productions of the play staged consecutively, this was set in a school. Puck, a winged school-boy of the immediate postwar years, stands over a model of the set, a school, also seen back-projected behind him.

3 *King Lear*, directed by Suzuki Tadashi, Toga Shin Sambô, 1997. The old man (Nakayama Ichirô) who imagines himself to be Lear, and his nurse (Aiba Chisako).

4 *The Chronicle of Macbeth*, directed by Suzuki Tadashi, Playbox Theatre, Melbourne, 1992. Carillo Gantner as the Cult Leader leads his followers in chanting "Farewell to History."

5 *The Chronicle of Macbeth*, directed by Suzuki Tadashi, Playbox Theatre, Melbourne, 1992. Ellen Lauren playing Lady Macbeth's breakdown in the sleepwalking scene.

6 *Arigachina Hanashi* (The Same Old Story), directed by Suzuki Yumi for Jitensha Kinqureat Company, Ginza Hakuhinkan Theatre, 1991. The quotation of Zeffirelli's film is undercut by the contemporary gossip of Juliet's fat aunt Elizabetha.

7 *Romeo and Juliet*, directed by Shibata Yukihiro for Takarazuka Review Company, Takarazuka Theatre, 1990. Death scene.

8 *Ninagawa Macbeth*, directed by Ninagawa Yukio. Hira Mikijirō as Macbeth. Director Ninagawa melds Shakespeare's text with Japanese theatrical elements in this intercultural production. Nissei Theatre, Tokyo, 1980. Program cover.

order to extract its essential elements through making drastic cuts and rear-rangements of lines, scenes, and characters. Kent must be cut, so must the reconciliation scene between Lear and Cordelia (*King Lear*, 4.7) as well as their joint captivity (5.3). These are some of the precious but ineluctable sacrifices offered to the altar of Suzuki's kind of "theatre of cruelty."

On the other hand, however, it would be rash to complain that Suzuki's vision is simply too gloomy and cruel to let him retain any episodes that might hint at hope of redemption. For instance, it is not true to say that at the end of the blinding scene Suzuki has cut, out of wilful cruelty, the concluding lines spoken by Gloucester's two loyal servants: "I'll never care what wicked-ness I do, / If this man [Cornwall] come to good." Peter Brook, in his famous 1962 production of *King Lear*, also cut the same redeeming lines. Both Brook and Suzuki are justified in following the text of the First Folio rather than the 1608 Quarto. (Suzuki, admittedly, has gone a step further in making Gloucester himself give Cornwall a wound; but this, I believe, is due to the necessity of reducing the number of characters.)

Or take the final scene. Belying our expectation, the dying Edmund is allowed to say the repentant lines: "Some good I mean to do, / Despite of mine own nature." Most importantly, the entire dramatic action, from the entrance of the Old Man as Lear carrying Cordelia in his arms through his col-lapse on top of her body, is enacted with full sincerity, with no tongue in cheek. There seems to be nothing to undermine the belief that the emotion welling up in the audience's mind is genuinely tragic, except for the fact that Cordelia is actually played by a bearded male actor – or does the fact bother the audience? It is my impression that the audience has long since ceased to be alienated by it. Even the Nurse herself, we observe, joins the others in watching the death of the Old Man/Lear with what looks like a serious expression.

But the point is that the play does not really end there. We see that the death of Lear, as enacted in his fantasy, coincides with the actual death of the Old Man himself on the stage. (The perfect doubling here reminds me of the effect caused by Samuel Beckett's novel, *Malone Dies*, in which the hero-narra-tor seems to die precisely as he narrates the death of the hero of his story.) Or, for that matter, it could be interpreted that both deaths coincide with the Nurse coming to the last page of the book. All the characters that have so far been real only to the Old Man, having played out their roles for him, must now disappear. The stage is left empty save for two presences – one is the body of the Old Man on the floor, and the other is the Nurse sitting with the book in the chair, which had been occupied by her patient at the outset of the play. Then, finishing the book with great relish, and closing it with a bang, she bursts into another of her unstoppable laughs. This is the last of what we see and hear as the stage dissolves into darkness.

The total impression of this ending is absurdly comic without ceasing to be frighteningly tragic, or rather tragedy and comedy here passionately and separately assert themselves, insensible to each other. It may be argued that Suzuki here pushes the absurdist vision of Jan Kott wildly beyond the point that Peter Brook reached in his production. It is as if Suzuki were determined to go against Aristotle, refusing to build up tragic emotions of fear and pity, which the audience needs to taste to the full in order to be released at the end of the play. What he compels us to experience is not a tragic emotion as such but a kind of tragic emotion that simultaneously comprises critical re-examination of itself. The framing device is particularly effective for this purpose. The juxtaposition of the Nurse's comic absorption in the book of *King Lear* with her professional indifference towards her pathetic patient generates a savagely conflicting effect.

Yet it will not do either to look upon *The Tale of Lear* as a comment on the inhuman system of modern hospitals or to read it as an iconoclastic parody of the classic play. It is rather an unflinching anatomy of the human psyche by means of a dramaturgy that can both move us towards a tragic emotion and, at the same time, cast a cold eye on it.

The same goes for the question of "stylization" mentioned earlier. It must have been far too easy for Suzuki, should he have been so minded, to create a self-contained beauty of stylized acting such as we encounter in Noh and Kabuki. What he does is to keep de-creating the stylized beauty that he has just come closest to creating.

The use, for example, of Handel's *Largo* and Tschaikovsky's *La Danse espagnole* might sound beautifully harmonious with the stylized motions of the actors, but we cannot readily yield to the beauty, conscious as we are of the sobering onstage figure of the Nurse. *La Danse espagnole* might be arguably a pathetic evocation of the bygone splendor of Lear's royal court, but we must also admit the helpless sentimentality of nostalgia: the meaning of that splendor has obviously grown as incomprehensible to the Old Man as to the audience, as evinced by the indecipherable finger-signs of the dancers. The whole point seems to me to lie in the ironical gap between the signifier and the signified. The costume of the courtiers also thrives on the ambiguity of its semantics: it looks vaguely medieval, neither Japanese nor western, suggesting both regal splendor and beggarly tatters. The fact that it does not relate to any specific culture is stressed, paradoxically, by its flagrant contrast with the universality of the modern uniform worn by the Nurse.

The points I have made, however, may not be so obvious to some (if not all) western spectators as they are to some (if not all) Japanese ones. It is interesting to compare differences in the reactions of American and British critics when the play toured North America (1988) and London (1994), bearing in mind the fact that the American tour was English-speaking with an all-American cast and that the London one was Japanese-speaking with an all-Japanese cast.

On the whole, the Americans were more receptive of, in the words of one critic, "Shakespeare the likes of which you've never heard." Though baffled by the "cerebral, and surpassingly strange adaptation of *King Lear*," the critic of *The Washington Post* is able to see the performance as "a meeting place of ritual, reason, and madness." The Nurse's "discomfiting laughter" does not prevent him from taking it as Suzuki's device for maintaining "an ironic distance" from the text. Another critic, writing in *The New Republic*, admits that he finds some parts of the work "a bit too technical and somewhat exotic," but he is surprised to find that the western actor is "perfectly capable of subduing ego and vanity to an Eastern discipline"; he is open-minded enough to marvel at "how much we can learn from the Orient about our own traditional masterworks." A third reviewer (*Time*) denies that this is an "auteurist direction run riot," stressing that the work "focuses its innovations more on the play's psyche than on the director's." He, too, concludes, "for the most part this work sparks the audiences to think anew about Shakespeare's original intent."[3]

By comparison, British critical reactions were strikingly hostile: "Something coals-to-Newcastle about importing foreign language productions . . . listening to the matchless poetry in an incomprehensible tongue" (*The Daily Telegraph*); "Does the world need another Japanese production set in a mental hospital?" (*The Times*). The *Guardian* critic writes: "Where Shakespeare's *Lear* offers us a fluctuating image of moral chaos, Suzuki's implies that we are all mad or spiritually crippled. It reduces the multi-dimensionality of Shakespeare."

I have, in a way, tried to refute some of these objections in advance. I hope to have shown that Suzuki's power to arouse strong antipathies both abroad and at home derives from his uncompromising questioning of theatrical art. In a Japanese context, however, it may by now be safely surmised that he has traveled so far in his quest for a new dimension of theatricality that few but the die-hard purists among critics would talk about his desecrating the holiness of traditional forms. It would no longer be possible to categorize his style as either Japanesque or westernized.

It would, then, be a pity if, in the Occident, Suzuki's refusal to join in Bardolatry should be taken to mean disrespect. On the contrary, *The Tale of Lear* should be regarded as a unique way of paying a profound homage to a great western dramatist who excelled supremely, among other things, in the art of making drama out of meta-theatrical questioning of drama. It is, in a sense, another attempt to prove the truth of the poet Ted Hughes's definition of Shakespeare: a "quarry of raw material."[4]

Postscript

(1) *The Vision of Lear*, an operatic version of *The Tale of Lear* on which Suzuki collaborated with Japanese composer Hosokawa Toshio, saw its world premiere as the opening piece of the Munich Biennale Festival in April 1998. The opera is unique in that, reversing the customary order, here theatrical direction has preceded musical composition. Hosokawa has composed the music to suit the details of Suzuki's *Lear*, with the differences that the Japanese text used by Suzuki has been replaced by Shakespeare's original English, and that the roles of Lear's daughters were performed by female singers. The cast, chosen after auditions for the Munich production, comprised various nationalities: American, German, Japanese, etc. They had undergone a month of intensive workshop and rehearsal in Japan, immersed in the "Suzuki Method," and learning every physical movement from Suzuki's original cast on what might be called a "man-to-man (or in some case, man-to-woman)" scheme. The impression I received from the last dress rehearsal in Japan in March, 1998, was that Hosokawa's music as embodied by the singers succeeded, despite (or because of) its hyper-modern ring, in producing movingly emotional effects at the same time as it made the opera look even more hypnotically ritualistic than the drama.

As for the Nurse, Suzuki and Hosokawa agreed that she should be the only character in the opera who did not sing: she was played by the same Japanese male actor who had played the part in the drama. (Incidentally, I should add that, already in the last dramatic version as well as in this operatic version, there appeared on stage a second Nurse, also played by an actor, the first Nurse's minor double, as it were, with no lines to speak, augmenting the grotesque and the comic. I will here refer to the two Nurses collectively as a singular presence.) Her function remained the same as I have described above, both alienating and highlighting the poetic tragedy with her comic guffaws. The German critical responses, of which I have read seven examples (*Berliner Zeitung*, *Frankfurter Allgemeine*, *Süddeutsche Zeitung*, and others), seem to have ranged from rave to puzzled wonder.

(2) In September 1997, there was an important production of *King Lear* in Tokyo. Realized after three years of incubation, and sponsored by the Japan

Foundation, it embraced a multinational team of Asian artists. The play, re-titled just *Lear*, was written by Kishida Rio (Japan) and directed by Ong Ken Sen (Singapore). Musicians were mostly from Indonesia. Lear was played by Umewaka Naohiko (Japanese Noh-actor), Goneril by Jiang Qihu (Beijing opera actress), Cordelia by a Thai actress (Regan was cut), and Fool by a Singapore actor. Given such different nationalities, the unity-in-diversity of the total effect of the stage was surprising. This is Suzuki's bilingual *Lear* writ large, and the success (call it so in view of the enormous difficulties besetting the project) would seem to open new possibilities of international collabora-tions in theatre.

One of the striking alterations in terms of the narrative was a distinctly feminine twist. The playwright Kishida says that she was deeply moved by the German production of *King Lear* (directed by Robert Wilson and played by the actress Marianne Hoppe), which she saw in Berlin in 1990. Her main theme as playwright had long been that of parricide, but she now started to think not only about the daughter's parricidal passion, but also about her mother or Lear's absent wife. It is the latter, the female figure, who appears as a ghost in response to Lear's agonized cry for help. The feminine is here represented not only as a destroyer (whose enemy has always been both the father and the Imperial system of Japan), but also, for the first time in Kishida's writing career, as a figure of salvation. It would be interesting if Shakespeare, by dint of his apparently total obliviousness to Lear's dead wife, has somehow sug-gested a revitalizing idea to a remarkable female dramatist in Japan, contrib-uting thereby to setting the audience of this Asian production thinking afresh about the significance of the female in Asian cultures, or indeed about whether one could talk of Asian cultures in this context at all.

NOTES

1   Watanabe Tamotsu in SCOT: *Suzuki Tadashi's World* (a brochure published to cele-brate the 10th anniversary of The Toga Festival), 1992, 52–55.

2   Suzuki himself, in a television interview, says that the Nurse is reading the book aloud to the Old Man, which, however, does not accord with the details con-firmed by the videotaped production.

3   The above quotations from the American and British press, which follow, are taken from the anniversary brochure mentioned above, 51.

4   Ted Hughes quoted by Michael Kustow in his article in *The Independent*, November 19, 1994. A lone voice among London critics, Kustow deplores the devastatingly negative reception by the British critics of the foreign produc-tions (a German *Romeo and Juliet*, an American *Merchant of Venice*, Suzuki's *Lear*, etc.) presented in the "Everybody's Shakespeare" Festival at the Barbican. He

wonders whether the British critics are "maidenly" in "preserving our classical heritage intact" or, rather, "skinheads warning off trespassers." He quotes Ted Hughes who came to see Suzuki's *Lear*: "Our resistance to foreign innovations in Shakespeare production has to do with the way we internalise the complete works as a national sacred book of rites."

10

The Chronicle of Macbeth: Suzuki method acting in Australia, 1992

IAN CARRUTHERS

By Suzuki's standards, the structure of The Chronicle of Macbeth is much simpler than any of his other adaptations of Macbeth.[1] The project was initiated by Carrillo Gantner of Playbox Theatre in Melbourne, the idea being to open up new approaches to performance in Australia through the use of Asian theatre training systems such as Suzuki's. For this reason it was technically a beginners' piece for actors with only two or three months' experience of Suzuki training.[2] However, as Suzuki explained in interview, another important factor was that "With Shakespeare the story is generally known, so the audience are able to see what's done to that story. They can enjoy that; it's a deeper experience to compare their own perceptions of that story with the presented version onstage."[3] Indeed, this was one of the drawing cards of the production. Working with a cultural icon would allow audiences to assess the relative abilities of the actors using Suzuki's acting method as well as Suzuki's approach to the play.

In stripping the play down to the story of the Macbeths, and relegating all of the other parts to members of a chorus, Suzuki wanted to recast it structurally as a postmodern Greek tragedy. A part of this strategy was that it would allow two major actors 'star turns', while not over-taxing the inexperienced. The approach had worked well for Shiraishi Kayoko, Kanze Hideo, and a young chorus in Night Feast 3. Unfortunately, the ambiguity of the contract, as to whether this was a Suzuki production with Australian actors or a Playbox production with a guest director from Japan, and union regulations that hampered selection of experienced Suzuki-trained actors from Sydney, limited his options.[4] In interview he commented, "What's important is the selection of the actors . . . [But here] It's as if the casting had already been done before the selection process began. Bringing Ellen into the production was one thing that was necessary" (213). When asked to explain how things had changed from his original expectations, he replied, "Especially in terms of the playing of Macbeth, a lot of things changed. And Lady Macbeth became a stronger character. In the Japanese version she doesn't bring the sword to

Macbeth. So there were alterations"(219). In effect Ellen Lauren, with her eight years of Suzuki training and stage-experience as Agave in Suzuki's 1991 production of *Dionysus*, became the production's locomotive.

The Chronicle of Macbeth is faithful to the core of Shakespeare's play (the story of the Macbeths) and respectfully preserves Shakespeare's poetry; however, as in *Night Feast 3*, it makes radical contemporary use of the witches as murderers (symbols of Macbeth's passion and energy), unmooring the "Double, double toil and trouble" speech for choral use in scenes 4 and 10. It also transposes the action of the play to an institutional space that could be seen as the meeting hall of a New Age religious cult, a prison, or an infirmary.

A huge inverted double cross hung over a raised central entrance, down the steps of which spilled a blood-red carpet. Asymmetrically arranged rows of white chairs glowed incandescently in the dark, as if waiting for aliens to be beamed down onto them. Like Ionesco's chairs they took on a mysterious life of their own, especially during the Banquet scene in which they all – not only Banquo's seat – remained empty.

Scene 1 began with Serge Aubrey's "The Burnt Garden" played at deafening volume to suggest a certain fanaticism, while figures in black kimonos and nun-like wimples moved from the wings across stage, clutching copies of *Macbeth*. Reaching their chairs on the fourteenth musical beat, they turned as one, and sat. Downstage right, in front of the rest, sat an old man (who was to play the role of "Macbeth") on a golden chair. As the last bars of music ended, two cult leaders (The Reverend Father and Mother, played by Carrillo Gantner and Ellen Lauren) appeared on a blood-red rostrum at the back of the stage to lead their followers in a solipsistic liturgical chant called "Farewell to History." It seemed to refer to their reading of *Macbeth*, for they held their closed books at chest-level while chanting "But this one [this reading] is different from always / Finish this one / Then there can be rest." They then opened their books on the Reverend Mother's cue, "Today we shall do *Macbeth*. Begin reading!", and started to intone the "Tomorrow, and tomorrow, and tomorrow" speech in unison (v. v, 19–28). "Out, out brief candle!" was delivered individually in quickening succession until it became an overlapping babble of experiential difference – only to subside into the undertow of uniform experience on "life's but a walking shadow / Full of sound and fury / Signifying nothing." The music swelled trumpet-tongued as the words died, the cult leaders disappeared back into the darkness under their inverted double cross, the chorus rose slowly, turned, and exited, still mouthing the words of the text which they read as they walked. The man called "Macbeth" now rose and began "If it were done when 'tis done, then 'twere well / It were done quickly" (I. vii).

Complex things were going on here. Some sense of the technical difficulty – and dramatic power – of Suzuki's approach to the play is given by the director's note to Peter Curtin (Macbeth) at this point:

Peter, when you're sitting there as this little old man who is in trouble, as the music comes in for Scene 2, your transformation as the warrior Macbeth must take place . . . Standing up needs to be indicative of something big happening inside, not just 'standing up' . . . Construct forms, sculpt movements. How many steps, how far back do you go behind your chair? (239)

Suzuki also side-lit his actors to give them greater presence, lifting out their movements from ground and background in order to make them seem as if – in this deluded old man's fantasy – they were floating in space. The slow-motion *ten tekka ten* exercise became Suzuki's basic grammar with which he "raised the stakes" of the Farewell Cult entrances and exits. Instructions for this were to maintain an even, slow-motion walk that would defy physics in its smooth tautness of line.

As Ellen Lauren (Lady Macbeth) points out,

All of the exercises . . . are basically impossible. What Suzuki is asking you to do are movements that are not seen in daily life . . . that take the body out of a habitual way of moving. Then he asks you to maintain an equilibrium and steadiness as if you held a glass of water inside the body which you don't want to spill . . . So you wilfully create a collision in the body and try to control it, keeping a very strong specific outward focus at the same time . . . Suzuki thinks the actor should do something extraordinary on the stage, something that not just anybody can do. (221)

In the intimate spaces in which the production played around Australia, audiences quickly became aware of the extraordinary difficulty of what they were seeing, for they were close enough to feel the electrical energy pouring off actors' bodies and glistening on their skin as sweat. Peter Curtin vividly describes the experience from the actor's point of view in the opening minutes of the play:

Imagine that you are in this position (demonstrates and holds a low knee-bend, feet wide apart). You seem to be sitting on a chair, but you're actually not; you're taking all the tension here – the *hara* – to guarantee the correct intensity for delivering your lines. So that chair can be taken away at any time and you're still 'sitting' there. Imagine that you have committed yourself to this position and you're going to hold it for probably three or four minutes before your next soliloquy. Just to your left are the equivalent of about six car headlights on high-beam, and you're looking into them, and not blinking [so as to hold your focus and concentration]. Imagine that you are also listening to nine witches coming on, smashing the floor with staves. While this is happening, you count the beat so that, when they have smashed the

9 *The Chronicle of Macbeth*, directed by Suzuki Tadashi, Playbox Theatre, Melbourne, 1992. John Nobbs as Banquo's ghost.

floor thirteen times, that's when you'll give up this position, and start to make your move across the stage, When they hit the floor for the nineteenth time, you'll know there's going to be silence and you will be there with your line. (139)

Suzuki was well aware of the difficulty of what he was demanding of his actors – testing their very reason for being onstage. In interview before rehearsals started he had insisted that, "Until they've actually done *Macbeth*, they won't have a clear sense of what it is they're trying to do" (205). Hence his insistence on the importance of Suzuki training, which was undertaken initially for two weeks in Toga in August 1991, for a further two weeks at November auditions in Melbourne, and then right throughout rehearsals in February 1992 and the entire run of the play (March–May). Early on in the rehearsal period he provided his actors with the conceptual grammar of his method:

My argument with the ideas of Stanislavski is that Stanislavski does not provide a good way to deal with the moment when we must see that which cannot be seen. So we need to develop a system to do that. As actors, the first thing we must do is throw off that which is unnecessary, that which we bring from our daily lives. Of course there is a minimum of behaviour that is dictated by the action of the script, for instance the actors' entrances. But if movement is used just to explain the words, we must get rid of it. Then we must look at ourselves from the audience's point of view to see if what we are doing is effective. In Rodin's sculpture "The

Thinker", the movement of thought inside is obvious. Yet no-one actually sits in this position when they want to think. Rodin has effectively lied in order to show us the truth.

Sitting in a chair is not just daily life behaviour. We can take this formalism of sitting to express something to the audience that they cannot see. What then is the man-made structure we must impose upon this action to make it clear? . . .

When working out what you're doing there can be changes made within the structure, but these must not be improvisational changes. You must have the structure before you can really begin to rehearse. Your concentration should be on doing things as well as possible. We're all human, and we all come to rehearsal in different states each day. When we're not in tune physically it's difficult to get quickly to the required level because this kind of theatre requires great intensity. This is why I stress the idea of exercises and training before each performance. (236–38)

Along with a basic grammar of stylization, Suzuki also provided his actors with a set of hypotheses within which to understand their function within the frame story:

(1) The play is the evocation of the memories, the consciousness of the person we're going to call "Macbeth."

(2) This person exists within an organization (religious, terrorist or otherwise) called "The Farewell Cult," and is to be destroyed somehow.

(3) What we have to realize are the visual workings onstage of that person's spirit; that is, everything that takes place behind "Macbeth" onstage exists only in his fantasy.

(4) Real present time begins on the two occasions when "Macbeth" sits in his chair downstage (during the "Farewell to History" chants at beginning and end of the performance).

(5) The person in the cult who facilitates "Macbeth's realization" is The Reverend Mother (who plays "Lady Macbeth" in the play-within-the-play).

(6) This space is where The Reverend Father (who role-plays "The Illusion or Subconscious of Macbeth") performs psychoanalysis on the man called "Macbeth." (233–34)

The model Suzuki gave his Australian cast for the *modus vivendi* of The Farewell Cult was the mass indoctrination leading to group suicide of Jim Jones's Guyana cult. In 1992 David Kuresh's fiery shoot-out with the FBI had not yet taken place in Waco, Texas, but the "doubling" of such scenarios throughout recent history suggests the uncanny potency of Suzuki's updating of *Macbeth*.

It was the framing device's ability to turn *Macbeth* into a play-within-a-play, and the support of a coherent anti-realist acting method which were so powerfully new in their Australian combination. In order to expand on the kind of experience that the Suzuki Method was opening up for actors and audiences, I shall concentrate on the two climactic scenes of Suzuki's production: scene 11 (v. i, 1–72) and scene 12 (v. iii; v. v, 1–28, 51).

Most scenes and passages from *Macbeth* were chosen by Suzuki to show the old man drifting in and out of his "Macbeth" visions (created by unsatisfied desire). The effect of this was most fully realized in the rapid and unpredictable oscillation from one state to the other. At the end of scene 10 (IV. i), the Witches, standing on their chairs to suggest their visionary status, show "Macbeth" a line of kings (disembodied voices projected by chorus members from different parts of the auditorium). "Macbeth" bravely attempts to face his fears but, despite a fierce struggle, is inexorably bent by his paranoias. These culminate in a vision of "the spirit of Banquo" (played by John Nobbs) at which "Macbeth" finally quails as he realizes the futility of all his struggles. (See photo 9.) Reawakening at "Where are they? Gone!" (133), the old man returns exhausted to his chair, and immediately – perhaps this is a dream projection or displacement of his own guilt? – envisions scene 11 (Lady Macbeth's sleepwalking) taking place behind him. The fact that he stares glassy-eyed out into the audience while they see "Lady Macbeth" glide forward out of the darkness behind him suggests a summons from the depths of the unconscious. In a note to Curtin, Suzuki put it this way,

Each Apparition is a more difficult opponent, so you must really build. A snake, even when defeated past hope, still tries to strike. So long as we're struggling, there's something healthy about us. When the battle ceases, senility sets in. Think about the structure of this. You wring out your last energy in the struggle against the witches.

It's the death of your partner that causes you to give up . . . Make it very clear that the "brief candle" is your wife . . . This theatre is the world of your heart, which it encompasses . . . Something we weren't conscious of becomes visible. You face your internal world. (244–45)

The emotion-charged strangeness of scene 11 is heightened by the appearances of the Doctor (David Pledger) and Gentlewoman (Katia Molino) who tiptoe furtively from empty chair to empty chair in a farcical ballet of fear. They are dressed absurdly: the 'Gentlewoman' like a maid from a French farce in frilly pinafore and cap, the Doctor with raybans, stethoscope, white coat, gartered socks and black shoes – but no trousers. Their intonations are quite unnatural, stylizing the cracked, scurrying voices of their mounting fright as they approach the blood-red carpet of light down which "Lady Macbeth" (Ellen Lauren) will travel. Suzuki reinforces our sense of this as "Macbeth's vision" by setting it up as a two-camera shot. They look front and see her coming through the audience, which reverses what the audience sees: Lauren entering behind them.

Though dream-like, there is a visual logic at work, Suzuki using lateral crossing of the stage for the Farewell Cult's narrative in scenes 1 and 13, diagonal crossing for the dynamic, violently aggressive stamping marches of the witches in scenes 4 and 10, and vertical upstage-downstage movement along the central blood-red carpet for moments of trance-possession and vision. When the little old man who sits DSR travels into his own nightmares, he has to move laterally across to the "river of blood" and make a right-angled turn onto it "as Macbeth" in order to play out his desires – the murders of Duncan and Banquo. Up this river, beyond the dais and under the sign of a "double cross" lies the darkened "room of power," where the murders of Duncan and Banquo take place, and from which issue the Reverend Father and Mother, whether as their Cult "selves" or as The Illusion of Macbeth and Lady Macbeth.

This carpet, then, is the runway where Suzuki's actors must "make visible the invisible". When in scene 5 Macbeth emerges from the dark inner room with "I have done the deed" (II. ii) he must be able to convey to the audience a vivid image of precisely what has taken place there. By taking Peter Curtin physically through a range of possibilities in front of the other cast members – sitting on his chest, covering his mouth and slitting his throat, or plunging an imaginary dagger up through his rib-cage to the heart as he tried to sit up – Suzuki encouraged him to put the precise and unmediated physical horror of the offstage moment so vividly into his body that it would become visible onstage in the motor-memory's traumatic nervous discharge.

The Sleepwalking scene was another such moment of "traumatic discharge," this time displaced in "dreams that shake us nightly" onto Lady Macbeth. "Out, damned spot!" was delivered in visceral anguish out of a cavernous darkness lit, apparently, by the single candle in Lauren's hand. On the line "Hell is murky," she sank slowly into a low crouch, seeming, because of the looseness of her robes, to compact down as she moved from rostrum to the front of the stage, getting smaller and smaller in terms of height – but somehow more dense in her compactness as she approached audience-space, as if about to implode under the gravity of her guilt. Physically, this was real, the scene being, for the performer, a litany of screaming muscles that replaced any need for psychology. "Lady Macbeth's breakdown is terribly sad, but you can't *play* sad," was Lauren's response to my question about this in interview; "what you can play is struggle, and you don't manufacture that struggle on a presentational level; you actually put your body in the position where you're struggling" (233–34).

The parameters Suzuki gave her to work within were also clear and precise:

This sort of mad person isn't locked into a single concentration. You're doing one thing and suddenly a completely different sensibility is there. Separate movement from speech. The order of how things happened is confused, out of context. Everything happens suddenly, jerkily, cut from what came before. The changes are very quick, but give them time to happen. You get smaller as you approach the front, more condensed. (241)

Lauren herself described the experience in this way:

What happened in rehearsal was that, when I began to isolate movement from voice, I got into a rhythm that drove Suzuki up the wall, a *predictable* rhythm of move then speak, move and speak. So then I had to begin the process of "shattering time" if you will. . ., trying to jumble the timing sequence so I could keep the audience from knowing what was going to happen next. I chose to defy everything he told me about moving and then speaking. And that's how I began.

He likes it when you throw things back at him. All his tenets and rules are simply to give rise to freedom for the actor. So I began by saying "Out, damned spot!" while moving. Then I isolated it down to "Out, damned . . . spot!", in which "spot" is said in the stillness. From there I decided moment by moment how to structure my body in space, the physical impression I wanted to make, and then how much time each structure and transition would take, as in a dance.

But please understand, it's not simply about movement – the body is there to determine the voice. I literally counted out beats – how long in the stillness I would hold before the voice would come out of the body. You're working with your breath to create a great deal of tension and energy in the body but you've also got to be preparing to speak right away, without losing that energy. This takes enormous breath control.

Suzuki's greatest actress, Kayoko Shiraishi, was once asked how she was able to change the sensibility of the three very different characters she was playing in *The Trojan Women* [Hecuba, Cassandra, and a contemporary bag lady]. She simply answered, "I change the way I breathe." I understand now a little bit more about what she meant. Breath is a powerful force inside the body. By the audience watching you fight to control the uncontrollable, in a sense you begin to control their breathing – and indeed, when I watch SCOT company performing, I find I often hold my breath for long periods of time. (222–23)

The most breathtaking moment of scene 11 occurred in just this fashion. At "Banquo's buried. He cannot come out on's grave," the Doctor, hidden behind a chair, blurted out "Even so?", rose – and then froze in horror, hand-to-mouth, as Lady Macbeth slowly turned to look in his direction. Lauren describes the subtext of this moment:

Suzuki sets up this incredible woman going through this crisis with this French farce on the side . . . and then suddenly he slams the two worlds together. Lady Macbeth hears something and turns and looks at them. Only what you realize is that what Lady Macbeth has heard is something very different *inside* herself. It's an enormous moment. It's funny, it's horrific. I did it one day in rehearsal almost by accident. And then Suzuki said, "Really look at them", so I looked at them and turned back and he said, "No, no, no. When you look at them, hold it for a very long time, because that's the only way the audience will know you *don't* see them". . . So now I literally count to 9 – and it's killing me (laughs) because I'm really low to the ground, and then I turn back.

Suzuki then says, "When you turn back, you've held time in a way that you've *created* something, and when you turn back the idea isn't that you've turned your body back to the audience; your centre of gravity, here [in the *hara*], grabs the audience and turns *it* around so they can see with your eyes."

What I've described creates a very different physical reality in the body. Among other things, it creates a great amount of tension, and this is one of the great problems when you start working with this method. Without proper control, it creates constriction and tension and a flat-line machine-gun vocality which is probably what you hear in *The Chronicle of Macbeth* with some of the actors who've just begun this training. Like anything objective and difficult, it takes a long time to gain enough control to begin to compose inside this sensibility. It takes enormous mental as well as physical tenacity. (224–25)

As Lady Macbeth glides back into the darkness and the Doctor cries "God, God forgive us all!" (crossing himself with his stethoscope), Scene 12 begins with a return to reality as sudden as anything in *The Singing Detective*. Seyton-the-cook (Joel Markham) – in fat-suit, chef's hat and clogs – rolls in a meal-on-wheels for "Macbeth," who returns to the state of being an institutionalized old man. Suzuki's note to Markham was that he should play Sancho Panza to this institutionalized Don Quixote.[5] If the first transformation in Scene 2 from little old man to "Macbeth" was heroic, this reversal is tragically pathetic, and the sympathy of "Sancho Panza" helps to underline it. Everything said has a "Double, double" *entendre* as Shakespeare's words pull away from the action. "Macbeth" comes out of the trance in which he "saw" Lady Macbeth's anguish, stares at his plate, up at the cook as if to say "Where am I?", gulps down his soup ("I have supp'd full of horrors" is suggested), and then returns to his fantasy with "Bring me no more . . . reports." His abuse of the Maidservant, "The devil damn thee black, thou cream-faced loon" builds for several lines as he rises, waving fork in the air. Each line of verbal abuse seems to hammer her further into the ground, as she cowers back, fearful of being speared by flying cutlery. Our attention is divided between admiration for Molino's physical virtuosity as she bends deeper and deeper backwards, and concern for her safety in the face of a nursing home tyrant. "Macbeth" disappears as, on "Take thy face hence," the fork clatters to the ground and the old man turns to his friend the cook for sympathy with "Seyton! – I am sick at heart." He sits at "This push will cheer me ever, or disseat me now" (reinforcing the chair-of-power image) and complains feelingly, "that which should accompany old age . . . I must not look to have." Another of Shakespeare's rapid mood swings is reinterpreted at "Give me my armour!", the old man shaking his arms in a towering impotence of rage like a child "spitting the dummy." Seyton's refusal, "'Tis not needed yet," is motherly in its concern, but when the old man demands again, "Give me mine armour!", his response is to take the napkin that has covered the food, and tie it round "Macbeth's" neck like a bib. The petulant demand, "Give me my staff" sees the fork returned carefully to the geriatric warrior's waving hand in such a way as to suggest that the big baby should finish his meal; and the old man's whispered, "Doctor, the Thanes fly from me," has a wonderful resonance somewhere between pleasure and despair at gaining attention but losing respect – an effect latent in *Macbeth* but released with shocking freshness in this estranging institutionalized context.

Finally, at "Wherefore was that cry? – The Queen, my lord, is dead," the old man's nightmare returns to claim him. The music of Serge Aubrey's "The Burnt Garden" returns, and the Doctor, Maidservant, and Cook creep off.

Scenes 12 and 13 conclude the play, in circular fashion, by repeating scene 1. On a signal from the Reverend Father, the chorus of believers, which now includes a broken "Macbeth," rise from their chairs to chant "Double, double toil and trouble." One significant change is that staves are no longer needed to pound the floor at this point; the same stirring motion is made, but, this time, book in hand: Shakespeare's *Macbeth* is used as the ladle with which to stir the institutional soup of history. A final surprise remains. The lights dim as the chant continues. When they come back up, and before the audience can begin clapping, the Reverend Mother announces sternly, "This concludes today's labours. Thank you. You may go home."

Suzuki's contemporizing of the witches as members of a New Age religious group may have been pin-point accurate in the context of *Macbeth – The Rise of the Farewell Cult*, for shocking events involving Aum Shinrikyo were continually bubbling up to the surface of Japanese public life between 1990 and 1996. However, for many Australians, the chief value of *The Chronicle* seemed to lie, not so much in its offering of yet another interpretation of the play – though it was controversially that – but in its introduction of a new performative approach. Judging by audience responses to *The Chronicle* at the 1992 Mitsui Festival in Tokyo, seeing Australian actors working to fuse Shakespeare's original words with Suzuki's performance style was as much a point of interest in Japan as it was in Australia.[6] While almost all could appreciate the qualitative, stylistic differences between the performances of Peter Curtin (Macbeth) and Ellen Lauren (Lady Macbeth), the explanation of the critic Uchino Tadashi is perhaps the most even-handed. According to Uchino, though "she obviously does not have training in Shakespearean acting," Ellen Lauren offers "one of the best examples of how Suzuki method can be applied to Shakespearean acting." On the other hand,

It is interesting to see the actor of Macbeth who tried to preserve his Shakespeare training. Obviously he is not very young and his Suzuki training is a new input. These two different kinds of physical acting are struggling within him, and never integrated – and this too is good.[7]

NOTES

1   *Yoru to Tokei* (*Night and the Clock*) Tokyo, 1975; *Utage no Yo 3* (*Night Feast 3*) Toga, 1978; *Macbeth – Osarabakyô no ryûsei* (*Macbeth – The Rise of the Farewell Cult*) Mito, 1991; and *Sekai no hate kara kon'nichiwa 1*(*Greetings from the Edge of the World 1*) Toga, 1993. According to Suzuki in conversation, *The Rise of the Farewell Cult*, was "basically the same play as *The Chronicle of Macbeth* but with a much bigger cast."

2   In 1992 most members of the SCOT Company (The Suzuki Company of Toga) had worked and trained together for ten years or more.

3   Ian Carruthers ed., "Reading Suzuki Tadashi's *The Chronicle of Macbeth* in Australia" (unpublished manuscript), 209. Page numbers for all subsequent references to this manuscript will be given in brackets after each quotation. All quotations from *Macbeth* are from the Arden edition, Kenneth Muir, ed. (London: Methuen, 1972).

4   Something similar had happened in *The Tale of Lear* but there he had been able to replace his first Lear, when he proved inadequate to the task, with the actor he initially wanted, Tom Hewitt.

5   Suzuki emphasized to Peter Curtin, "In this structure, you must be the strangest. You're the most recent convert [to the Farewell Cult] . . . There has to be evident your folly of taking every little thing and blowing it up. What we want to get at is that the followers are *more* radical than the leader in their simple-mindedness. These are not people being dragged in against their will. The mob is *more* frightening than the dictator . . . What I'm giving you is the throughline of fanaticism through idealism." Personal notes taken in *Chronicle* rehearsals, Books I, 15; II, 42.

6   For audience response in Tokyo, see Tony Chapman's and Zi-Yin Wang's video

documentary on the production of *The Chronicle of Macbeth* entitled *One Step on a Journey*, SBS, 1992. For the extraordinarily positive response of Australian audiences as opposed to critics, see Patricia Mitchell's "Responses to a Questionnaire distributed at performances of *The Chronicle of Macbeth*," in Ian Carruthers and Patricia Mitchell, *Theatre East and West: Problems of Difference or Problems of Perception? (Suzuki Tadashi's Australian Macbeth, 1992)*, La Trobe Asian Studies Papers (Melbourne: La Trobe University, 1995), 20–30 and 40–43.

7   Uchino Tadashi's review of *The Chronicle* provided by Peter Curtin (no publisher or date given).

The rose and the bamboo: Noda Hideki's
Sandaime Richâdo

SUZUKI MASAE

When Noda Hideki started his wild adaptations of Shakespeare in the late 1980s, it was a time when various styles of Shakespearean productions or Shakespeare-based plays seemed to have become acceptable in Japan. Deguchi Norio had completed producing all of Shakespeare's plays in Jeans style in the underground theatre JeanJean using Odashima Yûshi's translations.[1] Productions like *Ninagawa Macbeth* and Suzuki Tadashi's *The Tale of Lear* had had their international debuts, and various experimental fusions of western and Japanized styles were emerging. Using Odashima's translation as a base, Noda produced *Twelfth Night* (1986), *Much Ado About Nothing* (1990), *Sandai-me Richâdo* (Richard III, 1990) and *A Midsummer Night's Dream* (1992). Since he had a reputation as an original writer, Japanese audiences already took for granted that substantial textual changes would be made without any implication of "blasphemy."[2]

Among all his Shakespeare-based plays, Noda's *Sandai-me Richâdo* is particularly distinctive for showing how his consciousness as a writer overlaps with his own understanding of Shakespeare as a fellow-writer. Inspired by the episodes of Shakespeare's imaginary love life in Anthony Burgess's *Nothing Like the Sun* and also by the mystery presented in Josephine Tey's *The Daughter of Time*, Noda imaginatively fuses the accounts of Shakespeare and his own younger brother Richard with the Yorkist Richard's alleged crimes. Above all, it was the complex and ironic character of Shakespeare's *Richard III* that made Noda write *Sandai-me Richâdo*.

When asked what he has in common with Shakespeare, Noda once answered "Our love for the theatre that overcomes our grudge towards and hatred of society."[3] He later explained in an interview,

I meant to explain why Shakespeare's villains are attractive. If the hatred of the society were greater, the author would have given heavier punishments to his villains. Also, the plays would have been too argumentative and less interesting . . . I feel the same way in reading Kabuki plays. Kabuki plays also include some morality and punish evil at the end, but they wouldn't be interesting without their villains.[4]

It can be said that Noda finds certain hero-villains attractive for their playful-ness, for their bloody but merry pranks, and because they inspire what Noda calls his own "wild fancy"[5] as a director/playwright.

Another reason Noda seems to have become interested in this particular work of Shakespeare is the hero-villain's relation with his "lost" nephews, as well as the metaphors of flowers and plants in the play. In his earlier original works, Noda had often expanded his "wild fancy" by creating historical or fictional villains stamped as "kidnappers" or "child-killers." At the core of those plays with a villain-motif was also a motif of "lost children." Noda prefers to recreate such hero-villains with something of the innocent mischievousness of little boys, whose sometimes cruel jokes and ambitions take the form of outlandish children's games.

A good example is *The Prisoner of Zenda – The Night of Our Mossy Infancy* (1980), his representative play in the 1980s. In this play, a comical but enigmatic character called Omoto, whose name is derived from a plant, which can be literally translated as "Forever Blue," plays a crucial role. According to Noda, this character was modelled on Gilles de Rais (1404–40), the French marshal who once was regarded as a hero for his battles against the English, but who later became known as "Bluebeard" for his alleged murder of 140 children. To Noda, both Richard III and Gilles de Rais, with their alleged crimes as child-killers, are characters caught up in "wild fancy," as writer/directors are. "Wild fancy" is also the source of children's games.

In this essay, I would like to focus on the play-within-the-play element and the strategy of localization in Noda Hideki's *Sandai-me Richâdo*, together with his imagery of plants (especially the symbolic use of the bamboo tree as an emblem of "wild fancy") via punning and radical word play. My aim is to show how all these elements are interwoven into a "wild" reinterpretation of Shakespeare's Richard as a villain-hero who recuperates the spirit of childhood adventure.

The first trial: the play-within-the-play and the strategy of localization

In *Richard III*, Shakespeare created a scene in which the ghosts of the villain-hero's victims remind him of his alleged crimes and foretell the final act of justice (5.5). The scene is likely to have been created to make the audience feel relieved that the order on which their society is based revives on stage with the victory of Richmond, the founder of Tudor England. However, through-out the stage history of *Richard III*, audiences have tended to be fascinated by the villain Richard's merry pranks, sympathizing with him, rather than with his victims. Are we not tempted to imagine what would have happened if Richard did get a horse in exchange for his kingdom? Noda wants us to imagine just this.

The opening scene of *Sandai-me Richâdo* takes the form of a radical departure from Richard's famous line at the climax of the play, "A horse, a horse! My kingdom for a horse!"(5.4.7). It starts in a tent in Bosworth Field where Richâdo (Richard) is rolling in agony, as if he were seeing a nightmare.[6] Hearing Richâdo's cry, three characters, namely Mâchan (who later reveals himself as Shylock in *The Merchant of Venice*), Chiropractic (a character later superimposed with Buckingham), and Shinri (Truth) – the Daughter of Time, who is also elided with Hastings in the course of the play – appear in front of Richâdo with the galloping sound of horse hooves. Calling themselves Richâdo's defenders, they show him a contract which offers him the chance to repudiate his reputation as a villain. The contract signed, the scene changes into a trial.

"Shakespeare,"[7] the author-and-prosecutor, is seated with his family opposite the defenders, Mâchan, Chiropractic, and Shinri. Twelve seats in the audience become a jury box. The Chief Judge, seated with his brother, the secretary Irudake (The-Clerk-Just-Sitting-There), announces that Richâdo is accused of "massacre, including the child-murder in the Tower of London." The alleged crime is re-enacted as a play-within-the play, according to the record of the prosecutor (the play by "Shakespeare").

The defenders try to attack the weak points of the record, often using syllogisms and various other specious tactics to influence the audience, so as to change the course of the play-within-the-play. For example, when the murder of Aka-bara Ô (The King of the Red Rose) is represented (the murder scenes of Henry VI and his son Edward are combined into one), the defenders claim that political murder during time of war is a heroic deed and not a crime. When the prosecutors accuse Richâdo of enjoying the murder itself, thus of having a cruel nature, the defenders quote Richard III's line, "Take that, to end thy agony"(*Henry VI Part 3*, 5.5), to claim that it was in fact a mercy killing. The defenders further twist the convention of soliloquy or "asides." They point out that the information in Shakespeare's record concerning Richard's hunchback, lame foot or any of his crooked intentions to murder his brother or wife appear only in his "asides," to which nobody else could have listened. Therefore, they say, this must come from the writer's own imagination and cannot be counted as a valid record of the prosecution. This argument can develop into a criticism that recorded history depends on the politics of the time, but Noda does not go far into that and emphasizes the show element of an open trial.

10 *Sandaime Richâdo* (adaptation of *Richard III*), directed by Noda Hideki for Yumeno Yûminsha, Tokyo Globe-za, 1990. The trial scene.

The trial further develops as a "family matter." First "Shakespeare's" boyhood days and married life are briefly introduced. Also introduced are his family and his wife's relations who also serve as prosecutors. These people are supposed to be from Stratford, but they speak in Kyûshû dialect (that of Noda's home region). During the intermission, they discuss the strategy to appeal to the sympathy of the jury (audience), and decide that "localization" of the play-within-the-play is necessary (scene 7):

MAJODAI   (I'm-A-Witch) We shouldn't depend just on Shakespeare's script.

SUTORAGIGÎ   (Cunning old man) Let's adapt it.

SHAKESPEARE   What do you mean?

SUTORAGIGÎ   We should rewrite it and make it something even fools can understand.

MAJODAI   In the first place, the characters' names are no good. Edward, George, Morton, and Buckingham, Norfolk, Hastings, and Stanley. And their titles are Baron, Count, King . . . And the names of [King] Edward's sons are Edward and Richard!

OBA-DE-WARUKA-KA   (What's-Wrong-Being-Her-Aunt) Aren't names given as signs to avoid confusion?

MAJODAI   Even "Richâdo Sansei" (Richard III) sounds like a very dignified villain.

SUTORAGIGÎ   How about calling him "Sandai-me"?

SHAKESPEARE Sandai-me!?
MAJODAI Sounds good.
SUTORAGIGÎ Good.
SHAKESPEARE But "sandai-me" (third generation) of what?[8]

Here we can see the basic idea behind Noda's localization of western classics. The suggestion is that it will be difficult to make the concept behind the words understood if they sound unfamiliar even to himself, and that the play will work better if it is drawn closer to the world of the audience. In a memo dated January 20, 1990, Noda contemplates how to localize Shakespeare's world for his audience and names the worlds of Kabuki, the tea ceremony, flower arrangement, Sumo wrestling, and the Yakuza in present-day Japan as something equivalent to the social hierarchy in Shakespeare's time, for tradition and heredity systems can still be found there.[9] For this reason, and because of its association with the Wars of the Roses, he chose the world of flower arrangement for his *Sandai-me Richâdo*. The Japanese *sandai-me* (the third generation), which betokens a tradition of succession, can be used for the head of the "family" of the world of traditional arts or the head of a Yakuza "family," which may "war" against different "families."

Thus, from scene 8, the character corresponding to King Edward of the White Roses in Shakespeare's *Richard III* is introduced to the jury as "Iemoto (a title given to the head of a school of a traditional Japanese art) Ikenobo-the-Sick," the head of a prestigious flower arrangement school. His wife, corresponding to Shakespeare's Queen Elizabeth, is transformed into proud "Madam Iemoto," who raised herself from the position of a mere tea-serving assistant clerk, but claims to be of the lineage of *Sen-no Rikyû* (who raised tea ceremony into an art form in sixteenth-century Japan). Instead of the Tower of London, prisoners in this play are led to the Tower of Kenzan, named after the metal base with spikes upon which flowers are arranged.

The names of the characters have much to do with their destiny in this play. "George Ikenobô," brother to both the Iemoto and Richâdo, is arrested not only because his name starts with a "G," as in Shakespeare's *Richard III*, but because Madam Iemoto predicted that a man with a foreign-sounding name would ruin the Ikenobô clan. "Richard" is, of course, also a foreign name, but his name in Japanese translation is pronounced as "Richâdo." What's more, in this play, it is not even transcribed in *katakana* as is the case with most words of foreign origin, but written in *hiragana*. Transcribed in this manner, it not only looks Japanized, but even suggests a character out of a children's picture book, since books for little children are written only in *hiragana* and are usually about heroes, fairies, and innocent characters. Regarded from this point of view, the *hiragana* name "Richâdo" may even suggest that he is a

character out of a boy's adventure book sharing something with the two
innocent but mischievous boys he is alleged to have murdered.

The imagery of the garden and the flowers

Noda's verbal alchemy in *Sandaime Richâdo* seems to work well because of his
highly original use of the rich imagery of flowers and plants in Shakespeare's
text(s). Needless to say, the historical name "The War of the Roses" suggests
flower personification anyway, and the metaphor of the "sick garden" is
generally familiar in Shakespeare's history plays. The garden is the kingdom
and the king is the root of a hereditary tree, as is suggested by Queen
Elizabeth in Shakespeare's *Richard III*, when she laments the death of King
Edward:

> Edward, my lord, thy son, our king, is dead.
> Why grow branches when the root is gone?
> Why wither not the leaves that want their sap? (2.2.40–43)

Thus King Edward's transformation into Ikenobô-Byôjaku ("Ikenobo-the
Sick"), head of a Flower Arrangement Family, is convincing. Furthermore,
the transformation of the intrigue and conflict in the British royal family into
those of a Japanese Flower Arrangement family allows the story to become
more than that of a struggle for power. The suggestion is that the hatred
incited by Madam Iemoto among the young princes is rooted in their conceptual differences concerning the art of arranging flowers, which is to say, in
their different ideas of a "kingdom":

MADAM IEMOTO The way of flower arrangement is not a way of war. It repre-
    sents peace. First, we'll make a circle, and then, we'll add a branch symbolis-
    ing heaven . . . and then we'll put another branch to crawl on earth, then create
    a triangle from half of a regular square, in which the third branch represents
    mankind. Heaven, Earth, and Man. This is harmony. This is the pattern of
    flower arrangement. This is an ideal kingdom . . .
RICHÂDO I wouldn't say so.
MADAM IEMOTO What would you say?
RICHÂDO Branches are not for decoration. They are for climbing.
MADAM IEMOTO For climbing?
RICHÂDO There may be a kingdom above the trees. We climb up branch after
    branch. It goes snap! . . . But we continue climbing. Then we hear the birds
    singing. The last branch breaks. We will brush it off. Then appears the blue
    sky. It's like a hole we wish to fall into. It's the kingdom over the trees.
    Compared to this, Iemoto's work is a garden in a box. A rotten utopia![10]

Madam Iemoto's utopia represents the traditional idea of flower arrangement, while Richâdo's idea is that of a wild children's game. Together with
George's wild flower arrangements titled "Dammit! I'll Kick Your Ass!" or
"Mind Your Own Fucking Business!," Richâdo's idea may be too radical for
Madam Iemoto. In the actual production, both Madam Iemoto's traditional
idea of flower arrangement and George's avant garde flower arrangements
were physically expressed on stage by a group of actors acting the parts of
flowers and plants. This visual emphasis on the difference between the brothers' wild spirit and their sister-in-law's rather serene version hints to the
audience (the jury) that Madam Iemoto had more reason to hate George than
Richâdo did.

A pun on the word "flower" (*hana* in Japanese) is also used to claim
Richâdo's innocence. When the defenders, Mâchan, Chiropractic, and
Shinri, appear in this play in the roles of courtiers on Richâdo's side and try to
make him look innocent, the prosecutor "Shakespeare" objects that they are
distorting his record. Chiropractic counters with a playful "message game"
based on the nature of distortion:

CHIROPRACTIC Honourable members of the jury, I'll whisper a sentence to the
    person at this end, and you keep whispering the message to the next person . . .
    Tell it exactly as you heard. The course of the play depends on your accuracy.
    Now, the last person, what did you hear?
THE LAST PERSON Richâdo is a hunchback . . .
CHIROPRACTIC All right. The sentence I whispered to the first person is this.
    [He gives a memo to someone in the audience.] Read this aloud.
ANOTHER PERSON Richâdo was not a hunchback.
    [A tumult in the court.]
CHIROPRACTIC He was not a hunchback. But he was turned into one in a
    minute or so. So if it comes to a rumour five hundred years old . . .
SHAKESPEARE Please stand up and tell us the truth. What did you hear? Wasn't
    it whispered to you that he was a hunchback from the beginning?
THE FIRST PERSON Yes.
SHAKESPEARE See? This is the true face of the defendants who are wearing the
    masks of conscience. Speaking of history? No, their words were lies from the
    beginning.
MÂCHAN Well said . . . Yes, it was the fruit of a lie . . . the message I wanted to
    deliver was that no matter how accurately the words are told, history will lose
    the fruit of its meaning if the flowers are false from the beginning.
HAHABAI You are losing the debate, Shakespeare.[11]

There is a pun here on the Japanese sound "*hana*" for the two different *Kanji*
characters meaning "flower" and "beginning," which are homonyms.

Whereas the point of this child's game apparently was to prove how the first message was distorted during the play-within-the play, the defenders claim that it was to prove that certain information can be controlled from the outset. In *Richard III*, Shakespeare shows his hero-villain manipulating the people around him by giving false information and controlling public opinion. But, as proposed in Tey's *The Daughter of Time*, Shakespeare's history plays on The War of the Roses themselves may be based on false information that Richard was a villain and a hunchback. Noda's pun on the word "flower" is apparently a mere nonsense, but he is again playing with the notion that recorded history depends on the politics of the time and that the playwright could have just made use of false information.

Destabilizing the boundary between illusion and reality

Feeling in the course of the trial that he will lose the debate if some proof that Richâdo is a child murderer is not shown, the prosecutor ("Shakespeare") decides to transgress the boundary between illusion and reality by entering the play himself. In the play-within-the-play, "Shakespeare" persuades Richâdo to sneak into the tower as "Kurogo," a conventionally invisible stage assistant dressed in black in Japanese Bunraku or Kabuki. Richâdo lays his hand on the imprisoned child, but "Shakespeare's" hand is laid on top of his. Just before the child is killed, the defender Mâchan catches the hand. But is the hand Richâdo's or "Shakespeare's"? Is it the hand of the playwright, or was the character moving his hand by himself? The jury is certainly confused by this transgression of boundaries. More confusing is that the defender Mâchan at this stage reveals himself as Shylock. "Shakespeare," feeling his position as the writer usurped by the fictional characters he created, pleads to the emotion of the jury that their kingdom, or the world of reality on which their happiness is based will be in danger if Richâdo is proved innocent:

SHAKESPEARE   I gave him (Richâdo) a heroic death as a villain. The defender
    Shylock gave him a horse and brought him from Bosworth Field to the court.
    What for?
SHYLOCK   To save him from false accusation.
SHAKESPEARE   No, because he took an interest in the kingdom he offered for a
    horse. Such a merchant is he. He had tried to buy a man's heart with money.
    Now he is here to take over our happy kingdom. That is why he is bringing in
    the shadows that do not exist[12]

Richâdo is finally proven guilty and is sentenced to end the play in his traditional role as a villain on the battle field. But does Shakespeare really prove his superiority as the writer of the play? As "Shakespeare" has noticed, Shylock's (Mâchan's) aim of offering Richâdo a trial was not to prove his innocence, but to revenge himself on "Shakespeare," who he thinks mistreated him in *The Merchant of Venice*. The boundary of reality and illusion is already blurred on stage.

It is then revealed that there had been another contract stating that Shylock can cut off one of "Shakespeare's" feet if Richâdo loses the trial. "Shakespeare" announces that no blood should be shed because it is not offered in the contract, but Shylock outwits him by pointing out that if he is hung upside down, no blood will drop when his foot is cut off. Thus, "Shakespeare" is stripped of his confidence as the god-like author who controls the characters and events in his plays and is imprisoned in the same cell as Richâdo. There "Shakespeare" finally recognizes Richâdo as his lame brother.

The twist that Noda has adopted from Anthony Burgess's novel is that "Shakespeare" has been jealous of his younger brother because he had set off to realize his boyhood dream in spite of his lame foot, while "Shakespeare" had stayed home to support his large family. In their childhood, they have shared the same dream of the kingdom above the skies, and "a foot" had been a code word for the brothers to symbolize a step towards the kingdom. In other words, "a foot" (which is interchangeable with the word "a horse") is connected with the power of creative imagination, which explains why Shylock, who sees "Shakespeare's" imagination as the source of the misery of the mistreated characters in his plays, threatens to cut off his foot.

The second trial: the bamboo of wild fancy

Now comes the phantasmagoric climax of the whole play in which a grove of bamboo trees moves toward "Shakespeare" and Richâdo. It is an echo of the opening scene of the play where Richâdo had been suffering from a nightmare, fearing the shadows of his alleged victims. But the bamboo trees seem to be moved by the characters "Shakespeare" has stamped as villains in his plays. The scene also reminds one of the scene from *Macbeth* where the forest of Birnam advances on the hero-villain, and also the final scene of Teshigawara's movie *Rikyû*,[13] in which the hero is surrounded by an uncountable number of bamboo trees, some of them hanging from the air like spikes, while he moves toward his death ritual as if walking in a dream. Because of its pliant nature, bamboo is used in many traditional Japanese crafts including tea-ceremony utensil making. It is also the best material for various childhood toys like "bamboo dragonfly," "bamboo swords" and "bamboo guns."[14] Yet the bamboo grove is profoundly mysterious, for it seems to grow endlessly toward the sky, and its white flower is rarely seen.

The particular species of bamboo surrounding "Shakespeare" and Richâdo is called *Môsô-dake*, which can also mean "mere wild fancy," for the sound "môsô" also means "illusion" or "wild fancy" in Japanese. Richâdo and "Shakespeare" start climbing this Bamboo of Wild Fancy to search for "the kingdom above the trees" they have been dreaming about in childhood. But wild-fancy is not only the source of creative games. It is also something that can turn into a nightmare if the person gets too much involved in it. If the children were left in the fields or in a tree after dark to play games forever, what would happen? It is this nightmarish side of wild fancy that "Shylock," the one accusing "Shakespeare" for his imagination, bitterly feels. The Judge and his brother ("the lost children") announce that climbing the Bamboo of Wild Fancy is part of the second trial given to Richâdo and "Shakespeare":

SHYLOCK   Keep climbing the Wild Fancy. Up, up. Keep climbing for a thousand years. In a thousand years you'll almost reach the white flowers. But when you think you've reached them, the tree will have already grown another thousand years . . . You keep climbing and all you see is our wild fancy. Only the agony of climbing remains.

WASUREGATAMI (Judge)   So this is the Last Judgement of the Wild Fancy.

OTÔFU (Clerk)   This is the Millennium of the Wild Fancy.

Both WASUREGATAMI (Judge) and OTÔFU (Clerk)   Here we close the trial of wild fancy.[15]

If one chases one's "wild fancy" forever, without knowing where the goal is, will that be joy or pain? This is also the trial every playwright of his type, Noda seems to say – including "Shakespeare" and Noda himself – must go through.

The revenge of the shadows versus the spirit of boyhood adventure

With the second cry of the cock, the bamboo tree "Shakespeare" has been climbing is torn down, and he finds himself at his desk where he has been writing a play. There is another meaning here, for the Japanese phrase for "kingdom above the trees," *jujô no ô-koku*, can also be read as "*kijô no ô-koku*," which means "the kingdom on the desk." The pun here leads to the conclusion that the kingdom the boys have been searching for above the trees could be seen as equivalent to the kingdoms that poets and playwrights create at their desks. This poet/playwright's reign is what Shylock and his troupe of shadows (the characters in Shakespeare's plays who had been destroyed as "villains" by the author) regard as their source of misery and try to usurp. In Shakespeare's *Richard III*, the villain-hero Richard was trying to be something like a playwright, confident in controlling the destinies of the people around him till he is threatened by the ghosts of those he destroyed.

But in *Sandai-me Richâdo*, it is Richâdo who saves the writer/director "Shakespeare," who has been threatened with usurpation by the characters he destroyed. Both Richâdo and "Shylock" share the bitterness of being turned into villains by "Shakespeare," but in the case of Shylock, his grudge is so deep that in the final battle scene he reappears endlessly from "Shakespeare's" desk no matter how many times Richâdo kills him. On the other hand, Richâdo's playful love of adventure overcomes his hatred of those who have created him as a deformed figure, which reminds us of Noda explaining that what he has in common with Shakespeare is "our love for the theatre that overcomes our grudge and hatred towards society" and also that if hatred were greater, "the plays would have been too argumentative and would have grown less interesting." To Noda, "love for the theatre" is also related to his playful spirit of adventure, as Richâdo answers "Shakespeare" when asked whether he had killed the two little boys and what the true nature of his war was:

RICHÂDO   The boys are only held captives by the shadows-without-substance.
SHAKESPEARE   Held as captives? Are you going to rescue them?
RICHÂDO   To rescue the spirit of adventure. That is my ambition.
SHAKESPEARE   So my story of the flowers was false from the beginning. With
    my wild fancy underneath, I have made a false story on the desk.[16]

At the climax of *The Prisoner of Zenda*, the Lucifer-like Omoto descends from heaven to hell announcing that he is sacrificing himself to "give buoyancy to the lost child(ren)," and the play ends with the scene of a child-hero rising above the sky. In the same manner, in *Sandai-me Richâdo*, Richâdo cuts off his own foot and descends from the bamboo tree, asking "Shakespeare" to free the Adventurous Spirit imprisoned only in Wild Fancy (*Môsô-dake*), which takes the form of his lost young nephews. After all the quick-changing scenes and logic jumping, Noda ends the play with a quiet image of a bamboo tree reaching out to heaven and the silhouettes of the two lost children, who are identified with "Shakespeare" and Richâdo. Thus, with the elements of a play-within-a-play, children's games, and the imagery of nature associating Richâdo's ambition with that of a child's fantasy, the audience can experience a feeling of resurrection instead of guilt about sympathizing with this alleged child-killer.

To Noda, Shakespeare is not a foreign rose to be planted in a pot but a soil to nourish a new form of indigenous plant. The bamboo tree of "wild fancy" suggests that Noda's localization is not only aimed merely at simplifying the play for the audience's sake, but that it is a fantastical meditation on his own position as a writer/director. To him, "translation" is an impossible exercise if considered merely as an importation of a Shakespearean world into Japanese, for the very process of searching for genuine Japanese equivalents of Shakespearean names, images, localities, etc., takes us impossibly far. Noda the "adapter" abandons himself to a jouissance of punning and infinite deferral of meaning, infinite play. It is how Noda interweaves the images of his own understanding of the world – or himself – into his source materials that the audience is to anticipate. The more he adds his own elements of fancy, the more refreshing and creative are his plays. In other words, to him, western plays, including Shakespeare, are not to be used as models, but to be digested as a source of inspiration. Traditional culture is equally a source of inspiration for him. However, he will not accept it as a potted *bonsai* pine to be tended, but as a playground where bamboo grows wildly. With the image of the bamboo associated with playfulness and natural growth, Noda has certainly found a new type of fascination with Richard's status as hero-villain.

NOTES

1 For the Odashima translation, see "Introduction, p.3."

2 In an interview held on May 9, 1996 at the Cocoon Theatre, Shibuya, Tokyo, Noda explained that he thought it appropriate to change the word order and introduce word-play when adapting translated works because they are dislocated already. He further hinted that he felt this especially when using Odashima's Shakespeare translations.

3 Noda Hideki's answers to my Questionnaire, February 8, 1996.

4 "Interview," May 9, 1996.

5 "Wild fancy," the literal translation of *môsô* in Japanese (and a keyword in this play), is the term Noda uses almost as a synonym for "a playwright's imagination." Noda also associates the term with the mysterious atmosphere of a bamboo grove or the pliant nature of its stems.

6 In the first version of the play, later included in *Mawashi wo Shimeta Sheikusupia* (Tokyo: Shinchô-sha, 1994), Noda started the scene with Richard (Richâdo) dreaming of a lame foot, while sleeping in a hammock. In the stage production in 1990, however, it was revised as a dream scene in which bamboo branches move towards the hero, suggesting the ghost scene, Act 5 scene 3 of Shakespeare's play.

7 In this essay, "Shakespeare," the character in Noda's play will be in quotation marks.

8 *Sandaime Richâdo*, scene 7, p. 179. All the quotations from the scenes of *Sandaime Richâdo* are from *Mawashi wo Shimeta Sheikusupia*. All English translations in this essay are by the author.

9 See Hasebe Hiroshi, ed. *Teihon: Noda Hideki to Yumeno-Yuminsha* (The Complete Album: Hideki Noda & Yume no Yûminsha), (Tokyo: Kawade-shobô-shinsha, 1993), p. 340.

10 *Sandaime Richâdo*, Scene 9, p. 183.

11 *Ibid.*, pp. 184–85.

12 *Ibid.*, scene 21, p. 217.

13 *Rikyû*, directed by Teshigawara Hiroshi, was released in 1989. There is no evidence that Noda had seen the movie before he wrote the play, but both Teshigawara and Noda made good use of the mysterious profundity of a bamboo grove for expressing nightmare.

14 *Sandai-me Richâdo*, scene 23, pp. 224–25.

15 *Ibid.*, p. 225.

16 *Ibid.*, scene 24, p. 228.

Shakespeare reinvented on the contemporary Japanese stage

MINAMI RYUTA

Recent translations of Shakespeare into modern and colloquial Japanese have encouraged theatre professionals, not only to stage the plays with minimum textual alterations, but also to refashion them with considerable alterations of their texts or settings. Prime examples are Ninagawa Yukio and Suzuki Tadashi, who are internationally well known for their original stagings of *Macbeth* and *King Lear* respectively. But the late 1980s and early 1990s saw other, younger directors and playwrights using Shakespeare as a vehicle to project their contemporary problems or concerns. It will not be amiss to think that they regard Shakespeare not as canonical, but as a material resource to exploit. Their textual alterations of Shakespeare are sometimes so radical that their works can be treated as new plays rather than adaptations. This article examines Noda Hideki's *Twelfth Night* (1986), his *Midsummer Night's Dream* (1992), and Iijima Sanae's *Arigachina Hanashi* (The Same Old Story: an adaptation of *Romeo and Juliet*, 1991) as notable examples of such radical recreation.

I
Noda Hideki's *Twelfth Night* (July 1986)

Noda Hideki has so far produced four Shakespeare plays – *Twelfth Night* (1986), *Much Ado about Nothing* (1990), *Richard III* (1990), and *A Midsummer Night's Dream* (1992), all of which were captioned "Noda's" to underscore the alterations he made. His *Twelfth Night* is a comparatively faithful presentation of the translated text with little change in the time, setting, and the characters of the original. But what is noteworthy are the scenes he added before and after the play proper.

The production starts with a statue of an androgynous Venus emerging vaguely at the stage center in the darkness. The darkness changes into the sea, in which appears a huge dragon surging high and low around the statue, and next the dragon gradually divides itself into two dragons, which disappear into the darkness again. In the meantime, the statue of the androgynous Venus also splits itself into two bodies, a man and a woman. Noda, at the very

11 *Twelfth Night*, directed by Noda Hideki for Tôhô Company Ltd, Nissei Theatre, 1986. Cesario/Viola stands in front of giant masks.

beginning, clearly implies that all the following mishaps, misunderstandings, and false expectations are caused by the division of a dragon as well as that of Venus, both of which symbolize the end of a happy state, or humans ceasing to be androgynous anymore.

Noda reconstructs *Twelfth Night* as the story of an androgyne, who, being divided into twins, Viola and Sebastian, goes back to an original androgynous state as Cesario. He adds some scenes in order to highlight this. After the first meeting with Olivia, Cesario is addressed as "*Andorogyunusu*" (androgyne) by a Sphinx in the sea. There is also a scene in which Cesario tells Orsino why a man and a woman fall in love. Cesario says that there used to be complete androgynous human beings called "*andorogyunusu*" in the sea, but as they grew so arrogant as to defy the gods, they were divided into two bodies, male and female. Thereafter, men and women sought their other halves. Cesario concludes that men and women are twins born out of the sea and that love was also born in the sea. As the play unfolds, it becomes clear that Noda sees the sea as a happy or Edenic state in which humanity is not yet divided into genders.

Noda ends the production, after the original denouement of the play, by showing the reunion of the two halves into the body of an imaginary Cesario that must be discarded and forgotten in the end. Obviously, Noda is more interested in the reunion of the divided halves of an androgyne in the sea than in the reunion of Viola and Sebastian that leads to their marriages on the land. Noda presents, as a mime, the imaginary androgyne Cesario left alone at stage center, as if staying peacefully on the seabed at the very end of the play.

What is interesting about this production is that the play appears more like Noda's than Shakespeare's, although Noda retained seventy to eighty percent of the original in translation. Partly, this is because Noda's *Twelfth Night* was performed with the eloquence, extreme speed of acting and linguistic puns which are the hallmarks of Yume no Yûminsha; but it is chiefly because "androgyny" and "twins" are ideas that frequently appear in Noda's plays.

In *Zendajô no Toriko* (*The Prisoner of Zenda*), for example, Noda presents a character named Akazukin, who goes down the ladder of evolution through retrogression, and finally becomes an androgynous angel at the end of the play. Here the boy Akazukin, played by an actress, is saved as an androgyne free from evil and sin. In some of Noda's plays, the androgynous state of being is represented as a kind of primeval Edenic state.[1]

As for the theme of twins, a telling example can be taken from *Han-shin* (Half Gods), first performed in the winter of 1986. *Han-shin* centers around Siamese twins, who will both die unless they have an operation to divide them. The twins live simultaneously in the world of human beings and that of gods taken principally from Greek myth. During the operation, the twins go back to the primeval world of legendary gods – one then returns to the world of human beings, leaving the other behind. In this play, Noda presented the dividing of the twins' bodies as analogous to man's parting from the mythically pristine, happy state.

Just as one of the twins goes back to the human world while the other remains in the mythical world in *Han-shin*, so Viola and Sebastian stay on the land, while Cesario goes back to the sea in this *Twelfth Night*. Yet Noda is more concerned with Cesario. In this sense, Noda's *Twelfth Night* can be summarized as a play that starts with the arrival of an androgynous Venus dividing into two bodies and ends with Venus's departure as a complete androgyne.

Noda introduced his usual themes into *Twelfth Night* with relatively few alterations to the original. The play was set in Illyria, and the characters are all taken from the original with no alterations. Yet, given the unmistakable hallmarks of his style, this *Twelfth Night* is a Shakespeare à la Noda.

Noda Hideki's *Midsummer Night's Dream* (August 1992)

Unlike his *Twelfth Night*, Noda daringly transferred the time and settings of Shakespeare's *Midsummer Night's Dream* into Japanese versions. He changed the court at Athens into a Japanese-style restaurant called "Hanakin," while the forest set in Mount Fuji was almost like an amusement park with carnival lights and a roller coaster. Naturally, the characters are completely transformed. Demetrius becomes a cook called "Demi" and Lysander a cook called "Rai." Hermia becomes Tokitamago, who is the only daughter of the owner of the Hanakin. Helena becomes Soboro, the daughter of a cook.[2] Demetrius and Lysander fight with swords in the original play – Demi and Rai, their counterparts in Noda's version, fight with kitchen knives. Noda's transformation of the dramatic world into the world of Japanese cooks worked very well, not only to represent the patriarchal structure of the original, but also to add comedy and vivacity to the verbal exchanges between the lovers. When Noda directed *Much Ado About Nothing* for the Tôhô Company in 1990, he first thought of replacing the words of love in the original with those of food, though the play was recontextualized into the world of sumô wrestlers. Noda jotted down a memo as follows: "28th Dec. 1989. What will it be like if I replace 'to love' and 'to like' with 'to want to eat'? To change the relationship between to love and to be loved into the relationship between to eat and to be eaten."[3] The idea is successfully applied to his *Midsummer Night's Dream*. One example will suffice to show how he carried out this plan. When Lysander wakes up and falls in love with Helena in the original, he exclaims:

> . . . run through fire I will for thy sweet sake!
> Transparent Helena! Nature shows art,
> That through thy bosom makes me see thy heart.[4]

Noda's Lysander (Rai) puts it this way:

> . . . run through fire I will like *shabushabu* for thy sweet sake!
> Beautiful *Soboro*. You're as beautiful and transparent as
> *shirataki*. My bosom is pierced through like *yakitori*.[5]

While trying to retain the words and phrases of the original (the translation by Odashima Yûshi), Noda weaves names of foods into the lines. Since love and sexual desire are projected upon appetite in Noda's version, love is always talked about in metaphors of food and eating. Consequently, the exchanges between lovers aroused laughter thus preventing them from getting too romantic.

In addition to the transference of the play to a Japanese setting, Noda not only transplants Mephistopheles from *Faust* into the play, but also incorporates *Alice's Adventures in Wonderland*.

Noda presents Mephistopheles (Mephisto) as a character who picks up man's conceived but repressed and unuttered desires and realizes them. Mephisto takes up and gratifies the lovers', Oberon's and Titania's repressed

12 *A Midsummer Night's Dream*, directed by Noda Hideki, Nissei Theatre, 1992. Fantasy scene with lovers on a Japanese Chopping Board.

desires, thus bringing confusion and hatred to all in the forest. One of Noda's intentions in introducing Mephisto into *A Midsummer Night's Dream* is to show the darker side of man's dreams and desires. Yet, what should also be noted about Mephisto is his playing the role of "Puck." Mephisto is obviously aware that he is intruding into the world of Shakespeare's play. Mephisto says, "Instead of my cousin Puck, I will show a midsummer night's dream to humans."[6] Puck protests, "He's stolen my lines. He is going to misappropriate my part as well as my lines."[7] Both Mephisto and Puck share an understanding that the role of Puck and the lines to be spoken by Puck were written beforehand. Noda's *Midsummer Night's Dream* is a self-conscious or meta-theatrical play in that Noda's Puck and Mephisto are very conscious of Shakespeare's original play.

Noda introduces *Alice's Adventures in Wonderland* as a play performed by Soboro, Otemoto, Fukusuke, Kôri-ya, and others at the wedding reception of Demi and Tokitamago. Yet the episode of *Alice's Adventures* expands beyond the frame of the play-within-the-play and covers almost the whole of the play. Soboro, in the end, turns out to be the heroine of *Alice's Adventures*; it also turns out that all the nightmarish experience in the forest was brought about by Mephisto as a realization of Soboro's conceived but swallowed desires. Soboro stands in between and connects *Alice's Adventures* with the experience in the forest.

Towards the end of the play, as a result of Mephisto's intrusion into the fairies' world and the lovers' world, both worlds reach crisis. Owing to the lovers' hatred of one another, the forest catches fire. Soboro learns that "Kinosei" (fairies of trees/ because of groundless fears or imagination)[8] will disappear without the forest; that Tokitamago, Demi, and Rai hate one another; and that she herself is the cause of all these crises.

SOBORO   The forest will be burnt to ashes.
MEGAWARUISEI   We "Kinosei" will lose our home.
MIMIGAWARUISEI   If "Kinosei" disappears from this world, a midsummer
    night's dream will be ruined.
MEGAWARUISEI   If "Kinosei" be gone out of this world, the world will become
    boredom itself.[9]

Here Oberon and Titania encourage Soboro to evoke the power of words, narrative, and imagination. Soboro carefully fabricates a story out of her unuttered/swallowed words, and the story brings rain to the forest.

TITANIA   The fire of the forest is going out.
PUCK   The forest of a midsummer night is saved.
SOBORO   But I know that if it rains, I will have to say farewell to "Kinosei,"
    "Natsunosei" [fairies of summer/because of summer] and "Yorunosei"
    [fairies of night/because of night].
OBERON   Why? Come back to the forest whenever you want to.
SOBORO   The fairies are wearing the ashes that enable them to become visible to
    humans. The ashes will be washed away by the rain. When the ashes are thor-
    oughly washed away, I can never see the fairies again.

This situation is reminiscent of Noda's other plays. Soboro and other humans cannot but lose the mythical and Edenic state where humans and fairies live together. Soboro finally regains the power of words and imagina-tion at the expense of the world of fairies. In many of Noda's early plays such as *Shônen Gari* (Hunt for Boys), *Hashire Merusu* (Run Merusu), *Koyubi no Omoide* (Memory of the Little Finger), or *Nokemono Kitarite* (Descent of the Brutes), Noda presents a character who, seeking to go back to his ideal and Edenic state, is forced to face a ruthlessly damaging reality and to bid farewell to the Edenic state. But the loss of such an Edenic state also suggests the beginning of a new one.

Noda frequently introduces a fire towards the end of his plays. *Hashire Merusu* and *Koyubi no Omoide* are good examples. In such plays, as Hasebe maintains, "flames do not only mean disruption or destruction. Rather, they give the feeling that purification by flames will lead to the emergence of a new world where renewal and construction will take place."[10] In Noda's

Midsummer Night's Dream, the sense of renewal after purification by fire is suggested by Puck and Oberon:

PUCK Before long, the invisible fairies in the ground will go up through trunks and turn into fresh green leaves.
OBERON And when young lovers walk through the forest, those fresh leaves will rustle and bless them (you) all with the sunlight through the leaves.[11]

When the fairies are no longer visible, another relationship between Soboro and the fairies starts. This feeling of the beginning at the end of the play is the very feeling audiences experience at the end of *Koyubi no Omoide* and *Hashire Merusu*.

When Noda directed his *Midsummer Night's Dream*, he was also preparing a new play for his company. Interestingly, he incorporated the motif of his next play into this production. Noda writes about the new play, *Tômei Ningen No Yuge* (Steam from an Invisible Man):

People are getting haunted by an invisible power. As the logocentric Western values have collapsed one after another and the world seems to have crumbled, people have begun to rely on an invisible (mystical) power that has not been believed in this world . . . But very few people are aware that the colossal invisible power lies in words. This will be, after all, the motif of my next play *Tômei Ningen no Yuge* [Steam from an Invisible Man]. Now I can reconsider *A Midsummer Night's Dream* from this point of view.[12]

Noda intends to present *A Midsummer Night's Dream* as seen by Helena, "who benefits a great deal from an invisible power."[13]

It will be obvious that Noda presented *A Midsummer Night's Dream* as one of his own plays in terms of its dramatic structure and theme. However, it must be noted that Noda retained more than fifty percent of Odashima's translation in his version, and, particularly, that the first half of the play develops just like Shakespeare's original play. Noda once said in an interview:

For the last several years, I have written plays with motifs taken from works composed by authors such as Sakaguchi Ango, Hagio Moto, and Shakespeare. This is because I felt I had developed some mannerisms in my work. When I have completed a play, I always think it a good one. But when I mount it on the stage, I cannot but notice that it is almost the same as the previous one. That is why I create plays with outlines of others' work.[14]

Noda's plays are often labeled as "amusing but hard to understand" because his plays usually have two or three seemingly unrelated plots that proceed simultaneously and turn out to be a coherent whole only at the end. But working with the framework of Shakespeare's play, Noda created a play that is impeccably Noda's though easily understood by its audience.

13 *A Midsummer Night's Dream*, directed by Noda Hideki, Nissei Theatre, 1992. Closeup of Lysander and Hermia.

As mentioned above, Noda transferred the time and settings of the original to Japan and transformed the characters into Japanese. Yet, this does not mean that *A Midsummer Night's Dream* was localized or "Japanized" in the same way that *Macbeth* was by Ninagawa. The warriors in Ninagawa's *Macbeth* wear Japanese armor and look like samurai in a fairly naturalistic way; in Noda's play, the costumes worn by the four lovers and the mechanicals are symbolic of their roles at a restaurant and far from realistic. Also, names such as Soboro and Tokitamago, as well as Demi and Rai, are not realistic at all. In other words, the Japan in which Noda sets the play is a conspicuously fictitious Japan, and this is the very setting in which Noda's plays always take place. Noda's *Midsummer Night's Dream* is a Noda à la Shakespeare rather than a Shakespeare à la Noda.

II
Jitensha Kinqureat's *Arigachina Hanashi* (November 1991)

Jitensha Kinqureat, a company founded by seven girl students in 1981, is one of the leading companies in the so-called fourth generation of the Shôgekijô Undô or the Little Theatre Movement. The company chiefly stages Iijima Sanae's plays, which graphically depict young people's daily life in contemporary Japan from a girl's point of view.

Arigachina Hanashi (the same old story) describes the everyday life of contemporary Japanese young lovers in the framework of *Romeo and Juliet*. Or, it would be more appropriate to say that *Arigachina Hanashi* represents Romeo and Juliet as young lovers in contemporary Japan. What makes this production different from other recent Shakespearean adaptations is that Iijima retained the time and settings of the original. What Iijima writes about the play illustrates her approach and the company's to *Romeo and Juliet*:

> None of Juliet's friends appears in the original, but we thought she should be an ordinary fourteen-year old girl who surely had some friends to have a chat with everyday. This is why we invented Juliet's friends. For example, we know Romeo suffered unrequited love for Rosaline, who is only mentioned in the original. But we wonder how Rosaline felt when she found that Romeo, whom she believed was in a one-sided love-relationship with her, had fallen in love with Juliet, and died. Amongst Juliet's friends, there may have been a girl who secretly loved Romeo, a girl who admired Paris, or a girl who was dating with Tybalt. We also wonder what Juliet had been talking about with her friends before she fell in love with Romeo. What did they think of Romeo and Juliet's love and death? They may have envied the lovers or merely thought them stupid.[15]

This remark shows that Iijima regards Juliet as an ordinary, modern Japanese girl, and that she intends to depict Romeo and Juliet from their friends' viewpoints as well as in relation to their friends.

In order to underline the contemporaneity of *Romeo and Juliet*, Iijima, or director Suzuki Yumi, starts *Arigachina Hanashi* with a dance at a disco before the play proper. This dance scene, performed in modern clothes, not only presents all the actors/characters as contemporary Japanese, but also somewhat foreshadows what is going to happen in the following scenes. This scene starts with the entrance of the actress who is to play Juliet. She first dances alone at the stage center, but soon the actor who is to play Romeo joins her. When they are dancing alone, they suddenly find themselves surrounded by hostile-looking people who try to capture them; they run away in different directions only to get cornered, and then the couple disappear. That the first dance scene performed in modern clothes parallels in some way the story of *Romeo and Juliet* will serve to lead the audience to see a contemporary couple projected upon Romeo and Juliet.

Iijima invents four friends of Juliet's: Rosaline, Flora, Bianca, and Ottavia. Rosaline is a woman to whom many men, including Romeo, make advances, but she always brushes off the advances for fun. Flora is Benvolio's childhood friend and love. Bianca is Tybalt's love. And Ottavia admires Paris, though she already has a fiancé. Iijima also invents Juliet's aunt Elisabetta, who suffers unrequited love for Romeo. Elisabetta, played by a plump comic actor, repeatedly grieves over the possible obstacles to Romeo's falling in love with her. But, as she appears to be the last woman to be loved by Romeo, her worried look and anguish only provoke laughter. Since Elisabetta wants to attract Romeo's attention, she invites him to Capulet's house so that she can meet him. Like Elisabetta, almost all the young characters in *Arigachina Hanashi* make every effort to find and secure their lovers/love, and their behavior realistically represents those of contemporary young Japanese.

It is noteworthy that almost half of the play comprises Juliet and her friends' chatting or gossiping about boys and their lovers. As the audience hear and see the star-crossed lovers' behaviors as well as other characters' responses to them, they will be prevented from engaging with Romeo or Juliet.

Although *Arigachina Hanashi* is set in the time and settings of the original, the language the girls and the other characters speak is naturalistic and very colloquial modern Japanese, except for the scenes taken from the original in translation. The phraseology and the content of conversations in the play are similar to those of contemporary Japanese plays, but it would be pointless to criticize their anachronism, for Iijima intends to present the characters as modern Japanese. Yet, it is also pointless to try simply to set *Arigachina Hanashi* in today's Japan, because Iijima presupposes the audience's knowledge of *Romeo and Juliet* and wants them to recall it while watching this play.

Iijima retains the setting of the original in order to take advantage of the audience's expectations. As Susan Bennett remarks, audiences always bring particular cultural expectations to the production of Shakespeare's plays.[16] And such expectations are more likely to be prepared by previous famous productions. Jonathan Miller once said of reproducing classical plays: "The revival or re-production of a play could never take place in complete ignorance of its previous incarnations, so that although the text has remained unchanged by the vicissitudes of various productions, the memory of previous performances exerts a powerful influence on the shape of subsequent ones."[17] This remark holds true for the reception of classical or well-known plays like *Romeo and Juliet*. The audience of *Arigachina Hanashi* cannot appreciate the play in complete ignorance of its previous productions of *Romeo and Juliet*. Suzuki Yumi, the director of *Arigachina Hanashi*, was fully aware that one of the best known previous incarnations of *Romeo and Juliet* is Franco Zeffirelli's film, and she made her Juliet's costume and hairstyle reminiscent of those in the film. However, the "quotation" of Zeffirelli's film does not extend to its atmosphere. It is, rather, meant to raise among the audience some expectations that *Arigachina Hanashi* will readily disappoint.

What makes *Arigachina Hanashi* distinct from other Shakespearean adaptations is that Iijima retains several famous scenes of the original in her version, while eliminating the rest, and inventing quite new scenes. The well-known scenes that Iijima retains are the so-called balcony scene (2.2), the scene in which Romeo reluctantly parts from Juliet in her bedroom (3.5), and the scene where Romeo and Juliet die (5.3). Interestingly, these scenes, and some lines that Iijima keeps intact, are familiar even to those who have never seen or read *Romeo and Juliet*. While retaining familiar scenes of the original, Iijima reconstructs its world in a parodic manner, thus disappointing the audience's expectation or preventing the audience's engagement with the protagonists.

Iijima's intention to alienate the audience from the lovers becomes clear in the last scene, coming after the death of the lovers. In this scene, both Juliet's and Romeo's friends make frank comments on their death. Here it turns out that they are not very sympathetic to their "passionate love," and that they regard their death as an indiscreet, rash or even stupid deed rather than a tragic one. When Elisabetta says with a sigh of relief, "If Romeo had fallen in love with me, I would have been dead now," the atmosphere of the play becomes more comic than tragic.

Iijima presents Romeo and Juliet as seen through the cool eyes of contemporary young Japanese. The Jitensha Kinqureat company specializes in representing the urban life of young Japanese from a girl's viewpoint. *Arigachina Hanashi* reflects the company's usual productions in terms of its theme and theatrical vocabulary. In this sense, this production can be regarded as an example of localization of Shakespeare. Yet, what is to be noted about this production is Iijima's and Suzuki's manipulation of audiences' foreknowledge of the original, which is only possible with such a popular play as *Romeo and Juliet*. If localization of Shakespeare depends on the popularity of Shakespeare's work among its recipients, localization will necessarily presuppose the manipulation of its recipients' responses.[18]

III

Noda's and Iijima's Shakespearean productions reflect the taste of young Japanese audiences, who prefer laughter to seriousness. Their "Shakespearean" productions are Noda's or Iijima's plays in their own right, and Shakespeare's *oeuvre* only supplies these playwrights with a framework for their own plays. In other words, neither Noda nor Iijima serves Shakespeare. They use Shakespeare as a source material. This attitude towards Shakespeare will be different from that of some directors in England. The attitude of English directors is partly demonstrated by Jonathan Miller: "With texts that come from the more or less distant past, it is often claimed that their meaning inevitably changes with the passage of time, and that it is only profitable to read them for contemporary meanings or for meanings which are interestingly relevant to the modern imagination."[19] Noda and Iijima do not read Shakespeare for contemporary meanings, but they write contemporary meanings into Shakespeare. This difference between Miller and Noda or Iijima may not be definite, but it still holds good to some extent. And it is the variety of translations of Shakespeare that has enabled Japanese writers and directors to write new meanings into Shakespeare.

The reinvention of Shakespeare is indeed one of the noticeable tendencies on the contemporary Japanese stage. As Michael Billington once said about European Shakespeares, the current "Shakespeare-boom" in Japan can be understood as "a direct comment on the dearth of new drama."[20] However, when we discuss the reinvention of Shakespeare, we must also be aware and wary of the fact that we also witness Chekhov, Chikamatsu, and other classical playwrights reinvented. Reinvention of Shakespeare takes place more often than that of Chekhov or Chikamatsu, and this probably reflects only the differences in the distance between contemporary Japanese dramatic imagination and their works. The proliferation of Shakespeare in Japanese theatre shows Japanese theatre companies' dependence upon Shakespeare for their repertoire; yet, judging from Noda's and Iijima's cases, it does not necessarily mean "the dearth of new drama." The recent reinvention of Shakespeare suggests the changes in theatre professionals' attitudes towards Shakespeare, which seems to have enriched the dramatic imagination in Japan.

NOTES

1 *Nokemono Kitarite* (Descent of the brutes), which toured to Edinburgh, also depicts some characters' attempts at returning to the primeval state of being.

2 Both Soboro and Tokitamago are names of Japanese dishes.

3 Hiroshi Hasebe, ed., *Teihon: Noda Hideki to Yume no Yûminsha* (The Complete Album: Hideki Noda and Yume no Yûminsha), (Tokyo: Kawadeshobô Shinsha), 1993, 346.

4 William Shakespeare, *A Midsummer Night's Dream*, Harold F. Brooks ed., (London: Methuen, 1979), 2.2.103–05.

5 Hideki Noda, *A Midsummer Night's Dream* in *Mawashi wo shimeta Shakespeare* (Tokyo; Shinchôsha, 1994), 33. Translation is mine. Italicized words are names of Japanese food.

6 *Ibid.*, 31.

7 *Ibid.*, 39.

8 "Kinosei" means "fairies of trees" and "because of groundless fears or imagination." At the very beginning, Soboro says that strange things do not happen
   "because of groundless fears (Kinosei)," and that they are the work of "fairies
   of trees (Kinosei)" (7). Throughout the play, Kinosei means both "fairies of
   trees" and "because of groundless fears or imagination."

9 Ibid., 79–80.
   "Megawaruisei" means "because of bad sight," and "Mimigawaruisei" means
   "because of poor hearing." Yet, since "sei" means "a fairy" as well as "because
   of," Noda plays with the word "sei" here and makes them mean "a fairy of bad
   sight" and "a fairy of poor hearing," just as he does with "Kinosei." Japanese
   audiences and readers will automatically notice and recognize such verbal associations.

10 Hasebe Hiroshi, "The City of Vertigo – Hideki Noda or the Theatre of Speed,"
    trans. by Yoshida Mie, in Teihon, 477–87, 487 note 7.

11 Hideki Noda, A Midsummer Night's Dream, 81.

12 Teihon, 347.

13 Ibid., 348.

14 "Saturday interview: Noda Hideki san," in The Mainichi, August 10, 1991.
    Sakaguchi Ango is a modern novelist and Hagio Moto is a cartoonist.

15 Introduction written for the leaflet on the video of Arigachina Hanashi.

16 Susan Bennett, Performing Nostalgia: Shifting Shakespeare and the Contemporary Past
    (London: Routledge, 1996), 57.

17 Jonathan Miller, Subsequent Performances (London: Faber and Faber, 1986), 68.

18 This is also true of Noda's Shakespearean productions other than Twelfth Night,
    which is not so familiar to Japanese audiences. Thanks to the productions of A
    Midsummer Night's Dream at Theatre Cocoon for some consecutive years, as well
    as its long history of performances in Japan, Noda's adaptation somewhat
    expects its audience to share and appreciate its self-consciousness of the origi-
    nal. Since Much Ado About Nothing is rarely performed in Japan, Noda introduced
    into his version the well-known actions of Romeo and Juliet and of Iago from
    Othello to replace Don John. For example, Azami (a counterpart of Beatrice)
    gives her sister Hiro (Hero in the original) a medicine, which will bring her into
    a state of suspended animation for forty-eight hours. When Azami persuades
    Hiro to take the medicine, she speaks the lines of Friar Lawrence in Romeo and
    Juliet (Romeo and Juliet, 4.1.94–97, 104–06). As Suzuki Masae illustrates, Noda
    presumed the audience's knowledge of The Merchant of Venice when producing
    Sandaime Richâdo (Richard the Third).

19 Ibid., 71.

20 Michael Billington, "From the Stage of the Globe," The Guardian, April 18, 1991.

13

Juliet's girlfriends: The Takarazuka Revue Company and the *Shôjo* culture

OHTANI TOMOKO

I

The Takarazuka Revue Company's 1950 version of *Romeo and Juliet* presents several young ladies who accompany Juliet onto the stage. What is significant here is that the bawdy adult Nurse is replaced with sexless young ladies. In the scene after Juliet first meets Romeo at the ball, Juliet and these young ladies, separated from the other guests, appear in the garden and, to the faint sound of dance music, begin an intimate conversation about Juliet's marriage to Count Paris. Juliet's reluctance to marry without love invites discussion of their own marriage views:

ANNE   He adores me.
JANE   Did he propose to you?
ANNE   Of course!
AMELIA   Did you accept it?
ANNE   No, I didn't, but I don't care. I'm sure he will ask me again anyway.
DINAH   Do you love him?
ANNE   No, not in the least.
MARY   Then what made you think to marry him?
ANNE   Well, I think it would be better to marry someone I don't love.
ALL   How could you think in such an awful way?
ANNE   Because that will make things much more manageable.
ADELE   In that case, I agree with you.
JANE   So do I.
JULIET   I would never dream of that. I would rather die than marry without
   love.
ANNE   I can't be that sure. Nobody can be sure which is the better. Everyone has
   their own fate. Well, that's enough of that. Seize the day. Let's have fun, shall
   we? (Scene 2.41–65)[1]

While they respectively congratulate Juliet on her desirable position, none of them talks of romantic or transcendent love. It is an enviable match or marriage of convenience they unanimously desire. Whereas Juliet "would rather die than marry without love," one of them, Anne, believes "it would be better to marry someone [she doesn't] really love" because it would be easier to manage him. Pleasure, as a process without a subject or a *telos*, not sex-desire as the truth of self, seems to be mirthfully affirmed. Marriage is just another temporal topic amongst intimate friends, which is easily replaced with another amusement. They would rather make a commitment to easy opportunism than to ideal love. The young ladies demystify the ideology of romantic love no less than the Nurse does in Shakespeare's text: "Then since the case so stands as now it doth, / I think it best you married with the County. / O, he's a lovely gentleman! / Romeo's a dishclout to him'(3.5.216–19).[2] The scene of Juliet and her girlfriends rather serves to foster an extra-libidinal intimacy amongst the girls. This replacement of the Nurse with the girlfriends in this version of *Romeo and Juliet* represents the contingent relation between marriage and sex, a feature of the *shôjo* (young girls' or adolescent women's) culture.

The presence of these young ladies, then, might be explained by the history of the company. The Takarazuka Revue Company was organized by Kobayashi Ichizô, a Hankyû railway and department store tycoon, in 1913 as the "Takarazuka Girls' Opera Training Group"(Takarazuka Shôjo Kageki Yôseikai).[3] Kobayashi promoted the theatre as a "wholesome entertainment for the entire family." Regarding himself as a paternal figure for all the performers of the company, he saw the theatre not only as a place for entertainment but also for education. The characteristics of youthfulness, virginity, and unmarried status were required, probably because Kobayashi attempted to promote the ideals of the "good wife" and "wise mother." That each Takarasienne (so called after Parisienne) is referred to not as an "actress" but as a "student" perhaps reflects the same design – to mould her into a model of adult female subjectivity. However, the image of the Takarasienne eventually subverts Kobayashi's designs. *Shôjo*, a "not-quite-female female," resists becoming a fully female adult, because in Japan this involves marriage and motherhood. The core of the Takarazuka company is still comprised of such young girls. Takarazuka[4] functions as a cultural space where the inhabitants, Takarasienne, can remain young and unmarried as long as they stay within the theatre.

Yet in Britain the critical reaction to Takarazuka's London performance in 1994 was almost unanimously negative, many reviewers complaining of the absence of sexuality. The performance was a triptych: pseudo-Kabuki, an adaptation of an O. Henry short story, and a spectacular finale infused with Broadway musical features. In virtue of Takarazuka being a single-sex institution, the audience might have been led to expect "the Japanese counterpart of a radical feminist revue" or a "genuine homosexual subtext." The performance, however, offered them a very different experience: "extravagant showbiz pastiches." "It's not the gender-bending that's unsettling – not to people weaned on British pantomime, anyway"[5]: "Takarazuka's performance lavishly displays," Michael Billington insists, "Oriental kitsch and the overall effect is curiously sexless."[6] As Peter Popham put it, "this stage of black-suited non-men, with their little round heads and highlighted quiffs and cheeky grins, belongs in some limbo that never existed anywhere."[7] "Takarazuka," Benedict Nightingale also wrote, "inhabits a wonderfully innocent, strangely sexless dream world in which men are as they should be, not as they are."[8] The performance has been interpreted as suggesting "that Japanese women yearn to escape from their dominant menfolk into a world of colour, romance and spectacle, where relations between the idealized sexes are unimpeded by anything as threatening as carnal contact."[9] It seems that the fascination of Takarazuka is considered to be not so much artistic as sociological in the international or British arena.

Yet, as can be clearly seen from the free adaptation of *Romeo and Juliet* above, Takarazuka does not aim to produce a canonical and authentic Shakespeare, which requires a faithful translation of the text and expresses the English point of view on Shakespeare. This tendency can be more clearly detected in the company's more recent adaptations of Shakespeare's plays: *Love Adventurers* (*Twelfth Night*, 1980), *Sweet Little Rock'n' Roll* (*Much Ado About Nothing*, 1985), *Bay City Blues* (*Hamlet*, 1993) and so on. Perhaps the most conspicuous example is *Puck* (*A Midsummer Night's Dream*, 1992), which is tinged with a sentimental, dreamy fantasy: fairy Puck suffers from unrequited love for human Hermia. Is Takarazuka, as a specific form of popular culture, a pre-modern version of stylized or localized Shakespeare?

In the ambivalent world of transcultural discourse, the central objects in the western world become eccentric, accidental, and partial, and the body loses both its part-objects of presence and its representational authority. The culturally produced body splits under the globalized gaze of the international audience, displaced into signs of geopolitical, social tensions. It is then that the phobic myth of the timeless, universal Shakespeare is revealed.[10] Whereas the white's anxiety over the black is based upon blacks being excessively sexual, anxiety over the Japanese is premised upon their being "curiously sexless." Are these stereotypical images about sexuality not two sides of the same coin, the anxiety of modern western subjects over the Other? My aim here is to interpret the Takarazuka's *Romeo and Juliet* by reconsidering the structure of representation of that very anxiety. Through the image of Juliet's girlfriends, Takarazuka attempts to represent the purest form of social being in the contemporary capitalist society. First I would like to propose a positive interpretation of Takarazuka's sexlessness from the viewpoint of the *shôjo* culture.

II

The concept of the *shôjo* emerged in the late nineteenth and early twentieth centuries and has been rearticulated as a definitive feature of Japanese late capitalism, or what Asada Akira calls "Infantile Capitalism."[11] As John Whittier Treat remarks about Japanese consumer society, "In English, gender is binary, but in Japan, *shôjo* constitute their own gender, neither male nor female but rather something importantly detached from the productive economy of heterosexual reproduction."[12] Although it literally means young girls or adolescent women, translation of the term into any single English expression is misleading. The *shôjo* are different from the sexual subject, which, internalizing paternal "instance" through "Oedipalization," has learned to supervise itself through discipline and training. Not "the formation of the adult subject" but "the process of relative competition" is indispensable to capitalism:

> It does not matter whether the relationship becomes internalized or remains external. Clearly, the latter is the case with Japan. Thus in Japan, there are neither tradition-oriented old people adhering to transcendental values nor inner-oriented adults who have internalized their values; instead, the nearly purely relative (or relativistic) competition exhibited by other-oriented children provides the powerful driving force for capitalism.[13]

The *shôjo*, in such a cultural context, have been transformed into an abstract concept and a sheer sign of consumption.

Just as the *shôjo* have indeterminable gender, Takarazuka's *otokoyaku* performers, women playing men, represent a unique social being. In the discourse of Japanese popular culture neither "effeminate Romeo" nor "masculine Juliet" is necessarily received as a representation of homoeroticism.[14] The style of male impersonators is not that of a man nor of a woman, but of a molded, abstract being. It could be deduced that the *otokoyaku* of Takarazuka, in some way, also consume the idealized image of man on the stage as the *shôjo* do in the consumer society. In that sense, the performance of Takarazuka can be categorized as belonging to *shôjo* culture. A parallel phenomenon is reproduced in the hugely popular manifestations of cute culture, such as *shôjo manga* comics (comics for young girls), magazines, cute handwriting, fancy goods, cute clothes, cute food, cute ideas, and so on.[15]

"Cute" or "*kawaii*" is the word most often associated with this *shôjo* culture. This aesthetic value, directly linked to the sheer sign of consumption, the *shôjo*, is "one element of the vast popular culture that has flourished in Japan during the last quarter of a century, overwhelming and threatening traditional culture."[16]

Igarashi Yumiko, one of the most popular writers of *shôjo manga* comic books, adapted *Romeo and Juliet* from the viewpoint of Juliet's love story[17] (see photo 14). The story begins by introducing Juliet as a young girl with starry eyes who dreams of romantic love. Both the huge-eyed and non-Japanese looking Romeo and Juliet have the round, lovable and infantile appearance typical of cute cartoon characters associated with fancy goods. The appraisal of romantic love may allegedly make this version appear "romantic". Yet, the theme of *liebestod* is proved to be absorbed into the cute memoir of Juliet's love story. The action of star-crossed lovers ends up being a mere pastiche of the fatal tragedy in which the sexual revolution is rewritten in a manner suitable for a juvenile book. Most notably, the golden statues that Montague and Capulet promise to erect are transformed into "remembrances" or "souvenirs" of the enemy families. The metaphoric displacement of the lovers' erotic desire into such a cute image attests that Igarashi's version contains rather than affirms erotic desire: their romantic love is commodified. This kind of reified image or the content of the *shôjo* culture as such could be considered as an escape from reality. Nevertheless, the consumption of the sign rather than of the thing itself makes appearance and reality assimilated to each other in a world of sheer images and spectacles where any possibility of distinguishing between them is rejected from the outset.

On the other hand, modern interpretations of *Romeo and Juliet* have tended to focus on the two lovers' attempt to forge an erotic alliance beyond the physical and ideological constraints of patriarchy.[18] Their love heroism is certainly misguided and vulnerable, and they pay for their own sins of impatience, anger, and revolt. Yet the love between the two children of the enemy families, reversing the borders between life and death, reflects the contradictions and clashes in Verona's patriarchal system. It also leads to a subversion of the ordinary social and sexual roles: an "active, almost masculine Juliet" is presented against a "weak, effeminate Romeo." Nevertheless, "their transcendent love is ultimately shown to be contained within, and even invaded by," as Valerie Traub's shrewd insight shows, "the dominant ideology and effects of masculine violence."[19] Specifically, the subversive energy is absorbed into the social system by the closing lines in which the prince solemnly addresses the rest: "Go hence to have more talk of these sad things; / Some shall be pardoned,

14 *Romeo and Juliet*. The death scene in Igarashi Yumiko's manga cartoon *Romeo and Juliet*.

and some punishèd: / For never was a story of more woe / Than this of Juliet and her Romeo"(5.3.307–10). "Romeo and Juliet's erotic love, while liberated through the expression of spiritualized poetry, is ultimately doomed precisely because it attempts to exist outside of the material, political world."[20] Therefore, the very endorsement of their erotic power obscures the fact that the corpses of Romeo and Juliet make possible the union of the two opposing patriarchs.

In contradiction with these modern interpretations, the *shôjo* culture, and in particular Igarashi's Shakespeare, appears to be "entirely devoted to an escape from reality."[21] Yet the view that sees these cultural representations as "curiously sexless" is based on the seemingly commonsensical view of sex in the modern discourse of sexuality. It is probably true that, whereas the desire for sex is associated with the social value of adulthood, sexlessness is associated with that of childhood. The modern discourse of sexuality makes abnormal the failure of the sexless *shôjo* to grow up into the sexually mature being. To encourage the desire for sex apparently looks more liberated; but this encouragement, in fact, is a subtle ideological operation of sexuality. The representation of sexless *shôjo* thus should be reinterpreted as a counterattack on the ideology of the patriarchy.

III

Takarazuka, to some degree, shares features of *shôjo* culture with Igarashi's *shôjo manga*. However, the endings of Takarazuka's two versions disclose that Takarazuka's cultural translation of Shakespeare into the *shôjo* culture is not simply a Japanese version of postmodern culture.

In the 1990 version, the curtain is brought down after Juliet "stabs herself," and to resounding music the lovers are displayed lying "one upon another"[22] (see colour photo 7). Although Juliet's dying speech is retained, most of the last half of the final scene is heavily cut. Friar Lawrence's disclosure of the whole business is completely left out, and there is no mention of Romeo's letter addressed to his father. Thus no account of the two lovers' past is given. As for the 1950 version, the suicide scene is surprisingly altered as follows:

ROMEO 'Tis I, Romeo. 'Twas my voice that awoke you.
> *Juliet throws herself into Romeo's arms.*

JULIET O Romeo.

ROMEO Juliet, I thought you had already departed this life, so I took this poison.
> *He shows Juliet the bottle.*

JULIET What? Poison? This must be your timeless end.
> *They embrace each other . . .*

JULIET . . . O churl, drunk all, and left no friendly drop
> To help me after?
> *She throws the bottle away and takes her dagger out of her bosom.*

JULIET O happy dagger, this is thy sheath: *stabs herself.*
> *Romeo half raises himself. Juliet falls on him.*

ROMEO Juliet, give me your hand . . .

JULIET O Romeo, Romeo, I love you, Romeo.
> *They breathe their last in each other's arms.* (1.10.23–42)

Juliet awakes just after Romeo takes the poison, and the erotic power of their death is, thereby, transmuted into the romantic image of embracing lovers. The elements of the *shôjo* culture observed at the level of the action, however, seem to be contained in the end. Romeo and Juliet are withdrawn in their world of sublime purity, which renders them spiritually remote from other characters and the concerns of real life: the erotic energy is displaced into the corpses. The version apparently reinforces what Shakespeare's play seems to mystify: that patriarchy requires growing up into the gendered sexual subject.[23] The corpses of the youthful lovers, that is, the image of eternal infants, cannot but designate their failure to grow up into a mature couple.[24] This might lead the critical mind to conclude that the ending is complicit with the ideology of civil society as Shakespeare's text assumes the order of civic society and paradoxically discloses itself in the prologue: "civil blood makes civil hands unclean"(Prologue 4). Even the image of the Sovereign-Father in heaven is employed in the finale. Is not their death under the gaze of a patriarchal figure a triumph of the dominant ideology over individual desire? It may be supposed that Japanese collectiveness is apparent here, revealing the premodern element in the performance. Nevertheless, close attention to the framework will disclose that rifts between the prologue and the epilogue exist, and the containment is imperfect.

The image or figure of patriarchy structurally displays itself in the framework of Takarazuka's 1990 version. The epilogue is attached or supplemented immediately after the scene of the lovers' death. The representation of Romeo and Juliet in heaven is performed by the very person of the prince himself.

PRINCE Their souls, conveyed by the power of love, now ascend to the heaven. The energy lost on the earth will be revitalized there. All the households of both families should learn the lesson of young love. (Epilogue 1–3)

The spiritualization of the lovers, "[whose] souls, conveyed by the power of love, now ascend to heaven," serves an ideological function. The marriage in heaven seems not so much to recover "[the] energy lost on the earth" as to provide the two families with the lesson of civic society upon which patriarchy rests. The original prologue is also replaced with the completely different one in which a "male" orator affirms youthful passion and romantic love and gives an appraisal of youth. In this regard, the epilogue apparently meshes with the prologue, in which the authority of the transcendental world is asserted:

It is through romantic love that energetically active youth on earth dream a fantasy of being in seventh heaven, and even poor nameless youth can rapturously experience elevation. (Prologue)

The lines seem to eulogize the idea of romantic love, yet the elevation of "poor nameless youth" is associated with a worldly concern for personal advancement and elevation, or careerism in the social hierarchy of modern patriarchy.

Yet, to ground the principle of pleasure in the Sovereign-Father is not necessarily to surround desire with all the trappings of the order of the premodern form of power. By mediating the imaginary element of love, the law of patriarchy covertly expresses the contingent, multiple pleasures of young bodies in the immanent world of real life. Indeed, the declaration of a spectacular dream, "a fantasy of being in seventh heaven" in the prologue, has prefigured "the power of love" in the epilogue. Even before the action starts, the judgment about sexual love and death, about the lovers' souls in heaven, has already become a pathetic action that affects us, the audience, like a spectacular representation itself. The prologue depicts the subjects' inability to control their erotic desire: "How mysterious love is; such refractory, unruly passion inadvertently proceeds by its own logic with the subject left behind. The ardour is uncontrollable" (Prologue). As the rhetorical structure of the prologue shows, the circulation of passionate energy precedes intention; passionate love, inadvertently proceeding with its subject left behind, is uncontrollable for any single individual.

The turn towards principles of radical contingency, randomness, and pleasure is more apparent in the scene of Juliet's girlfriends in which the matter of love or marriage was mentioned in terms of a narcissistic economy of *shôjo* well-being: "A N N E: He adores me. / J A N E: Did he propose to you? / A N N E Of course! / A M E L I A Did you accept it? / A N N E No, I didn't, but I don't care. I'm sure he will ask me again anyway" (1. 41–45). Anne is adored by a man of status and yet playfully rejects his marriage proposal, because what she as *shôjo* desires is her narcissistically invested self-image, which assures her that she can win anyone's affection whenever she wants. Neither can a grown-up subject of herself nor a future husband become the object of desire because neither of them allows Anne the pure pleasure or randomness of her self-satisfaction at each moment. This sanction of the recourse to immanent judgment in the understanding of the subject of desire has definitively foreclosed the recourse to a transcendental source of authority, such as a prince, or God.

Furthermore, just as in the scene involving Juliet's girlfriends, the substitution of the young ladies for the Nurse designates not only a shift from the adult woman to the *shôjo* but also the transformation from the singular to the multiple and collective. Indeed, the power of love in the prologue is associated not with a single subject but with the collective energy of youth:

Here youthful power is represented: those glittering and sparkling youths that have infinite energy, burning passion and fervent desire for sexual love. The story of the young lovers praises such intense and ardent energy possessed by youth. (Prologue)

Significantly, the affirmation of young "fervent desire for sexual love" is unmistakably subservient to the play of the infinite energy possessed by youth. What is brought into focus here is not a single subject in love but "collective, energetic, and passionate youth on the earth," the impersonal force of collectivity. The story of "collective, energetic, and passionate youth" can never apply as such to any particular lovers, for instance Juliet. This absence or non-presence makes the *shôjo*'s desire quite literally unrepresentable or voiceless. Does the body of the *shôjo* possess an organ with which it can state the desire or pleasures of the *shôjo*? Only the individual patriarch such as a prince or God can have the sight and the voice that the *shôjo* lacks. But this individual's ability to judge depends on the metaphorical substitution of the *shôjo*'s own for the divine voice. Since the viciously circular structure of Takarazuka's romantic discourse, by its logic, requires as a thematic assertion the necessary reintroduction of the rhetorical figure that was banned at the start, it is entirely consistent that Takarazuka's version of *Romeo and Juliet* introduces the image of patriarchal authority in the epilogue and has to define it as a simulacrum.

The simulacrum represents something other than a process of "the return of the repressed," what can be characterized as collective catharsis. Here is not so much nostalgia, as a nostalgia aberrantly historicized. Neither is it the sentimental yearning for the lost culture of pre-modern society in which the overwhelming desires of young Japanese girls to escape from real life are reflected. Rather, the figure of the two lovers in heaven expresses the space of utopia or "heterotopia," which the *shôjo* are able to enjoy freely and playfully without any anxiety every moment of life. The eccentric historicity Takarazuka's recycling nostalgia represents in its performance is not without utility to open up the possibility of the changed relationship with the contemporary postmodern world that we the audience inhabit.

IV

I have been arguing that Takarazuka's simulacrum deconstructs and reconstructs the binary opposition between the premodern form of patriarchy and the postmodern cultural form of cuteness, thereby dialectically, manufacturing the hybrid images of collectivity. The *shôjo* culture is not directed to destroying the premodern order or hierarchy of patriarchy in order to conserve and perpetrate the subtle operation of patriarchal ideology. What is required of us is to invert the binary opposition between the model or origin and the copy or image, reinventing the residual form of premodern culture. The historicization of nostalgia itself in the Takarazuka version of Shakespeare, a lucid and remorseless dissatisfaction with the subject form and the ideological operation of subjectification, pushes the simulacrum to the point at which it ceases to be the image of an image. Rather, it substitutes the collective agents of cultural production of meaning for the private subject of ideological castration. The part our interpretative practice hopes to play in the present cultural studies is to project a collectivity of whatever kind, only insofar as such collectivities are themselves figures for the achieved utopian society.

At the same time, the difference between the western and the non-western world should be reconsidered beyond the binary opposition between the modern and the premodern or the nontemporal. Takarazuka's supplementary representation of Shakespeare will then become an eternal return of Elizabethan Shakespeare, that is, the untimely within the transcultural space–time of late capitalism. In the 1950 version, a strategic confusion of metaphor and metonymy is detected in the ending.

Astonished to see the lovers lying on the floor, Friar Lawrence stands still, then turns back, putting his finger on his lip to quieten the others. All the rest gather and kneel surrounding the lovers and wish them the grace of God.
The sound of the death bell resounds on the stage. From underneath the bell, sparrow-like figures, symbolic of the sound, come out dancing and fill the stage.
Romeo and Juliet stand on the white cloud, welcomed by *angels and gods*.
All sing "Hallelujah" in chorus.
The curtain falls. (Scene 10–12)

It is true that the transcendental source of patriarchal authority is metaphorically depicted through the ideological institution and discourse of the church, embodied by Friar Lawrence and the funeral prayer about "the grace of God." However, it is not God himself who receives Romeo and Juliet "on the white cloud" in the finale; the metonymically transfigured image of gods and angels with the sparrow-like figures symbolizing the sound of the death bell admits them into the utopian space of the other world. The image of patriarchy is rearticulated along the axis of metonymy, and thereby the singular form of God is replaced by the plural form. The effects of a simulacrum on the authority of patriarchy is profound and disturbing. For, in the transcultural representation of Sovereign-God in the west, the dream of Christian humanism alienates its own language of universalism and produces another form of power.

In such a transcultural encounter between the occidental presence and its oriental semblance, Takarazuka's simulacrum as the metonymy of presence is an aberrant, eccentric strategy of authority in transcultural discourse. In other words, the interpretation of the Takarazuka version of *Romeo and Juliet* as "curiously sexless" raises the question of the ambivalence of the simulacrum. The displacement of the whites' anxiety is easily detectable in their equally partial and aberrant representation of Japanese popular culture. Takarazuka's simulacrum, like camouflage, hides "no essence, no 'itself'" and differs from presence by displaying it, in part, metonymically. That form of resemblance, that is, the *shōjo*, is the most curiously glittering and paralyzing to behold. The split body of the other culture, taking the amorphously collective and multiple forms of Juliet and her girlfriends, is potentially and strategically a threatening and even insurgent counter-appeal to international audiences, radically deauthorizing the normative knowledge of the priority of the timeless, universal Shakespeare. The ambivalence of simulacrum suggests that Takarazuka's cultural translation of Shakespeare into the *shōjo* culture is, in fact, nothing other than a Japanese version of postmodern culture. Takarazuka's seeming occidentalism and "oriental kitsch" is the very sign of infantile capitalism or late capitalism in the global, transnational world. The possibility of cross-cultural Shakespeare in the twenty-first century, the present essay would like to propose, lies in this non-repressive production of contradictory and multiple beliefs that are constructed across traditional, cultural norms and classifications such as authentic Shakespeare or stylized and localized Shakespeare.

NOTES

I am especially grateful to Shibata Yukio and Tanaka Takusuke of Takarazuka Kagekidan for their kind help in providing the scripts, photographs, and videos.

1 *Kageki Romio to Julietto* (An Opera, *Romeo and Juliet*), (Takarazuka: Takarazuka Kagekidan, 1950).

2 Gary Taylor and Stanley Wells, *The Oxford Shakespeare* (Oxford: Clarendon Press, 1994).

3 *Takarazuka Kagekidan Hachijūnen Shi* (The Eighty Year History of the Takarazuka Revue Company), Takarazuka, Japan: (Takarazuka Kagekidan, 1994); Laurie Brau, "The Women's Theatre of Takarazuka," TDR 34 (1990), 79–95.

4 Hereafter "The Takarazuka Revue Company" is shortened to "Takarazuka."

5 Helen Adkins, *Sunday Times*, July 17, 1994.

6 Michael Billington, The *Guardian Weekly*, July 24, 1994.

7 Peter Popham, *Independent on Sunday*, July 17, 1994.

8 Benedict Nightingale, *The Times*, July 13, 1994.

9 Michael Billington, The *Guardian Weekly*, July 24, 1994.

10 Homi K. Bhabha, *The Location of Culture* (London: Routledge, 1994), 92. See also, Ania Loomba, "Hamlet in Mizoram," in Marianne Novy, ed., *Cross-Cultural Performances: Differences in Women's Re-visions of Shakespeare* (Urbana: University of Illinois Press, 1993), 227–50.

11 Asada Akira, "Infantile Capitalism and Japan's Postmodernism: A Fairy Tale," in Masao Miyoshi and H. D. Harootunian, eds., *Postmodernism and Japan* (Durham: Duke University Press, 1989), 273–78.

12 John Whittier Treat, "Yoshimoto Banana Writes Home: The *Shōjo* in Japanese

Popular Culture," in John Whittier Treat, ed., *Contemporary Japan and Popular Culture*, (London: Curzon, 1996), 265–308, 282.

13 Asada, 275.

14 For an interpretation of Takarazuka in terms of lesbianism, see Jennifer Robertson, "Gender-Bending in Paradise: Doing 'Female' and 'Male' in Japan," GENDERS 5 (1989), 50–69.

15 This brief summary of cute culture is indebted to the following articles: Sharon Kinsella, "Cuties in Japan," in Lise Skov and Brian Moeran, eds., *Women and Media and Consumption in Japan*, (Honolulu: University of Hawaii Press, 1995), 220–54; John Clammer, "Consuming bodies: constructing and representing the female body in contemporary Japanese print media," in Skov and Moeran, 197–219.

16 Kinsella, "Cuties in Japan,"252.

17 Igarashi Yumiko, *Romeo and Juliet*, Manga Sekai no Bungaku (Comic adaptation of world literature), 2 (Tokyo: Sekaibunkasha, 1995).

18 See, for example, Francois Laroque, "Tradition and subversion in *Romeo and Juliet*," in Jay L. Halio, ed., *Shakespeare's Romeo and Juliet: Texts, Contexts, and Interpretation* (Newark: University of Delaware Press, 1995), 18–36.

19 Valerie Traub, *Desire and Anxiety: Circulation of Sexuality in Shakespearean Drama* (London: Routledge, 1992), 2.

20 *Ibid.*, 2.

21 Kinsella, "Cuties in Japan," 252.

22 *Bow Roman: Romio to Julietto* (Romance at the Bow Theatre: Romeo and Juliet), adapted and directed by Shibata Yukio (Takararazuka: Takarazuka Kagakidan, 1990).

23 See Jonathan Goldberg, "Romeo and Juliet's open Rs," in Jonathan Goldberg, ed., *Queering The Renaissance* (Durham: Duke University Press, 1994), 218–35.

24 Michael Bogdanov's 1986 production also employs the commodified image of statues. In his production, the erotic energy of Romeo and Juliet is displaced into the statues and contained within not only patriarchy but also economic consumption. The story of the lovers is exploited by the mass media. "Reporters and photographers rushed down the aisles of the theatre to capture the story and Lord Capulet reads a prepared statement," Pamela Mason remarks in "*Romeo and Juliet*," "the uncompromising hostility of two families forbids the natural growth of a youthful committed love." In Keith Parsons and Pamela Mason, eds., *Shakespeare in Performance* (London: Salamander Books Ltd., 1995), 188–94. Thus, the elements of *shôjo* culture can be found even in western culture.

14

Directing "Japanese Shakespeare" locally and universally: an interview with Gerard Murphy

TED MOTOHASHI

I

A group of Japanese actors working with an English director to perform a Shakespeare play in Japanese translation is no longer a novel phenomenon in Japan. As far as Shakespeare's comedies are concerned, *As You Like It* has been staged most in this mode (a 1992 Rhyming production directed by Glen Walford using Odashima's version; a 1993 Subaru production by R. White and C. Sampsion using Fukuda Tsuneari's translation; and a 1994 Tokyo Globe Company production by Gerard Murphy using Motohashi Tamaki's new translation). Also popular has been *The Merchant of Venice* (Walford for the Rhyming Theatre Company in 1990; Murphy for the Tokyo Globe in 1993 and 1996; Walford again for the Shôchiku in 1994). *A Midsummer Night's Dream* (Stormare for the Tokyo Globe in 1993 using a new Takahashi version), *The Comedy of Errors* (Stormare again, this time using Matsuoka's new translation, for the Tokyo Globe in 1994) and *Twelfth Night* (a 1993 Haiyûza production directed by Michael Pennington using Mikami Isao's translation) have each been presented once in this mode.

Other Shakespeare plays staged in this manner include *The Tempest* (Lepage for the Tokyo Globe in 1993, using Takahashi's new translation), *Titus Andronicus* (Daniels in 1992 for Shôchiku), and *Richard III* (Brock for Shôchiku, and Edward Hall for the Tokyo Globe, both in 1995).

For my immediate purpose, the parade of productions I cite above discloses a distinctive pattern – a close association between particular English-speaking directors and Japanese actors/companies: Stormare and the Tokyo Globe (four productions between 1990 and 1994); Walford and Rhyming (four productions between 1990 and 1994); Brock and Shôchiku (four productions between 1987 and 1995); Lepage and the Tokyo Globe (two productions in 1993); and Murphy and the Tokyo Globe (three productions between 1993 and 1996). This last association is the main topic of this essay. Although Walford always used already available Odashima translations, in many cases, those productions were done in specially commissioned translations:

Takahashi's for Stormare and Lepage, Matsuoka's for Stormare and Brock (though he used Odashima for *Richard III* and *King Lear*), Motohashi's for Murphy. Thus, they attempted to break the hegemony of Odashima Shakespeare, which has dominated "Japanese" Shakespearean productions for the past two decades.

In this particular mode of Shakespearean production, directors tend to return to the same companies with which they worked in previous productions, and co-operations between specific directors (who have very little command of the Japanese language), actors (most of whom cannot communicate in English) and translators (who not only provide workable Japanese texts but function as mediator between the directors and the actors) have proven to be especially significant. I was fortunate enough to have opportunities to work in this fashion with Gerard Murphy for three productions of Shakespeare comedies, *The Merchant of Venice* in 1993, *As You Like It* in 1994, and another production of *The Merchant of Venice* with different actors in 1996, all for the Tokyo Globe using Motohashi Tamaki's translations. The following account, which includes materials from an interview with Murphy conducted in July 1997, is an attempt to demonstrate the viability of a particular way of doing Shakespeare in Japan that possibly exemplifies one of its more paradoxical intercultural aspects. My account may be loosely divided into three sections: the process of translation and search for appropriate texts; various aspects of intercultural relationship between the "English" director and the Japanese actors; and particularities of Murphy's Shakespeare within the genre of "Japanese Shakespeares."

II

In the course of our interview, Gerard Murphy admitted that he first found the notion of directing Shakespeare in Japan completely incongruous: "Having been fascinated by the visual theatre Ninagawa wonderfully created in his Shakespeare, I thought at first I had nothing to offer." It is important to realize that Murphy saw "Shakespeare in Japan" mainly in two aspects – its radical adaptation of the text for the sake of re-telling a familiar story, and its emphasis upon visual effects. Consequently, and somewhat paradoxically, his own contribution did have something to offer. (It would go against both of these trends.)

Textual exploration was the first step Murphy took in approaching his "Japanese Shakespeare." For, as a director who is also very active as an actor for major companies such as the Royal Shakespeare Company, he places the utmost importance on words in a text. To start with, Murphy felt it essential to have a fresh translation, and I worked with him making a "shortened" version based on his idea of cutting some of the rhetorical elements within the original text which would not have made any immediate impact on a Japanese audience's understanding of the story. Murphy's intention was to present the play without interval, so the imperative was to have a performing text which would be completed in two hours. When a viable version was accomplished, the actual work of putting the text into Japanese was carried out by Motohashi Tamaki in close consultation with Murphy and myself, and there were constant revisions of the text during the rehearsal period. As a result, in the case of *The Merchant of Venice*, approximately two-fifths of the original text was cut. Murphy is emphatically unapologetic about those cuts: "A lot of western references only interest western audiences, and, for the Japanese audience, do nothing but put pebbles in the smooth path of the play."

In practice, the cuts we made were basically of two kinds. One was of rhetorical passages, the absence of which would not seriously affect the audience's understanding of the story. A typical example occurs in the opening scene of *The Merchant of Venice* where Salerio glosses Antonio's "sadness" for eighteen lines (1.1.23ff). Here we cut Salerio's response to a simple statement, "I know, Antonio / Is sad to think upon his merchandise" (1.1.39–40). This excision of rhetorical bits can also be applied to clownish parts such as Launcelot and Old Gobbo, as we largely cut the latter part of their encounter in Act 2, scene 2, which seemed to be repetitious and tiresome.

The other target was expression, which might sound culturally obscure to the average Japanese audience. For instance, we filleted most of Portia's culturally discriminating remarks over her suitors in Act 1, scene 2, and kept them to a bare minimum: for the Neapolitan prince: only "Ay, that's a colt indeed, for he doth nothing but talk of his horse" (1.2.39–40) remains; for the County Palatine, Portia replies, "He doth nothing but frown" (1.2.45), then immediately dismisses the above two, saying, "I had rather be married to a death's-head with a bone in his mouth, than to either of these: God defend me from these two" (1.2.49–51); and so on, as we reduced fifty-two between 1.44 and 1.95 to twelve lines. However, it is not necessarily the case that we summarily eliminated rhetorical and culturally "western" expressions. We kept intact Bassanio's confession to Antonio (1.1.161–76) and the "in such a night" interchange between Lorenzo and Jessica (5.1.1–24), both of which include ample references to Greco-Roman mythical tales.

Murphy's belief in the need to edit Shakespeare for a contemporary production not only applies to Japanese Shakespeare. He rejects, in practice, any "orientalist" assumptions, which would regard "Japanese" art forms as exotic and "other," hence requiring a special treatment in terms of aesthetic consideration:

I recently had a chance to look at the text of *The Merchant of Venice* for an English production, and, interestingly, I found myself making similar sorts of cuts. As far as the Japanese audience is concerned, why should they know who Diana is? For a lot of English audiences, too, Diana is irrelevant.

During our own process of editing Shakespeare, however, we constantly resisted the temptation to add:

I'm very averse to this practice of adding, which is certainly fashionable in some quarters, because I believe that the job of directors, actors, and the entire production team is to serve the writer, and adding goes against that principle. The director-as-star is a fashion that I don't subscribe to.

The result of radical cutting and no adding, I would say, was to make his Shakespeare definitely more accessible to the ordinary Japanese audience, but at the same time, to maintain some vaguely "European" cultural distance.

III

Murphy's directorial method starts with actors and ends with them. As it happened, his three productions of Shakespeare in Japan were all low-key, low-budget, non-spectacular ones using simple but effective sets and costumes. In the case of *The Merchant of Venice*, Murphy opted for a rehearsal room setting where all the actors are present on the stage all the time, sitting on chairs surrounding the acting space and assuming the role of spectators while they are not "on." The lighting was plain white only throughout, with most of the house-lights up too, only to be dimmed very gradually as the play progressed to make the last act focused within the relatively darkened stage. Although our second Shakespeare in Japan, *As You Like It*, had comparatively elaborate set, costumes, and lighting, they were by no means decorative. Again, the directorial attention was largely upon the actors' rendering of the text and their performance relationships. However, it is not that Murphy is fundamentally averse to spectacular stagings, for, as he says, "When you start from the text, it doesn't preclude going in any direction: it may become visually spectacular or simple."

Murphy draws an interesting comparison with Peter Stormare's stunningly spectacular *A Midsummer Night's Dream*, with "oriental" costumes and sets, also for the Tokyo Globe Company:

One of the main differences between Peter's production and mine is that my attitude to working as a foreigner was to bring what I know, whereas Peter seemed to
try to absorb what he knew about Japan into his own production.

What emerges here is a point about cultural politics: how would English or
European directors be tempted to "Japanize" Shakespeare when in Japan?
Alternatively, how would they resist that temptation? Would we criticize a
production such as Stormare's as "orientalist" and pandering to stereotypical conceptions of the east? If so, why have equally spectacular productions
such as Ninagawa's *Macbeth* or *Tempest* full of "Japanese" images and stage
conventions attracted not only western but Japanese audiences? Murphy
himself regards Ninagawa's A *Midsummer Night's Dream*, set in a classical
Japanese garden, with kimonos, and a sumo wrestler, as "one of the best
Dreams" he has ever seen. This leads to a paradox. When Murphy uses the
comparison with Stormare to rationalize (normalize even) his "non-
Japanized" approach, his strategy seems precariously close to cultural essentialism, as he indicates that only a Japanese director can successfully
"Japanize" Shakespeare. According to Murphy, Shakespeare is an "English"
writer, and it would be safer, and ultimately more rewarding, for an "English"
director to produce it within that framework. Cultural translation clearly has
its limits, as far as Shakespeare is concerned.

How, then, did Murphy try to convey that knowledge, which was "written"
in English rather than in Japanese, to the Japanese actors in the rehearsal
room? Did he attempt a different approach to them?

The last thing I wanted was to make my actors behave like "western" actors. For
instance, I could tell them how an "English" sense of humour might work in a particular scene, but I had to work with them to let a new and unique sense of humour
emerge from their own bodies and sensibilities.

As a normal practice, Murphy talked with his actors through an interpreter, but he denied that it was difficult to communicate with them. His
main strategy was to emphasize his individual personality and physicality
before his ethnicity or nationality.

At the first meeting, I talked quite a lot, so that the actors could get used to the
sound of my voice, my physical presence and so forth. I used the whole first day of
our rehearsal for this kind of talk, in which the actors could also ask many questions, and we very quickly forgot that we talked in different languages. And if your
concentration is right, you can often ignore the interpreter. A strange kind of illusion is created in a rehearsal room through a strange kind of mixed tongue: that
each actually understands what the other is saying until you get to the pub after-
wards to realize you totally misunderstood!

So – it would seem to Murphy – the actors communicated through speech-acts and body language almost independently of verbal language. Although those aspects of speech-act significantly affect communication, they remain left out of the technical act of translation. What Murphy had to devise, through the rehearsal, was an individual aural and bodily grammar, that would be suitable for a Japanese Shakespeare, and the script translated into Japanese served a vital, yet only a catalytic, function in that process.

There was another, wider problem of socio-cultural difference which he had to contend with, a problem rooted in the contemporary Japanese mentality – the question of responsibility or good faith towards what you do and have done. This can become a serious problem when a director tries to assert his or her authority over the actors. Murphy had to steer his way through a foreign actor-culture:

Japanese actors are accustomed to not taking responsibility. In Japanese theatre, it seems to me, there are two extremes: one is the traditional theatre such as Kabuki and Noh, where there is no director; the other is the theatre where the director is a complete dictator and the actors will do exactly what they are told. Of course, I am quite tough about what I want at the beginning, but I expect that actors will take over responsibility and the play will be theirs at the end. Japanese actors sometimes found that strange: they prefer to be told what to do. It will bring problems, because being constantly told what to do means that you are always a step outside the play, evaluating, commenting on it.

There was also a managerial problem, which was also culturally based. For instance, the casting, especially in the case of *The Merchant of Venice*, was pre-determined for the most part. Another problem relevant to that of casting was a preconception among some actors that they could work only in the particular style of the company they belonged to. For Murphy, this didn't make sense, because he felt each production should develop its own style, and that this should involve actors sharing responsibility with each other. An interesting case in point was the casting (largely for commercial reasons) of a Kabuki actor, Nakamura Hirotarô, for the part of Orlando in *As You Like It*, whose "essentially different" style of acting Murphy and his company of co-actors succeeded in making an asset rather than a liability through refocusing its performance grammar.

I think Kabuki is by nature a very selfish art form. It's wonderful to watch, but not at all contributory to the sort of theatre I'm interested in as a practitioner. So the difficulty was the habit created within that actor. I encouraged him to relax, make a fool of himself, if necessary. His brain was telling him to do that, but his blood not to.

As he adopted an "individual" approach in the rehearsal room, the difference between "eastern" and "western" modes of communication – the latter being far more direct than the former – caused further confusion. As Murphy believes, his tone of voice – he's got a very loud voice, a necessity for a veteran actor who has played many times on the huge Stratford and Barbican main stages – to his surprise made the actors puzzled and sometimes upset. Murphy said he never got angry with the Japanese actors, but his remark reveals his directorial assumptions in dealing with actors, as he sometimes had to assert his authority across the language barrier:

> The second time we did *The Merchant of Venice*, I had a mixed cast of people who'd done it before and people who hadn't. On the second day of rehearsal those who had said to their colleagues, "No, it isn't like that. Do it this way," and so forth. I did have to get very tough on that. I remember saying to one actor, "If you want to behave like a dictator to other actors, you just take over, and I'll go back to Britain. Though we take a similar approach to the one adopted two years ago, we need to take a step further with this production with a new company."

Again, it was not only the language barrier but also the cultural one influenced by the social hierarchy in Japan in which Murphy was intervening.

How about differences in the method of actor training? Japanese actors in general have various backgrounds: a few have long years of training, but many lack a formal education. To my surprise, Murphy was not at all concerned with this lack of training, as he believes that all actors are training all the time. Being a music graduate, he himself received no formal education as an actor. He felt no disadvantage in this, and, in fact, if anything, welcomed it: "I loved the fact that almost all Japanese actors felt that they were learning all the time. And that was exactly how I felt."

IV

How unique and significant is Murphy's Shakespeare in Japan within the whole genre of Japanese Shakespeare? Take the use of music. This is a very important element in his production, as he used live music in both *The Merchant of Venice* and *As You Like It*. One can't, however, imagine Murphy using music in Ninagawa's way – as a set – because he would always concentrate more on the words, which are the music for him. Music must comment on words rather than compensate for them.

More generally, what is his opinion about the on-going geo-political shift in terms of Shakespeare studies and productions from Anglo-American "center" to Asia-Pacific "periphery," which a project like "Shakespeare in

Japan" forms a part of, and to which, hopefully, he feels himself to be contributory in fruitful ways? There still remains a huge imbalance of power and knowledge, where a number of western directors and companies have been invited to do Shakespeares in Japan, while no English theatre companies would yet dream of inviting a Japanese director to do a Shakespeare with English actors.[1] We would like to see the co-operation between Murphy and the Japanese actors contributing towards correcting this inequality, resulting in interactions rather than one-way imports. Murphy's comment is clear: "I wish we had more directors from other cultures working with western actors. There is a barrier to it, a barrier of fear, which I want broken down because I think that, far from losing one's own identity in the process, one adds to it."

"What was the thing Murphy had learned most from directing Shakespeare in Japan?" was my final question. His answer sounded at once localized and universal:

How similar we were. Of course, one learns about differences, but the actor-director relationship doesn't vary that much. We aren't aliens in terms of practicing theatre, though our cultural differences are sometimes edifying, sometimes mysterious.

NOTE

1   An important exception is Suzuki Tadashi, who has been invited to direct productions with actors in America (*King Lear*) and Australia (*Macbeth*). Since the completion of this essay, Ninagawa Yukio has directed *King Lear* for the Royal Shakespeare Company in 1999.

PART III

INTERVIEWS WITH DIRECTORS AND ACTORS

15

Interview with Deguchi Norio

(April 4, 1995, with Takahashi Yasunari, Anzai Tetsuo, Matsuoka Kazuko, Ted Motohashi, and James Brandon.)

MATSUOKA   I have the impression that the conditions for the new Shakespeare in Japan can be largely attributed to you in The Shakespeare Theatre. In your first period, dialogue was delivered very fast. Did you do that intentionally?

DEGUCHI   We were inexperienced young actors performing in jeans, without costume or stage settings. We started from there, creating vigorous, energetic, and fast performances in which we just kept moving around and shouting. Coincidentally, it was right at the time when society was going through a dramatic period of change in the mid-seventies. That was the time when people's lifestyles were shifting from the normal "nine to five" pattern to an irregular one. All-night convenience stores were starting business, and midnight broadcasting and disk jockeys were popular. Disk jockeys talked at high speed in those days, probably unconsciously reflecting the fast-moving images of the city. So the audience could identify with such things without having any particular knowledge (of Shakespeare). Our first production was *Twelfth Night*, and we had only about one hundred people at the first performance, but, day by day, it gradually increased until, by the fifth day, we had about 300.

We were surprised that we could do just one play for a run of five nights. It was unexpected. The audience was surprised as well, even though they were not sure what was going on. JeanJean projected a different landscape onto the stage of Shakespeare even though it was not a sophisticated one: an image of the city presented just as it was.

ANZAI   You used to work for the Bungaku-za and Shiki theatre companies before you went to JeanJean. Were there any continuities and discontinuities between the work you were doing there and later at The Shakespeare Theatre?

DEGUCHI   Since the time I was with the Bungaku-za, I wanted to break with some received visual and physical images but wasn't sure how. At that time, an actor with whom I worked, Emori Tôru, who played Andrew Aguecheek and Hamlet, blazed a new trail that was well received. Emori's way of speaking and acting was cool – not eloquent but cold – and gave an impression that he kept his distance from the audience. However, it was well accepted by the audience. Perhaps it was just a coincidence. When I was at JeanJean, I didn't depend on having good actors; rather I wanted to produce a larger-than-life image in a rough and fast-moving way.

ANZAI   In those days of student movements, the larger-than-life image was what audiences wanted. It was an image of the time.

TAKAHASHI   But Deguchi was different from theatre people who came out of the student movement. Kara Jûrô and Suzuki Tadashi, who came from Zenkyôtô (the New Left), tried to produce unreal elements and mythologize the body. But Deguchi produced an everyday image that made Shakespeare our contemporary.

MOTOHASHI   Mr. Deguchi, was there anybody, in terms of drama, who influenced you culturally or with whom you strongly disagreed?

DEGUCHI   Well there was Fukuda Tsuneari. I read his theories about Shakespeare very closely. His translations were available when I was about twenty-seven. I chose Shakespeare partly because I liked its poetic elaboration. When I was an assistant director at the Bungaku-za everything on set aimed to provide a detailed portrait of real life. I hated those stage properties! I thought that an open space where people could move freely would be more suitable for theatre.

MATSUOKA   Was it Fukuda who introduced you to Shakespeare?

DEGUCHI   Yes. I was fascinated with his Shakespeare theory. I still think his *Midsummer Night's Dream* is the best I have ever seen. Nowadays, people think that we should play Shakespeare in certain ways, but when I was at Bungaku-za and JeanJean, I did not have any model except Fukuda's Kumo Theatre Company. It was not easy to know how to speak and act. We did not have videos nor go overseas so often, and foreign companies hardly came to Japan. So we were ignorant and had to resort to trial and error.

TAKAHASHI   Perhaps, in a sense, that was a good thing. Until the very end, Fukuda felt that his experience of watching Shakespeare performances in London was a millstone round his neck.

MOTOHASHI   Were there any significant changes in terms of your directorial concepts while you were directing all of Shakespeare's works at JeanJean during those seven years?

DEGUCHI   It was good when I did those works unconsciously in one continuous rush of energy. It got worse when I became careful and self-conscious and tried to direct in better ways, or produce the inside psychology, or started thinking of figures of speech. My powers flagged. In other words, there was no acting or directorial tradition which could support those ideas. So it was better to do it on impulse. In England there is a long tradition of how to deliver Shakespeare's speeches, and there are many good Shakespearean actors. Here Shakespeare has been played many times, but still nobody has been acclaimed as a great Shakespearean actor from whom succeeding actors can learn.

MATSUOKA   I don't think we will have any in the future in that sense. We should see it as a characteristic aspect of our situation.

DEGUCHI   Yes, well, I think what we can do is to try our own way.

MATSUOKA   Was it planned from the beginning to have performances with live music at JeanJean?

DEGUCHI   Yes. Originally, JeanJean was a place where people came to listen to folk music. It was the owner's request to have live performances with a band.

MOTOHASHI   Was it an intentional choice to use Odashima's newly published translation?

DEGUCHI   No, it wasn't. He was there, and I was there. That's all! It was our plan to do the *Complete Works*. So we made a contract with JeanJean to use the place on the condition that we could do all the plays.

MOTOHASHI   Did you think that Odashima's translations matched your style?

DEGUCHI   No, it wasn't that significant! I don't know much about literary style, so I can't tell which is better when I compare different translations. But I was used to the Fukuda translation. So when I read *Hamlet* in Odashima's version, I thought it was very weak: in fact, it was terrible! For example, the lines "To be or not to be. That is the question," which resonated so deeply within us when we are young, were translated as "Is it all right if we continue as we are, or not?" It was absurd! What should I do to give this absurdly translated line theatrical impact? That was my starting point.

TAKAHASHI   Then did you get used to Odashima's style gradually?

DEGUCHI   Yes, gradually the translation and our performance style came to match. When we used his words to create our *mise en scène*, it produced a definite style. I found that reading words is one thing and performing them another.

MOTOHASHI   Was it possible that he unconsciously rewrote some parts according to your actors' needs?

DEGUCHI   Perhaps, but Odashima did not come to our studio. We did thirty-seven works, and he never came once.

MOTOHASHI   That's incredible!

DEGUCHI   He never came to see our rehearsals. I saw him only when he gave me copies of his books, and on opening nights at JeanJean.

MATSUOKA   Did you talk to him over the phone?

DEGUCHI   There was absolutely no relationship between the director and the translator. When we saw each other on opening nights, we just got drunk together! I never altered the translations. There's a difference between a literature specialist and a director. My principle is not to make any claims to translation. The stage is an ambiguous place. You can say things in one way or another, but not change it. A translator translates with a certain style. I think the translator's world must be consistent from beginning to end. Actors don't understand what a difference it makes when they change a line. It may be necessary to cut some parts to reduce running time, but I'm strongly opposed to changing the words.

ANZAI   What happened after the JeanJean period?

DEGUCHI   After JeanJean I thought there was something wrong with my established approach that "Shakespeare is our contemporary." I thought that I had done something irresponsible, just recreating the atmosphere of the time and being satisfied with that without approaching the core of Shakespeare. Those feelings came to me whatever I saw, unbidden. I was ashamed of myself for not being genuine but just creating gimmicks by following my feelings. So, whatever I now did, it became ambiguous and lost its power. After trying various approaches, I finally entertained the idea that Shakespeare should be treated as a classic. But I just didn't know what to do about costume. For about eight years after JeanJean, most of my works were failures. I had a lot of ideas, but they didn't work out well onstage. Sometimes, if you aim too high, you fail; it was like that. Everything looked artificial.

My experienced actors were gone, and new members were young. We were looking for something we could present naturally when we happened to play *Comedy of Errors*. I thought that the actors had uninteresting faces, that their noses didn't look right and so on. Then I had the idea that, if they wore masks, they could increase their stage presence. Also, I thought it would produce a distancing effect, which would remind the audience that this was a performance; then, they could watch without being disturbed by other considerations. Besides, *Comedy of Errors* has been played in *commedia dell'arte* style. That's also why I decided on masked performance.

MATSUOKA   I thought that the masks in your *Comedy of Errors* worked brilliantly, particularly the moment when the actors took them off. It had such a paradoxical effect, exploring what has been hidden until that moment. I'm not so sure about your use of masks in *Taming of the Shrew*.

DEGUCHI   In the first production it worked well. Putting on and taking off the masks could be done naturally, without difficulty. But, in the second and the third trials, we had to think carefully about when we should take them off. So, sometimes, we burdened the production with all sorts of unnecessary ideas. In *Comedy of Errors*, it was our first experience, so we just stuck to the basic idea. We had just the simple idea that, after putting them on, later we would take them off. So the actors took them off when they met again. It wasn't a significant idea. On the contrary, in my experience, elaborate directing is not effective.

I feel that it is very difficult to explain the qualities of Shakespearean performance, particularly to practitioners. It is real, but not real. If we try to bring in naturalism, it makes the play very boring. I do not know how to put this, but, if you don't have a kind of instinctive acting, it does not work. What I'm talking about is different from modern realism, different from "doing it naturally." For example, what I found difficult in *Taming of the Shrew* was to maintain the reality of the relationship between a man and a woman even though the story itself is silly and ridiculous. People may say, "a play is just a play," but I think we need to remember that it is also a refraction of life. Actors have to balance contradiction – that's what I want out of them. If actors don't have that in their blood, I can't do anything about it.

MOTOHASHI   You deny yourself the visual aids of setting and costume, which Ninagawa uses so effectively. Is that a general principle?

DEGUCHI   Well, I think it comes from my own experience. *Hana no yakata* (The

House of Flowers) by Shiba Ryôtarô was the first play I directed. It was a big spectacle performed at the Nissei Theatre with stage settings changing one after another, with a crowd scene involving forty actors; even the stage broke in half as a theatrical effect. I realized, then, that spectacle was completely useless! That experience was so dire that it still influences my thinking.

MOTOHASHI　You do make use of spectacle in works other than Shakespeare's. Does it mean that you choose not to, or that you cannot make use of it in Shakespeare?

DEGUCHI　Well, if it were necessary, I suppose I could, but I choose not to. I think, basically, it is not part of directing.

MOTOHASHI　But that doesn't mean that spectacular staging of Shakespeare is necessarily wrong, does it?

DEGUCHI　Of course not. Some (such as Ninagawa) are excellent. It depends on the style of the director. You can't generalize. Most directors already have established styles and have to follow them. If I produced a spectacle now, it would be bad. People who do are experts in their own field. It takes years to master. You can't expect to be successful on a one-time basis.

MOTOHASHI　Compared with the period of JeanJean, you use bigger spaces now. Certainly, the audience is different as well. What particularly did you want to change?

DEGUCHI　The quality of the actors; it is now much better than it was at JeanJean. But unfortunately, there isn't such a wide age-range to choose from today.

MOTOHASHI　Since the JeanJean period, generally speaking, your comedies have been well received. Some people say you are less successful at doing the tragedies and histories. Do you take the view that "Deguchi's trademark is comedy"?

DEGUCHI　No! I prefer tragedy! If people ask what is my magnum opus, I'll answer "The trilogy of *Henry VI*." Of course, I could concentrate on the comedies now, if I wanted. But they are getting less interesting for me. I want other challenges.

MOTOHASHI　Your recent *Comedy of Errors* and *Taming of the Shrew* were well presented. The quality of the acting seems to be improving.

DEGUCHI　Yes, on the whole they are getting better, but we have no outstanding actors. So it is not good for Shakespeare. In his work, there is usually one extraordinary character that stands out above the rest. The supporting characters around this main character have merely average qualities. So, if the company has nobody with an extraordinary talent, we can't produce a great performance of Shakespeare. You cannot stride freely in the great Shakespearean universe.

ANZAI　What about your use of stylization?

DEGUCHI　This is not about acting itself, but I can say one thing: a period drama bears elements of pre-industrial society within itself. This is especially true of a sentimental play. However, fortunately or unfortunately, our generation's society is not an agricultural one anymore; it has become urbanized. We are in a transitional period. In other words, we passed our adolescence at a time when society's emotional attachment to agricultural society was diminishing. Since the 1960s, when the high-growth period began, I think that Suzuki Tadashi and Kara Jûrô have perpetuated the agricultural society's forms within their work and have nostalgia for it. However, The Shakespeare Theatre has a sensibility that is totally urbanized. In this respect, there is a big difference between those two directors and me. We worked in the same period and even in the same small theatres, but with a different sensibility. It's not too much of an exaggeration to say that my plays were modern but theirs were not. That's my belief. It was said that they were the best of their generation, but I have observed that they did not keep abreast of the currents of the time. They continued to play in a way that was bound to diminish in popularity. In the 1970s, they still tried to represent the old popular culture that was rapidly disappearing in reality. They were regarded as ahead of their time, but, in reality, they were behind it.

It may sound arrogant, but I think The Shakespeare Theatre was quite detached from that agricultural sensibility. That's why our plays were light. In the middle of Shibuya, far from the countryside, they could not be emotional. It did not reproduce the realities of daily life; our acting style was abstract. There were some negative elements to it as well, of course, like our lack of a strong sense of local community. But we had the feeling of people who did not have to eat rice anymore, urban dwellers asserting themselves at a time when agricultural society was on the wane.

MOTOHASHI   It is interesting to think of the urban young coming to Shibuya seeking verification of their urban sensibility. But they also had remnants of the agricultural past of Japan hidden within them, and this ambiguity was played out in the small space of JeanJean. After JeanJean, you had to move to big new theatres. Capitalism must go on. So, The Shakespeare Theatre loses its ambiguity when it is played in a place that is clean and neat. Do you think Shakespeare's plays lose their power in a big theatre?

DEGUCHI   I don't know. The most difficult thing is trying to understand Shakespeare's ambiguous attitude towards his time. But I also think that people who do understand it can create something that will last longer. When I see the RSC in London, I know they face the same kind of struggle. They do not make much progress in real terms, I think. It's not a matter of a decline in the standard of their acting, but in their way of understanding Shakespeare; they are stagnating. For example, the *Henry VI* directed by Katie Mitchell was not Shakespearean. True, it was made quite scrupulously. But I think Shakespeare should be more direct. What I see in the play is something very oriental, suggestive of the world of reincarnation.

MOTOHASHI   Do you have any desire to change the current stagnant situation when you are directing at The Shakespeare Theatre?

DEGUCHI   If you play Shakespeare only occasionally, Shakespeare does not come easily. I want to have actors who are specialists in Shakespearean performance. I don't know whether this is the answer, but we have to begin from this point anyway.

TAKAHASHI   Does that mean that The Shakespeare Theatre itself has to produce actors who perform only Shakespeare?

DEGUCHI   It is impossible. But I think it is a good idea to try to do the impossible. To put it simply, famous people try to keep the world the way it is, while those who are unknown try to destroy it. But, also, it is not always true that the unknown are less talented. Famous people have a certain degree of talent. In other words, it is an issue whether we bet on their namelessness. Maybe it won't make it happen, but I want to bet on the possibility. When they create, they create something bigger than those who are famous do. What famous people do is to ripen the established world. Nameless people can do new things.

MOTOHASHI   In Japan, we have only a few drama schools. Do you think it is important to teach Shakespeare in those schools as they do in England?

DEGUCHI   I think the Globe Theatre should have such a school. They should make it a matter of principle to spend their money in Japan rather than inviting expensive overseas companies. Though we have the Globe Theatre Company, it doesn't have any substantial activities. What good is that? When they established the company six years ago, I told the manager to set up a school. Then they could have started from the beginning. But they took a different direction. If they had spent money on basic necessities and let people know they were specializing in Shakespeare, audiences would be flocking to see the company.

ANZAI   Foreign productions are not that exciting anymore. The problem is where we go from here.

MATSUOKA   I see Japanese productions of Shakespeare as much as possible, always thinking about them in the context of Japanese culture. Deguchi has tried to localize Shakespeare in a few productions. His *Midsummer Night's Dream* was set in a bar and in a school.

DEGUCHI   When I did the bar version of *A Midsummer Night's Dream* at JeanJean for the first time, I had some adolescent experiences in mind – such as when you get drunk and have a relationship with a woman whom you don't love! I used to go to a bar in Hongô, and the madam, who wore a black jumper, reminded me of Titania when she shook the cocktail shaker. There was no barman who looked like Puck, however. I just wanted to project the image of the madam and the space of the bar into the play.

On top of that, I remember two other things about the experience: I got drunk and did not know what was going on; and the madam was pretty. I wanted to take those experiences into *A Midsummer Night's Dream*. Another embedded experience occurs in the scene in which Duke Orsino comes out of the bath in *Twelfth Night*. When I directed at Bungaku-za and did not know how to do a scene, I often went to a public bath to have a soak. The basic point is that when people are faced with a problem, they take a bath. I really wanted to put that on stage.

MOTOHASHI   Your bath and bar settings derive from personal experiences, but at the same time, they are very Japanese. Didn't you think of them as cultural translations, Mr. Deguchi?

DEGUCHI   I have no desire to make the plays specifically "Japanese." When I directed the school version of the *Dream* some years later, I was ambitious to make it successful. Because I was presenting it at the large auditorium in Theatre Cocoon in Shibuya, I thought I had to do something unusual and spectacular.

MATSUOKA   It was the first of a very successful five-year series of *Midsummer Night's Dream* productions done by different directors. I thought it was interesting that the play carried the personal history of Deguchi on its time axis.

DEGUCHI   In those days, Shakespeare was becoming increasingly remote from our contemporary social reality. So I got the idea of pulling it back to our daily reality by returning Shakespeare to the level of my personal history. For me, making it "Japanese" is not the ultimate aim. The important thing is to find a place where I and the text can converge. I also know that you can't cross borders by "Japanization." "Making it Japanese" is already about marking a border where exoticism begins. But I think exoticism is partly due to the ignorance of other nations. If there were no such ignorance, mysteriousness would not exist. Once you know that, it becomes an ordinary matter. When people prostrated themselves before British productions, they were worshiping exoticism. Now we are used to seeing British companies, so there's no longer anything mesmerizing about them. For that reason, I don't think we should emphasize our "Japaneseness." The images most people have of Japan at the present time derive from the period when we were an agricultural society: that is, old Japan, the "so-called Japan."

However, today's Japan is only partly traditional Japan. It is difficult to give an exact definition; nobody can say, "this is Japan." But it is also true that if we presented Japan in all its ambiguity, foreigners would not understand. It means that "Japanese Shakespeare" production cannot be recognized unless we simplify our Japaneseness. I don't think that is universalization; Japanization is simply a particularization.

TAKAHASHI   True. When you say "Japan," we don't know to which period of Japan's long history you are referring. Ninagawa and Noda's sumô version of *Much Ado About Nothing* use some stereotypical images.

ANZAI   It's nonsense to play "Japanese Shakespeare" to the Japanese.

MATSUOKA   I don't agree. Ninagawa said he directed Shakespeare because he wanted to communicate the old legends of foreign countries to a Japanese audience. A side effect of this was that his productions were well received overseas even though they weren't made for export.

BRANDON   Did you see any Japanese traditional plays in your childhood, Mr. Deguchi?

DEGUCHI   Yes, I saw Noh. But it was an old memory, and my staging bears no direct relation to Noh. It's a completely different form. But I feel good when I use masks. In my childhood, I went to village shrines to see Nohgaku festivals at night. When I put a live band onstage at JeanJean, it felt similar. But it doesn't appear directly onstage; it is filtered. I can believe in that kind of universality. When it is presented directly on the stage, I can't stand it.

MOTOHASHI   The process of filtering is localization in a true sense. If you present it directly, it becomes a reassertion of stereotypes.

DEGUCHI   Yes. I feel so good when I use masks. So comfortable. When I think about the reason, it's because I can go back to my birthplace. But I didn't like Kabuki.

BRANDON   Why not?

DEGUCHI   It was so boring. They just talk endlessly. Maybe the actors who came to our village were not good ones! I fell asleep. So my aversion to Kabuki is rather strong. But my ancestor was the *dômoto* (producer) of Kabuki in Okayama.

BRANDON   When?

DEGUCHI   In the Meiji period. In Katsutamachi, in Tsuyama, in the mountains of Okayama, a revolving stage still survives. My ancestor was the producer there, and he used to book in touring Kansai Kabuki companies. However, he went bankrupt. Then they escaped their creditors in the mountainous areas of Chûgoku and retreated to the end of the Shimane peninsula. That was where I grew up! So, when I joined Bungakuza, nobody opposed my involvement with theatre. Later, when I asked them about it, I was told the story. There was a separation as well. Though my mother stayed in Tsuyama, my father and grandmother, holding my hands, hiked through the mountains of Chûgoku to get to Shimane peninsula.

MOTOHASHI   It sounds like *The Comedy of Errors*!

DEGUCHI   We lived in a strange place, being looked after by various people. In my childhood, I didn't feel like a local. In an agricultural society of farmers' and fishermen's villages, we had no land. In our village, people looked at us as outsiders. Like strangers. I didn't feel it so much at the time, but later I realized we were strangers.

ANZAI   Isn't this directly related to the isolation in city life that you were talking about?

DEGUCHI   Yes, it sprang from an awareness of difference from agricultural behavior. Because I didn't have any ancestral property, I don't have that agricultural sense myself.

TAKAHASHI   Shimane is a place where the old Japanese way of life can still be found.

DEGUCHI   Yes, but not in myself. I think Shakespeare was different. He was a native in Stratford.

BRANDON   How do you teach the actors of your company?

DEGUCHI   I use the Odashima translations of Shakespeare. His words are very logical. I tell my actors that they must first learn to speak logically. Then they can speed up later. I always say that to follow the flow of the meaning accurately is like making a sketch for a painting. You add the colors later: the situations, human relationships, and emotional changes. First, they must do the sketch, which is a simple reading to clarify the meanings. After that, they must paint with speed and variation. In Shakespeare, especially, there are many long speeches, but these must be developed at a rapid pace. If you don't have a sketch to start with, you'll get into trouble. That's a basic lesson at The Shakespeare Theatre.

At first, I did not think that way, so the actors did not make much progress. I teach them with a system now, which is why their skill-level is higher. But still, nobody is an outstanding actor. Nevertheless, the standard is much higher than in the JeanJean days.

MOTOHASHI   How about physical training?

DEGUCHI   Well, I teach them not to "sit down." I think sitting down betrays the customs of an agricultural society. Nowadays, people look smarter. In the world of Shakespeare, there are vigorous changes. Suddenly everything changes in a moment. Those changes are very important. We are doing a silly exercise nowadays, which is called "Becoming an octopus." While you are playing an octopus, suddenly you are told to become a globefish. The actors learn how to change from being soft to being hard. They love each other as octopi and hate as globefish. It's very important to learn the art of fast transformation. Speed and flexibility are the basic elements of acting in Shakespeare.

TAKAHASHI   Where do you think your method for physical training can be located within the tradition of Japanese theatre? I think that your idea is new. In Noh, nothing changes. In Kabuki, transformations are made on a larger scale.

DEGUCHI   Shakespeare was working during the transition from the Middle Ages to the Modern period. I'm sure their sense of time changed dramatically. It was a new age when everything, including ways of thought, was changing rapidly. To be able to act that, speed is not enough. One has to be able to change in a second. The exact transformation depends on each actor's instincts. Sometimes they must be bold and at other times subtle. There must be variation within the transformation. Flexibility and speed are the basics of Shakespeare performance. From our point of view, Shakespeare's way is extreme. It involves a change from extreme A to extreme B. When we try to do that, it looks unconvincing.

How can we fill the gap? I think the most important thing is what you can see. An agricultural society is a society in which all things have continuity. Spring is followed by summer, then autumn. Time flows slowly. But time in

Shakespeare is not the time of a purely agricultural society. It is different, an artificial time created by people. So it is not well represented by Ozu Yasujirô's acting. It is closer to the style of Kurosawa Akira. It looks paradoxical. Maybe it is changing underneath, but on the surface it doesn't move at all. It even looks stagnant. That's why I feel some reality in their plays where there is no obvious drama. They express an aspect of reality that is opposite to Shakespeare's. If we don't confront the sheer power of Shakespeare's style, it becomes unconvincing in our present.

MOTOHASHI   Would you deny spectacle as too artificial?

DEGUCHI   In the case of Noda Hideki, I think he aims high in the sense that he never lets the audience become bored at any moment. I'm impressed by that. I wish I could present Shakespeare in a way that's never boring. The quality of his productions is another issue, however. It does not help merely to proclaim that Shakespeare is great. Noda's technique is not very good. I'm not sure whether his work has improved since the productions in Komaba; I believe it's getting more sophisticated. But anyway, his style is different from mine, though I, too, have developed techniques to avoid boring the audience. But if you look closer at that way of attracting audience attention, it is a very shallow world. When you're no longer "hot," they don't respond to you.

BRANDON   Is there any work of Shakespeare that does not match Japanese feeling in its content?

DEGUCHI   No. Everything matches up!

BRANDON   Even when it is about British culture?

DEGUCHI   The most obvious examples are the history plays. For Japanese, they are easy to understand. In *Richard III*, the war of factions becomes a war among brothers, within the family. In *Henry VIII*, it becomes a fight at Court, deep within the institutions of government.

MOTOHASHI   Does translation help in this process of "matching up"?

DEGUCHI   Just after I did *The Winter's Tale*, it was played by a Romanian company and by the RSC. I saw both and was very impressed. But at the same time, I thought something was missing in each. The British performance was very mature. But they were not interested in the state of contemporary society. They presented the world of a mature, settled, unquestioning society. The Romanian production – of course in translation – was set in the present, but a present that isn't mature yet. When I saw the Romanian staging, I could see they were taking it into the political situation of the present. So there could be no settlement at the end. However, I think Shakespeare is bigger than that. In other words, he thinks about the entire span of human history, not simply the history of the last ten or fifteen years. Human beings have reconciliations as well as fallings out. In the long run, reconciliation is definitely possible. But if you bring the current political situation into the framework, the world becomes smaller. More serious, perhaps, but smaller. On the other hand, if we are only concerned with the possibly more mature long view, then it may lack vital seriousness. So I wonder how we can get the balance right with Shakespeare. There must be a way.

The Winter's Tale has a span of fifteen years, but it doesn't seem like a mere fifteen years. You have to think about the time of the play as the entire history of humanity. Doing that play, I realized Shakespeare is a greater writer than I thought. There is nobody like him. His vision is on the grand scale, even in the domestic arena. In *Comedy of Errors*, a family gets separated. Then they get back together again, and the effect is enormous. In *Hamlet*, which is of course a tragedy, the family is split as well. Hamlet tries to solve the problem, but it doesn't work out. I understand that the same power is needed to get the family back together in comedy and tragedy. In our daily life, it hardly ever happens that a family breaks up completely. But to bring it back together takes an extraordinary act of grace. This is very difficult to get across onstage. It is easy to understand in the text, of course. But to be able to convince an audience, actors have to rely on their fundamental powers of understanding as human beings. It is very important to illuminate ordinary speech. You do not see such things in modern theatre.

BRANDON   Do you use some stylization in your work?

DEGUCHI   Well, no, I don't. I think form means stagnation.

TAKAHASHI   Then there is no image that we can identify as Deguchi Norio?

DEGUCHI   There's no such thing. I just hope my work keeps developing, though I am not overly confident about it. My family did not have land in the village where I was born; so, always, my sensibility is a "floating world" one.

BRANDON   Do you have your own way?

DEGUCHI   Yes, I do, and there is something indefinable that comes out as a result. I hope it remains incomplete. I don't wish to finalize it, if possible.

BRANDON   If you discover something that is effective, does it become a form, a permanent feature?

DEGUCHI   Yes, it does. I hope it does. But I think it should not happen. I rather want to destroy it.

BRANDON   How are you going to pass your work on to the next generation (a feature of traditional theatre espoused by Suzuki Tadashi)?

DEGUCHI   I do not have any expectation of that. It will end in one generation!

BRANDON   No disciples?

DEGUCHI   No. Disciples are no good!

BRANDON   But if you create good things, certainly you want to keep them, don't you?

ANZAI   You shouldn't.

DEGUCHI   You should try everything; try, try, try! I also want to destroy.

TAKAHASHI   Mr. Deguchi, you don't usually talk like this, do you?

DEGUCHI   No, I don't. I am very modest. For me the happiest moments occur when the actors do something unexpected. I am moved by that. Those are the most exciting moments for a director. If my actors simply play according to plan, even though they do something a little bit different, I won't be impressed. When something unexpected results, I am happy – so happy – to find another valid approach. A production that has these moments is a good one because it contains the possibility for discovery. But, if there are actors who, from the beginning, won't take direction, that's no good either. They should have enough self-discipline to try whatever a director asks. I'm happy when such an actor does something totally different. It is a third-rate professional who does not want to do what he or she is asked and does not have the guts to try. They have to try first; then they should think about whether they can go beyond what they've been asked to do.

I think that in working with Shakespeare we haven't reached the depths yet.

(Transcribed by Inazawa Shôko; translated by Hashimoto Kayoko, Ian Carruthers, and Ted Motohashi.)

16

Interview with Suzuki Tadashi

(April 6, 1995; with Takahashi Yasunari, Anzai Tetsuo, Matsuoka Kazuko, Ted Motohashi, and James Brandon.)

TAKAHASHI When we looked at the list of your productions, we realized just how long you have been involved with Shakespeare. What kind of play was *Don Hamlet*?

SUZUKI It was produced in 1971 or 1972. At this distance in time, I'd be hard pressed to explain what kind of a play it was. As usual, I used *Hamlet* dialogues in combination with dialogues from other plays.

TAKAHASHI "Don" refers to *Don Quixote* doesn't it?

SUZUKI Yes. Usually an insane person is my main character; basically, the structure of my theatre is that a person with excessive illusions sits alone in a room in real time, sometimes accompanied by an assistant. And the texts of Euripides and Shakespeare possess him or her. When a human being is waiting for something, always that person is possessed by words, which trigger fantasies. I use unusual words, for example the speeches of Izumi Kyôka, to express that because I think it's interesting to try to visualize such a state of mind. In other words, it's not a drama in which the action follows chronological time. The real drama is what transpires in the consciousness of someone who may just be sitting quietly in one moment of time.

TAKAHASHI The concept is similar to that of Noh, isn't it?

SUZUKI Yes, it is. But, basically, I am a modernist and have a modern idea about humanity. Freud has the same idea. Like him I look at humanity in terms of individual consciousness. In modern drama, playwrights have tended to think about the dramatic in terms of extended narrative time. Their work is about cause and effect. I'm not interested in that. I would rather present one aspect in a given moment. I want to show time as circular, rather than extended. Nobody has mentioned this aspect of my work, but it is my basic point of view. In one body, there exist various levels of consciousness. While you are doing one thing, you can think of others, be it on different levels of reality. To my mind, that's what makes humanity dramatically interesting.

TAKAHASHI I would like to hear how Shakespeare's words are taken into the structure.

SUZUKI I found it interesting that in Shakespeare, words for the inner worlds are clearly indicated. For example, "Blow, winds" and "rage, blow." These are not so much expressions of anger or sadness as metaphors of an inner world – or they present poetically the condition that such an inner world produces. Shakespeare's poetry excels in this respect. In *Macbeth*, "If it were done when 'tis done" is not what you would speak consciously, but it is accurate as an expression of consciousness. A monologue is not a natural form. It is always the speech of a stage character. Shakespeare writes speeches that the characters themselves may not understand, but others do. In other words, there is a gap between the character Macbeth and what he says. I'm very sensitive to what lies in that gap.

MATSUOKA   When I first read *Macbeth*, I thought it was Shakespeare's poetry that made Macbeth spring to life.

SUZUKI   Yes, I agree. Monologue in a true sense is there. Ibsen is different. Ibsen makes the characters speak his own ideas. But when Shakespeare presents a character, he imagines their desire and inner sensibility. Then he finds just the right words to describe them accurately and creates a monologue. The most interesting thing is the power of Shakespeare to make the invisible world visible through the poetic use of words. That's what I feel is truly great about him; the rest is not so impressive.

TAKAHASHI   Is that why you cut him so boldly?

SUZUKI   Yes indeed!

MATSUOKA   Ian Carruthers has pointed out that you can play Shakespeare only in a stylized, non-realistic manner.

SUZUKI   It is not realism, but it is real. For me (a soldier like) Macbeth could never possess the imagination to utter the "Tomorrow, and tomorrow, and tomorrow" speech. He's not educated enough. Yet I also feel the sense of transience in such a moment, something universal that could happen to anybody. Shakespeare is great in creating such situations through his poetic power.

TAKAHASHI   So you are not interested in characterization as a mechanism to enable the development of story and plot?

SUZUKI   Well, not because I'm not interested, exactly. It is an important territory for actors. But, at present, I'm not interested in that. I want to see how those speeches of Shakespeare's which have universality stand out, and under what kinds of situations.

TAKAHASHI   In the case of your Shakespeare productions, serious scholars, and Europeans in particular, are shocked at your cutting of large parts of the original text.

SUZUKI   I have responsibly presented the aspects I'm interested in. What's most important is what stays in your memory. You want to give form to the part with which you were most impressed. However, generally it is believed that plays are complete wholes made up of causes and effects. So, if I cut them out, people don't understand. But for me, theatre is about being touched. So even when people say the character of Macduff is interesting, I still cannot remember lines that don't affect me. In that sense, for me Macduff is not an interesting Shakespearean character.

MATSUOKA   Then, you can never do any new plays. For you it is a precondition that the audience knows the whole story.

SUZUKI   But I think I'm also doing something that the audience doesn't already know. Even if I present only those parts that move me, that's all right as long as it is interesting.

MATSUOKA   You could say that. But, in reality, there are few new plays that you have directed.

SUZUKI   Not quite. I did Betsuyaku Minoru and Kara Jûrô. But, does it matter?

MOTOHASHI   I think I understand your idea. You are a director, and know how actors create their stage-world by using their bodies to create characterization. So isn't it possible that the characters that actors create go even beyond the situation in your context? What do you think?

SUZUKI   Adrian Noble said something interesting about that. He said my stage reveals a completely new form of acting. So, the more you see the style, the more you can see the actors themselves. In my opinion, he is right. In other words, you do not see Macbeth. Rather, the human being who performs the role shines through. The issue is how actors can present the real conditions of consciousness on the stage, using Shakespeare's words. What transpires is the actor's interpretations of the word in the context of stage conventions. The issue is how you can deal with the words, using an artistic form called theatre. First comes style. I create a certain style of staging intentionally – Kabuki does the same, so do Noh and Takarazuka. Then I want to show how I can deal with these famous speeches, using this style. I reverse the usual situation. That's the strength of the classics. But realism assumes that there is no style onstage. Some people think they should approximate daily life in the text, or believe that, by playing character, they can approximate the play's intentions or meaning. We don't fall into that fallacy. We have a style and a grammar. We try to show how we can deal with Shakespeare's words using them.

ANZAI   I would like to hear how the style was created.

SUZUKI   Well, it's my own synthesis. It has a basic grammar, which is close to Kabuki and Noh, and also owes a lot to accumulated company experience.

ANZAI   It is not Noh, Kabuki, or Takarazuka! What, then, is the necessity to have a Suzuki style?

SUZUKI   Necessity? I can't say. When we think of the establishment of Noh and Kabuki in terms of necessity, we could argue that they lacked economic independence, were patronized or oppressed by the samurai, and under such circumstances, struggled to realize what they desired. But what matters is the result. In my opinion, the Noh, Kabuki, Takarazuka, and Suzuki styles are the only solid styles!

MATSUOKA   I still remember vividly what you said a long time ago: "When actors are young, they are full of energy and easily become manic. Theatre is a kind of manic condition. But when they get older, it becomes difficult to be manic, so with a certain style they can still be manic."

ANZAI   What I would like to know is how the training methods that make up the Suzuki style were created.

SUZUKI   I use the terms "training" and "style" differently. Basically, training is necessary to help project the voice and to improve physical control. Style, on the other hand, is a form that has artistic and aesthetic elements. Talking about the style, I create a style appropriate for the acting of characters that present their fantasies and inner worlds onstage. Japanese critics often misunderstand "the Suzuki method," though some foreigners understand it more accurately. It is a basic training to increase focus and energy (and can be used with different theatre styles). I think it is different from "the Suzuki style" in an artistic and aesthetic sense. When people find similarities between my *King Lear* and *Dionysus*, they see "the Suzuki style" in both, because, for example, I use wheelchairs in both. Of course, some plays are suitable for this style, and others not. In other words, it would be very difficult to play Beckett in Noh style. But that is all right. We do not run a supermarket! Talking about what can be done in Suzuki style, the monologues in *Macbeth*, *Hamlet*, and *King Lear* are very effective. On the other hand, Ibsen is difficult.

ANZAI   I see. So behind Suzuki style, there lies a theatre metaphysics?

SUZUKI   It is a limited world that one style can deal with. There is something that Noh and Kabuki cannot do. However, it is the Japanese literature-oriented theatre (of Shingeki) which assumes that one style can do all. The "Suzuki style" includes the formal presentation of the inner world of a character possessed by illusions, and the acting style that supports that structure. They are part of my style. Its constituents are a concept of human nature and a view of theatre. That is why there is a limit on the number of plays to which it can suitably be applied. But some parts of Shakespeare's works do seem to me to lend themselves very well to it.

ANZAI   It is often said that your style has continuity with the Noh.

SUZUKI   Yes, but I did not take the style directly from Noh.

ANZAI   There are many common elements.

SUZUKI   Yes, there are. I admit that. What European theatre has done since its establishment is to reveal how Europeans looked at human beings. Pondering that, I thought about what aspects of human nature I could describe through theatre. How could one present the unconscious, which cannot be verbalized? I thought maybe I could do that using the forms of stylized theatre. I connected my way of looking at human beings with a new form of theatre. I'm simply saying that Suzuki Tadashi, who is a theatre person, wishes to present a way of looking at human beings using a form of theatre that has historic elements. I wanted to show this as a way of shedding light on our human and theatrical situation.

TAKAHASHI   Nevertheless, as was clearly shown by the critical reviews of *King Lear* in London last year, some audience members still say, "I want to see Shakespeare, not Suzuki's view of human nature."

SUZUKI   Yes, indeed! But what they want doesn't make sense. First of all, I believe in the power of the form called theatre. The point is what we can do with it today. It is the task of theatre artists to show what can be done. It is just too amateurish to remain within the bounds approved by literary playwrights. Professionals do not have to put up with that.

TAKAHASHI   Well, there are various sides to Shakespeare. Certainly, some parts have elements of realism and tell stories, but, basically, they have taproots deep in human nature. Even so, your way of dealing with Shakespeare's texts is radical. Particularly your cutting. In your *King Lear*, one of Shakespeare's most important scenes, the one in which King Lear and Cordelia meet each other again, is simply not there. Some people in London could not stand that. They could not understand why.

SUZUKI   No, and there is no Kent, either.

TAKAHASHI   You did not want to do that scene, did you?

SUZUKI   I understood that if I included the scene it would make sense of the story. But when I do *King Lear*, I assume that people already know the story.

TAKAHASHI   You rely on the memories of the audience.

SUZUKI   Yes. I think that is acceptable.

TAKAHASHI   It is a Copernican way of rethinking Shakespearean performance. Really, you don't care for inessentials.

SUZUKI   I have another reason why I became interested in Shakespeare. European theatre history can be seen as the spiritual history of its playwrights. From this point of view Euripides, Shakespeare, Chekhov, and Beckett are indispensable. Greek tragedy presents the conflict of different value concepts among groups. In the three plays of the *Oresteia*, this is expressed as a conflict between the patrilineal and matrilineal idea of the family; in *Dionysus*, it is between royal authority and religious power. In other words, the ancient Greeks saw drama as a way of presenting value concepts in conflict.

In Shakespeare, it is not like that. There is a principle of order in the commonwealth. So the Elizabethans found drama in situations in which an individual goes against the fixed order. It means that he does not see the so-called fixed order as unchangeable. *Hamlet* is that kind of drama. *Macbeth* and *Richard III* as well. These are individuals who will not admit that value concepts are collectivized; their drama is that of the outstanding individual who fights society and loses. In Chekhov, the drama focuses on the individual differences in an established civil society. In Beckett, there are no such value concepts. Difference is no longer a standard by which to objectify oneself to the outer world. For a Beckettian man, all is despair; he simply exists out there like a piece of stone.

Those Shakespeare plays that focus on the individual rebellion against an emerging or established order can still engage our present social concerns; they achieve a certain "universality." Because of this, Shakespeare is still powerfully attractive. In Beckett, a special kind of elitism is described. What we need now is to examine Shakespeare's vision and Beckett's. These two can survive as drama. One of them says that there are no value concepts with which to objectify oneself and the other describes human beings that challenge common value concepts. This is my understanding.

TAKAHASHI   It's a good explanation of why Beckett never became popular and why Shakespeare is still so popular. You have also done Chekhov in Suzuki style, haven't you? I think it must have been very difficult.

SUZUKI   He is different from Ibsen. In Chekhov, there is some subconsciousness left, and the separation of language and existence is described. There is a gap between what is discussed and the misery that people feel in daily life. I find it quite interesting.

TAKAHASHI   But when you concentrate on that gap, it produces something very different from Chekhov, as he is commonly understood.

SUZUKI   Yes, it becomes grotesque.

MATSUOKA   Is there any Japanese writer whose work you wish to tackle now?

SUZUKI   Well, I'd like to try Tsuruya Namboku and Chikamatsu Monzaemon. When I saw the plays by Kara Jûrô, Betsuyaku Minoru, and Shimizu Kunio the other day, I enjoyed what I saw, but their bases are different. Usually, I choose a theme, such as four playwrights who represent European spiritual history. When that's decided, I proceed. If I do not have a theme, I do not direct.

TAKAHASHI   But your thinking does not match up with received Shakespearean attitudes at all. I'm saying that Shakespeare can encompass a multiplicity of points of view. Shakespeare's best virtues are considered to be his variety and complexity. But when we watch Suzuki's *Lear*, we find these features are cut off uncompromisingly. It is presented from one particular angle. This encourages people to complain that this is not Shakespeare.

SUZUKI   I understand that.

TAKAHASHI   So there is no room for argument, is there?

SUZUKI   People who like those things should do them. The strength and greatness of Shakespeare lies in his ability to mean many things to many people. My way is to focus on one aspect as a specialist. So, to those people who expect me to deal with the complete work, I would point out that it's not something we are obliged to do in this day and age. I think it is important that people discuss Shakespeare from different points of view and deepen the possible meanings in their own ways.

MOTOHASHI   The idea of Shakespearean variety or richness is not 400 years old. It was invented in the particular environment, politics, and culture of the twentieth century. I think Suzuki's approach to Shakespeare is a reaction against a certain era. We do not have to accept the British concept of "Shakespeare's variety."

BRANDON   Mr. Suzuki, how does your style suggest your view of the world?

SUZUKI   I think I'm close to Beckett, in a sense. It means that there is no absolute standard which can objectify the self or establish one's identity. But I'm different from Beckett since I emphasize the importance of fantasy in human existence. In Beckett, people talk individually and move as they do in daily life.

But what I'm saying is that people, who live in the real world, also have fantasies and illusions. And I'm saying that these have no end and cannot be solved.
In other words, my sensibility is similar to that of Beckett, but I deal with
human fantasy, which looks insane on the stage.

TAKAHASHI   Since your view of human beings and dramatic style are as strong
as they are, the outcome is always the same whatever you do, isn't that right?

SUZUKI   That's fine with me. People say I had better try something else rather
than going on repeating myself, but that's just nonsense. They simply don't
understand artists. The assumption that directors are capable of anything at
all is a ludicrous misunderstanding. It's irresponsible to expect Ôe Kenzaburô
to write in the style of Mishima Yukio. If Ôe did such a thing, he could not be
Ôe any more! Innate talent can't be tampered with. I hope people can differen-
tiate between entertainment and art. Otherwise, artists would never be
respected. When foreigners come to Japan and say my staging is different, you
know you're in business.

MATSUOKA   You said that the Suzuki training method and the Suzuki style of
presentation are different.

SUZUKI   They are totally different.

MATSUOKA   But do you think the Suzuki method is the most effective way to
realize Suzuki style?

SUZUKI   Yes. I do it in the way I believe is best. The reason Kanze Hisao wanted
to work with me was because he thought he could best achieve what he wanted
with this style of theatre.

MATSUOKA   Then it's possible to change the combination, to present a
different form using the Suzuki method, or to describe the world of Suzuki
style with a different method, isn't it?

SUZUKI   Of course, it is.

TAKAHASHI   We are not sure whether Suzuki method and Suzuki style are new
or old.

SUZUKI   They are old. I think that I should present the basics. On my stage,
there is one central human being, and the action is his or her fantasy
described. But I also think that everybody is like that simultaneously. It would
be wonderful if I could put ten people onstage and describe ten fantasies
simultaneously, but it isn't easy to do. That is why I'm trying to present the
minimum structure at this moment.

TAKAHASHI   When you first directed *The Trojan Women*, you thought of that
simultaneity, didn't you? Shiraishi Kayoko, Ichihara Etsuko, and Kanze Hisao:
those three all projected their fantasies onto each other, all of them different.
That created a bigger scale.

SUZUKI   Well, yes, but it was amateurish. There was no depth. It created a powerful spectacle though.

TAKAHASHI   Certainly it was much more successful when you remade it with
Shiraishi Kayoko at the center – playing all three roles.

SUZUKI   Yes, it had a centripetal force. I present a basic structure as a director. Then, when foreigners see my plays, they can understand both their structure and their strength. I think you can say the same thing about Noh. I treat the quality of energy in the space, musical qualities, and physical control with a traditional sense of theatre. If you say my theatre is old in that sense, you are right.

TAKAHASHI   The idea that the actor is at the center of the theatrical experience is an old one. Recently, multimedia theatre, which is represented by Peter Sellars, has appeared, and some people think it is new. In that sense, Suzuki Tadashi is not avant-garde, but rearguard.

SUZUKI   Yes. There are other styles that are obvious at first glance. Robert Wilson's is one of them. But they were discovered through an interest in the theatrical. In a sense, directors compete with each other in rediscovering different forms of theatrical stylization. It does not matter what the tradition is.

TAKAHASHI   The conclusion is that there is no medicine for Suzuki Tadashi, who is either a genius or a fool!

SUZUKI   That's right! Claudel was very impressed by Noh, in which there is no movement at all, and in which the voice sounds as if it is pressed out from under a pickle stone. He found a different pleasure in theatre. Noh specializes within a very narrow range of the pleasures of theatre. The ability to appreciate such variety is good.

MOTOHASHI   It is a part of English national pride to say that Shakespeare is a world poet. If somebody evaluated Suzuki's *King Lear*, which is adapted from Shakespeare, as "Japanese Shakespeare," what would you think?

SUZUKI   It is clear that I am Japanese. But what I present on my stage is not Japanese culture so much as something produced by the culture of The Suzuki Company of Toga (SCOT). A group always has its own culture. I do not think we have to limit ourselves to races or nations. Theatre groups may be influenced by race and nationality, but they also produce their own theatre culture. So I call my theatre "Suzuki culture." If somebody says it exists only in Japan, I would agree, but it would be erroneous to call it "Japanese theatre." In the same way, it does not make sense to say Picasso's paintings are Spanish paintings. If a group culture is not apparent, then, for me, there is no individuality on the stage. What there are will be merely some idiosyncratic qualities of the originator. For example, in Noda Hideki's work, only his habits are distinctive. To make its theatre powerful, the group has to create its own culture. Knowing that, I carefully consider training methods, and style, and even the organizational system in creating my staging. This can be called Suzuki culture.

MOTOHASHI   Reflecting on that, it's obvious that, for example, Ninagawa is not creating a Ninagawa training method or a Ninagawa theatre culture. Would you criticize him for this?

SUZUKI   Well, to create a culture is a kind of fascism. If there is no strong group, no culture is produced. Japanese theatre is by definition a group activity; yet, it no longer seems to be able to create a distinctive culture. Bungakuza and Haiyûza once did something like that, but they collapsed.

Nowadays, nobody wants to come to Japan to study arts, because established culture in Japan is ignored. There are no Japanese institutes, or Japanese arts education courses, nor a Japanese group culture. Because Japan does not have cultural policies, Koreans and Chinese go to western countries to study. It is said that we should export our culture, but I want to ask why nobody comes to Japan to study. If an impresario creates a false impression abroad through lavish expenditure on publicity, we lose our credibility. It is much better if we accept people who want to come to Japan to work with us; that way, we can truly share something, and they can go home having had an intense experience. This is what culture is about. We have to create such a thing. In that sense, I want to create a "Suzuki culture." But that will be inseparable from the fact that I am Japanese; there's no denying that. My grandfather was a master of Gidaiyû, and I don't deny the fact that it has influenced me.

TAKAHASHI   It is opposite to Japanese orientalism, which uses exoticism as a weapon.

SUZUKI   Yes, it is. I want to be exotic to the Japanese as well.

TAKAHASHI   Originally, Shingeki directors labored under the delusion that European theatre was universal. They thought that if they performed in European realistic style, they would become modernists. It was people like you who destroyed the illusion. As you said, when Japanese perform Shakespeare overseas, now and in the future, they should do it with the conviction of their own style.

ANZAI   You went to the United States, trained American actors in the Suzuki method, and directed using an American staff. I would like to hear about that.

SUZUKI   There is always something that is common to both cultures in the theatre. So, if you have shared interests, you can do it either the Japanese or the American way, both of which we have cultivated. Americans still think Japan is exotic. So, first of all, I show Americans that we're not exotic but ordinary. We explain that our style is a little bit different, but that it can supplement their own practices and possibly create a new fusion. In order to do this, we should not think of the teaching outcomes, but discuss issues that can be shared, such as training methods and theatre theories. After clear explanations of these, I can tell them what Suzuki, who is incidentally a Japanese, thought.

ANZAI   What was the reaction of actors over there?

SUZUKI   They enjoyed it very much. I think I can say there are two basic types of people I come across when I train: one is a person who takes an active part in theatre in their home country after my training; another is a person who ends up with one more exotic experience. It is a matter of individual talent.

TAKAHASHI   How about Katie Mitchell as a director? She studied Suzuki Tadashi a little, didn't she?

SUZUKI   Well, it's up to you. Nobody has to use my method in a certain way. Faking it is fine. Everybody is a bit of a fake anyway. Me too. My training method is taught in many places like the Julliard, but I suspect that the quality must have changed. However, in the United States there are some good exponents.

MOTOHASHI   I would like to know how directors with particular styles of doing Shakespeare think about others. For example, what do you think of Deguchi, who faithfully follows the text and tries to present Shakespeare simply through actors' speech and movement rather than through directorial concepts? How do you think he would be accepted overseas?

SUZUKI   Honestly speaking, the most difficult thing is the text. I think it would not be accepted.

MOTOHASHI   You mean the Japanese language?

SUZUKI   Yes. Ninagawa was accepted simply because he had a power to command the space. If we heard only the words on the textual level, we would find them weak. If British audiences understood Japanese, they would think Shakespeare's words are dead. I honestly think so. But, fortunately, Ninagawa is a powerful director, and his work was well received. It was because of Ninagawa's talent as a *metteur en scène*. In other words, whether one is accepted in foreign countries or not greatly depends on whether one can fill the space with energy and create striking visual effects. There is no guarantee for success overseas even if a production is viewed as a successful staging in Japan. The reason Terayama Shûji and I could continue our activities overseas was the strength of our concepts. It is the concept that is most lacking in Japan. We must work with ideas nowadays if we are to generate a substantial quality in our stage productions.

TAKAHASHI   Your *King Lear* was well received in the United States. The concepts you mentioned were also well understood there. However, there were some rejections in England. Maybe it is also a cultural problem on the part of the recipient.

SUZUKI   That's fair enough. The important thing is to put forward concepts that explain relationships clearly. It is important to get a clear response, even if it's a rejection!

MATSUOKA   You mentioned Ninagawa and his use of space; your concept must also be presented visually in the space, mustn't it?

SUZUKI   Yes, indeed. That's why you must be able to see that it is a Suzuki piece at first glance. Its style must be clear, as I mentioned. If you present it transparently as "Shakespeare" or "Chekhov," it does not go down well. You have to put it in parentheses – as Ninagawa did with *Ninagawa Macbeth*. These days, it's very difficult to get noticed if you do not label your style and create strong concepts.

TAKAHASHI   Style and form have their own strengths and weaknesses. There is a danger that people will tire of this approach as manneristic. What would you say to that, Mr. Suzuki?

SUZUKI   Well, I am a bit odd anyway. But I want to make it clear that we have to show that the theatre, which we put in parentheses, is not transparent, but an artwork. The problem is that we Japanese people have not yet become comfortable with foregrounding our individuality. I do not think you will be well received in a foreign country claiming to reproduce Shakespeare. In the field of arts, it is no good if you cannot see the director's face. Just a vaguely positive evaluation does not help you to cross cultural borders, except on a superficial level.

MOTOHASHI   Is it possible that you will yourself direct RSC actors?

SUZUKI   There are some such plans afoot. These days, I have been busy training foreigners. But I would now like to concentrate on producing good productions in Japan. I think we should develop places – like Toga – that people from foreign countries find interesting. Then they can go home impressed. The time will come when going abroad is, in itself, not meaningful anymore.

ANZAI   I think that westerners haven't yet recognized that there can be commonality in theatre outside the west. For Europeans, theatre starts with Aristotle and leads on to Shakespeare and Beckett. Probably, for them, there is no such thing as the wider cosmos of theatre in which many cultures can share common elements.

SUZUKI   When Peter Brook does something in foreign countries, journalists go there from Japan. But even though people say Ninagawa or Suzuki are international, when we produce new works, no journalists come from foreign countries. They do not even come from Korea and China. So it is not true "international dialogue"! There are many political and economic obstacles to realizing that goal. The issue hasn't taken root yet.

When Peter Brook did a production of the *Mahabharata* at the Saison Theatre, he didn't come for the opening. Moreover, he did indoors a play that was originally done outdoors. It was made possible because Seibu put in a lot of money, and he didn't worry about the reception of Japanese journalists. Maybe I'd feel the same way if I was asked to do a play at a 50,000-seat auditorium in the Philippines which I had done at a small, 100-seat theatre in Japan. I couldn't do it in terms of artistic conscience, but if they paid me a billion yen, definitely I'd go. If there were the same request from Paris, on the other hand, it would be impossible. Peter Brook understood that very well when he put on his production at the Saison. He knew that it was the victory of money over art. So he did not want to come for the opening. Why then, we should ask, did he do such a thing in the first place? Because, I think, he looks down on Japan artistically. There are many things that we have to fight as Japanese.

I'm trying to create a situation (with the 1999 International Theatre Olympics Festival in Shizuoka) in which foreign festival directors will actually come to Japan in order to see if there are Japanese productions good enough for them to feel like booking. I wish you luck in your attempts to balance the equation.

(Transcribed by Inazawa Shôko; translated by Hashimoto Kayoko, Ian Carruthers, and Takahashi Yasunari.)

17

Interview with Ninagawa Yukio

(July 4, 1995; with Takahashi Yasunari, Anzai Tetsuo, Matsuoka Kazuko, Ted Motohashi, and Ian Carruthers.)

MATSUOKA   We would like to begin by asking you how you met your producer Mr. Nakane and why you started directing Shakespeare's plays. I remember *Romeo and Juliet* was the first play you worked on together, wasn't it? Were you already interested in Shakespeare, and had you read his plays before you started directing?

NINAGAWA   Well, yes, I often saw theatre companies from overseas. Of course, I saw Peter Brook's *A Midsummer Night's Dream* and Trevor Nunn's *The Winter's Tale.*

MATSUOKA   And, also, *Twelfth Night*, I believe?

NINAGAWA   Yes, I saw most of what came to Japan.

MATSUOKA   How about Japanese Shakespeare productions?

NINAGAWA   I saw Akutagawa Hiroshi in *Hamlet.* Also *The Merry Wives of Windsor* with Senda Koreya as Falstaff. They were really good productions.

MATSUOKA   So, when you watched them, were you thinking of directing Shakespeare yourself in the future?

NINAGAWA   Well, I was an actor at that time and not anxious to direct. But I was reading some Shakespeare plays – not all of them, just the major ones.

MATSUOKA   When you first became a theatre director, you were working with Shimizu Kunio, the playwright, weren't you?

NINAGAWA   Yes, that's why I never thought about directing translated plays by myself. I had the idea of adapting some Japanese classics, such as *Yotsuya Kaidan* and *Chikamatsu Shinjû Monogatari.* Anyway, I never thought consciously about directing Shakespeare.

TAKAHASHI   What was the reason you came to direct him then?

MATSUOKA   Nakane got you to consider it, didn't he?

NAKANE   Yes, I was a fan of Peter Brook's plays. In the sixties, I was studying abroad, and, at that time, Zeffirelli was also one of my heroes – I thought his *Romeo and Juliet* was great. I had the feeling Shakespeare's plays were very entertaining, and the impression was confirmed when I saw that production. So, I promised myself that I would put together a Shakespeare production the like of which had never been seen in Japan. The play would not be for snobs but for ordinary people. However, I was working for Tôhô at that time and I never had a chance to produce the kind of play I wanted. Then, one day, the Nissei Theatre offered me the opportunity to produce anything I wanted, so I decided on *Romeo and Juliet.* I was considering several directors, but when I approached Ninagawa, he agreed right away. Of course, at that time he suggested *Hamlet* rather than *Romeo and Juliet*.

NINAGAWA   That's right.

NAKANE   I was really surprised when he said that if we were going to produce *Hamlet*, it would have to be done in *Hinamatsuri* (Girls' festival) style. Then I said, "Well, if we decide to do *Romeo and Juliet*, how would you direct that one?" First, he said the play should begin with Elton John's music, as if he had been planning this for a long time. And he wanted to use dwarves, and flaming torches in a dance scene. I said I wanted to produce the play in a big theatre and felt the story should be intellectual but entertaining. Ninagawa said he was also thinking about directing a big production. It was easy for us to decide to work together when our two approaches matched so unexpectedly.

NINAGAWA   It was in 1974. I had been working in Shinjuku in 1973, at a theatre company called Sakurasha that succeeded the Gendaijin company, and it was on its last legs. One day during the run, I came in to see the play I had directed, and thought, "This is hopeless." So, I told Shimizu our collaboration wasn't working anymore and that we should break up the company. That was my situation when I got Nakane's proposal to do a Shakespeare play. I started thinking about directing Shakespeare after my work with Shimizu had failed. So the *Hamlet* that Nakane mentioned gave birth to the *Hinamatsuri* idea. On the night of the festival, Hagiwara Ken'ichi (Hamlet) would appear like a ghost. I thought that, if we could play it this way, we could better express our own despair at the declining theatre scene and could find a way to revive my theatrical activities.

When we play Shakespeare in Japan, it usually has to be educational and explanatory. Past productions had aimed to introduce two things to the Japanese theatre scene. The first was the dramatic value of the play and the second a new style of playing. The key reason for using Hagiwara Ken'ichi was to overcome this "educational" type of Shakespeare as practiced in the past. Because he was a rock star and a cultural hero to the young, nobody would think he had any chance of playing Hamlet. I hoped this casting would create a timely problem for my theatre company to tackle and that, in this way, we could revitalize its declining energy.

The (Sakurasha) company's plays had been definitely stage-oriented, not meant to be purely literary texts. But I had come to feel this approach wouldn't do. Instead, I needed to have Shakespeare's play performed with very long lines and powerful expressions, or with lines in the classical style. I had asked Shimizu to write the script in that way. I was thinking about doing it with a play on Masakado, who rebelled against the establishment of the time, somewhat like Macbeth. It would be about a lost war leader's revival – the story of a leader who died in Kyoto, and whose head suddenly appeared in Ōtemachi in Tokyo. I wanted the story of a leader's revival to connect with our theatre company's revival. What I was asking Shimizu to write was quite different from what we had been doing before. While we were considering it, I received the good news from Nakane that I was to direct a Shakespeare play.

NAKANE   It was good timing for us. Theatrical fashion at that time was quite different from what it is now. For example, while Kabuki was appreciated for its style, and modern plays (Shingeki) for their words, there were also underground theatre groups focusing on using the body for expressive rather than narrative purposes, and commercial plays which relied on the actor's presentation of personality in a character role. All of these approaches existed, but almost without connection to each other. So I wondered if I could mix them together in the same production. However, there wasn't a single playwright available who could write for such a new genre.

That's how I came to realize that only Shakespeare was powerful enough to pull together all the elements in the Japanese theatre scene into one production. That's why I wanted to work with Ninagawa to combine classical stylization and the pop culture embodied by Hagiwara within the framework of Shakespeare. It was a chance meeting of two related ideas.

When we cast the play, we decided that Ichikawa Somegorô (now Matsumoto Kôshirô) would be Romeo and Juliet would be Nakano Yoshiko. Back then, we could not cast the actors we wanted because I didn't have enough power in the industry. When I approached some actors to play roles in our play, they didn't trust me.

MATSUOKA   I am not sure about *Romeo and Juliet*, because I didn't see it, but having seen most of your other productions of Shakespeare, with the exception of the recent *Othello*, they strike me as having a distinctively Japanese visual style. Did you consider this when you first did *Romeo and Juliet*?

NINAGAWA   No, because it was the first time we had done a Shakespeare, and it was as a consequence of taking on this production that we realized it wasn't going to work. We couldn't do the European style better than the European theatre companies themselves.

MATSUOKA   Did you realize this after you had finished the play?

NINAGAWA   No, I realized it when we were preparing the play. To be exact, on the second day of rehearsal! The reason I wanted to use Elton John's music was to popularize the production. I told reporters I wanted the audience to come in casual clothes as if they were coming to see a movie. I was actually trying to hide my own personal interpretation.

In the early seventies, I used Mikhail Bakhtin's *Rabelais* as a medium for thinking about the popular revival of Japanese theatre. And I showed Fellini movies, not Shakespeare, to the actors. So everybody was surprised. I wanted that kind of performance from the actors, but they were too rough, and the commercial actors didn't remember their lines. When they read a line, it sounded like stereotyped samurai speech. The lines just didn't mean anything. So I thought I should submerge them under Elton John's music. Then you wouldn't hear anything when the play started, only sound. I wanted strong contrasts, such as people running, with music coming from everywhere – a sort of visual rhetoric. Otherwise, it would need a rhetoric that comes from Europe or Greece that we don't have naturally. I still feel that way about it now; I'm still struggling with this disadvantage in our culture – we don't have a definite "self," "self" as an agent, an assertive, aggressive self. The core of my artistic struggle is actually to discover such a self.

I think understanding of self is basic to the idea of realistic acting, but many people are not educated that way. Besides, on a more practical level, there was the problem of how shabby the actors looked in tights! So I made the theatre really dark. The other reason for doing it this way was that the words were not getting through to the audience. If you read the play, you may understand, but when you actually say the words, they start to lose meaning. And also, actors can't project the self for long. They can hold it for maybe two lines but not for five. They need physical strength and a strong personality to maintain a strong, self-conscious presence.

Then I thought I had to find a technique which would connect with the thought-patterns of Japanese people by rearranging the play to use visual images in a Japanese style, without changing the words from the original except to take some proper nouns out of the play. This is why I get angry if somebody describes my plays as "Japanesque." I have attempted to introduce to a Japanese audience my impression of Shakespeare and analyzed how to achieve this.

MATSUOKA   What Ninagawa created for the Japanese audience unexpectedly became accepted internationally. Kurosawa's *Kumonosu-jô* (*The Throne of Blood*) was like that, too. Do you see that as ironic or happy chance?

NINAGAWA   The aim was to produce a Shakespeare play that could be understood by ordinary people. I wasn't thinking about appealing to the international market while I was producing the play. But Nakane was interested and suggested we go abroad.

To return to the matter of western rhetoric, take Juliet's lines in the third act of *Romeo and Juliet*: "Gallop apace, you fiery-footed steeds, towards Phœbus' lodging; such a waggoner as Phaethon would whip you to the west, and bring in cloudy night immediately." Not many Japanese can understand what these lines are saying. Even when you explain that it's an expressive way of saying, "Hurry up," it's still hard to relate to Japanese tradition. "O fiery red sun galloping like a chariot towards the horizon where night begins, please hurry; I want to sleep with Romeo." We can't understand rhetoric like this when it's translated literally because we don't have these figures of speech. I use visual images to make it easier for Japanese to understand the meaning of the scene. Of course, if I produced the way Suzuki does and used only easily manageable scenes, rather than the whole play, it would be totally different.

TAKAHASHI   You are very faithful to the original text. That might explain why Ninagawa is misunderstood by some people; for example, your remarks about the Japanesque. Some people say your *Macbeth* was intended for an overseas audience.

NAKANE   They say that a lot.

TAKAHASHI   You think it unjust, I suppose?

NAKANE   Very much so.

TAKAHASHI   Have you always believed in not changing the text?

NINAGAWA   My concept of never deviating from the original text started when I became a theatre director. I wouldn't direct a play just for my own convenience. However, I often rely on my imagination to try to understand something. For me, the most important thing in Shakespeare is the play within the play. *Hamlet* is a good example. The final decision to take revenge is made after the play within the play. And in *A Midsummer Night's Dream*, the revival of love occurs after watching the play within the play. You can't take out the play within the play without damaging the complex structure of dream layers within the play as a whole. So, you just have to be patient.

NAKANE   The reason I took Ninagawa overseas was because he was doing something totally new. Even if a production of Shakespeare is created in an Asian culture, it can be a genuinely persuasive piece of theatre for Europeans. Ninagawa's *Tempest* can be set on Sado Island in the Sea of Japan and still be real Shakespeare. When we brought our *Tempest* to England, it was seen as universal. I simply wanted to demonstrate the universality of his production.

TAKAHASHI   So, are you saying that your play becomes universal only through particularization in the paradoxical way that most art does? And that, if you had tried to achieve an unspecified universality, it would not have succeeded anywhere?

NAKANE   Yes, we have noticed many productions with that kind of mistaken perception!

TAKAHASHI   In all of your productions of Shakespeare, the world of the play – its setting – is very clear, and the concept is very sharp. It surprises us. I think that would be the most important feature of the production. So how do you decide on this? Is it just inspiration?

NINAGAWA   Well, it's certainly the result of a desperate struggle. Actually, it can't work well every time. Our *Hamlet* for this autumn has changed three times already.

NAKANE   *Macbeth* was the first play in which you transposed the setting completely to Japan. I first had the idea of setting the play in Azuchi castle. I thought the setting would be good for *Macbeth* because it was created by Oda Nobunaga (the first warlord to reunify Japan in the late sixteenth century).

NINAGAWA   But when I went back home and opened up our family Butsudan (Buddhist home altar) to light a candle and pray for my father, at that moment, I thought, "this is the right image." I had two overlapping complex ideas: ordinary people watching *Macbeth*, and a Japanese audience looking at the stage and seeing through it to our ancestors.

When I was in front of the Butsudan, my thoughts were racing. It was like I was having a conversation with my ancestors. When I thought of *Macbeth* in this way, I thought of him appearing in the Butsudan where we consecrate dead ancestors. Then we could change the setting when the witches appear, as in the Japanese expression, "To be tempted by time." We could create a setting like dusk, neither night nor day, when, according to a Japanese tradition, one often meets with demonic beings.

I was thinking about the scene of Birnam Wood too. In that scene, they carry Kadomatsu-like tree-branches (New Year's gate decoration of pine sprigs), which looks a bit funny. I thought I could change the setting to a lot of cherry blossoms moving, suggesting that the season is changing. As spring arrives, the whole scene would change, and the doors of the Butsudan would turn into the great gates of a castle, and the shelves within the Butsudan would turn into its stately staircase. Everything would connect together in this way. I thought the Butsudan idea should be the *leitmotif* of the play and, as I was wondering about it, we received an advertisement for Butsudans at home. So I thought that was a divine blessing.

The Tempest was also conceived like that. Some suggested that the Bermudas would be the best setting, and that I should travel abroad for fresh inspiration. I hate travelling, and I was not really anxious to go, but I did. However, I didn't feel good and just stayed in the hotel for two whole days thinking about the setting for the play: should the exiles' setting be The Bermudas? A South Pacific island? An island where convicts were exiled? Then I thought Sado Island in Japan should be the place! Zeami (the Shakespeare of Noh theatre) was exiled there. For the Japanese, Sado Island is also a place where convicts were sent. Then I wondered, "What would *The Tempest* look like if Japanese performed it?" So, I developed the idea of setting the whole play within a rehearsal – which I thought would reduce the incongruity of the play being done in Japanese. If we set it during a rehearsal, we would be signaling our pretence. We wouldn't need blond hair. Everything could overlap between play and rehearsal. We could remain Japanese but suggest Miranda or Prospero in any style of clothing. It would be a sort of play within a play.

With this decision made, I came back to Japan, then set straight off to Sado Island. I discovered there are thirty-two ancient Noh stages on the island, all of them open to the elements. The roofing was of straw and the whole stage shuttered because disused.

MATSUOKA   Hearing what you say, I feel you must always be searching for connections between the world of Shakespeare and your own world.

NINAGAWA   That's right, I am; and I also need to be impressed by something. Actually, when I was directing *The Tempest* I was slightly depressed.

NAKANE   Heavily!

NINAGAWA   The usual mid-life crisis. That's the way I was: not seeing anyone and thinking about retirement. My own situation at that time seemed to relate to Prospero's thoughts in the play when he says, "Our revels now are ended." I was convinced that I had lost my talent for directing and that this would be my last chance to make a successful production. If it failed, I would retire. You see, I can't start work until I've found some hook in the play that catches my imagination.

NAKANE   *The Tempest* was performed in 1989 wasn't it? We actually planned the play in the seventies, but you weren't interested at that time. Because you weren't depressed enough.

NINAGAWA   When I was producing *The Tempest*, I felt challenged by the shipboard scene and the need to assemble a ship. I wanted to use found objects from the old Noh stages on Sado Island: things such as old tatami mats and sliding doors. I actually tried to use this stuff to make a ship in the play, but it didn't work. It became too Japanese and didn't suit Shakespeare at all. I was dumbfounded. I thought I had created the image of the old ship in my mind, building it in a completely Japanese style to suit Sado Island. However, it didn't suit Shakespeare's gorgeous lines. Even the music, such as the sound of Japanese drums, didn't suit them. Such surface things cannot evoke the depth and vastness of the world of Shakespeare. I had found out these things by actually trying them. That's why I decided to give up using a purely Japanese style in my productions. I was surprised at myself, realizing I couldn't simply change the setting to a Japanese one. For example, my use of Fauré's music side by side with sutra chanting wasn't because I was trying to do something ostensibly very different. The power of the word in Shakespeare's plays is very strong, and one play runs the whole gamut, from the prose of daily life to the most beautiful and lofty poetry and philosophy. One of the most interesting things about directing Shakespeare is that you can't use only one tactic.

TAKAHASHI   Listening to you talk about *Macbeth* and *The Tempest*, I feel as if we are allowed to witness the secrets of your creative process. In fact, we have only observed their consequences, but they were surely good examples of the success of your ideas. How about *Hamlet* in that sense?

NINAGAWA   That was a failure.

TAKAHASHI   Why was that?

NINAGAWA   The reason was that we didn't have a concept powerful enough to make all the different images cohere. We tried, but something was always missing when we were producing *Hamlet*. It's a very difficult play. I feel ashamed that we made three passes at it. I thought it would improve if I could do it three times, but every time I tried something new, it failed. The acting and music just got worse. I knew my productions of *Hamlet* and *Othello* were failures.

People say there are no clowns in the play, but I perceived Hamlet as, in some ways, playing the clown. If I over-emphasized this, the character of Hamlet as a chosen, exceptional individual would fade. The contrast between Hamlet and other characters like Rosencrantz and Guildenstern would also diminish. So it depends on where you focus. I try to get the best balance as a cormorant fisherman does. You need to control the cormorants to catch fish.

NAKANE   One other thing we have to consider is that you have to make adjustments depending on which actor you are going to direct. In this play many of the characters are ambiguous, not only Hamlet. We need to ask actors to play well-rounded, complex characters, and if they can't act like that, we can't maintain the perfect balance in the play. That's the situation now in Japan.

NINAGAWA   Also, we are trained in Shingeki so, when we produce Shakespeare or other translated plays, it tends to show our bad side. We shy away too much from the intention to educate the audience, and we often run to the other extreme – of entertainment. Shingeki has had a kind of unfortunate culturalism, and, as a rebel against that sort of respectability, I tried hard to destroy the snobbism in it; but now, I need to get over both that cultural cringe and the heady revolt against it. The sixties style of producing had its own limitations. It tried to destroy the culturally received intellectual image.

MOTOHASHI   When the Japanese produce Shakespeare's plays, whether they use a visually Japanese style or not, they still have the problem of using the Japanese language. You can't escape from producing the play in Japanese. This suggests that the major reason your Shakespeare productions have success overseas is that your *mise en scène* is so masterful. What do you think?

NINAGAWA   I'm not sure. My productions don't work the way Suzuki's do, and, in my case, I don't start with a theory of drama. First, there's the play; I get an impression from it and think how I can express that impression. That means the style or method of the production must differ, depending on my impression. So, style is secondary in my case. I don't usually watch other people's plays. In particular, I don't see any play that I might be producing later because it's dangerous to do so; I don't want to be influenced. When I go to England, I don't watch any other Shakespeare productions. For these reasons, I can't really answer your question. However, when I think about stylization, I always consider how the body can incarnate the words that were first experienced in a reading. In order to give life to the words, we need to have complex personalities; otherwise, we won't be able to present Shakespeare's full range. This is because he includes everything from everyday speech to symbolic imagery, and if Japanese want to convey it, we have to twist ourselves, so to speak. We have to twist the core of our beings. But if you twist them too much, you will become like Suzuki's actors: too peculiar, too far away from the words of Shakespeare.

I don't care what other people say, but I want Shakespeare's words to become mine. However, because of differences in grammar, inversions in syntax frequently appear in the translation of heightened poetic expression. If we want to make these rhetorical expressions our own, we need to work with them until we can realize their effectiveness. So we have to create the structures to twist ourselves. You have to torture yourself a little bit in order for the play to work. In *A Midsummer Night's Dream*, for instance, I told all the actors to lower their center of gravity a little. I'm not sure if this is part of Japanese or Asian character, but we turn inside ourselves and hold in the energy.

In my opinion, the Japanese don't have the same style of communication that European people are trained in. Europeans use their words to debate and convince the opposition of their ideas. Japanese society doesn't have such an aggressive style of communication. But if you go to Europe to work, you have to persuade other people of what you want, otherwise they won't work for you. Yet, our approach can't be so definitely based upon the words as theirs is.

I have been denying the values of Shingeki. However, when I took up Shingeki, I was trained to analyze drama by Kurahashi Takeshi. He created subtext for even Abe Kôbô's dramas from beginning to end. In fact, his subtexts were often longer than the original plays. He trained me in thorough and consistent analysis of a drama and liked to refer to Frances Ferguson's concept of "the idea of a theatre." When I went to Europe, this training helped. I have a habit of analyzing what I read, so I was very confident about providing subtext, and I could argue with my European staff on an equal footing. So I was helped by the very thing I have been trying to get away from.

Because of this early training, I don't have any problems when discussing text with English actors. They require copious explanations, and if we can't explain something, they won't respond. If they ask, "Why do we have to sing in this scene?" they won't be satisfied if I simply answer, "Because Ibsen says so!" I have to give them a thorough explanation of why they need to sing in the scene.

For the English, entrenched in an attitude of positivism, or for people with ideas based on realism, we have to explain everything.

TAKAHASHI   How did you get the idea of using a Japanese style rock garden as the set in *A Midsummer Night's Dream*?

NINAGAWA   I always wanted to produce a play set in a rock garden. I'm a person who loves to stay inside all the time. The Ryôanji rock garden is an enclosed universe. When I go to Kyoto, I always visit the Ryôanji garden and look at the garden from the *engawa* (balcony). Then one day, I got an idea for a play set there. When the curtain goes up, the setting is at court, and the players will come out onto the *oshirasu* (raked white sand). I imagined the scene of Egeus and the young couples in the opening scene as done there. I thought it was a perfect situation and since then haven't changed the idea.

TAKAHASHI   Some people might say the idea is designed to appeal to the export market.

MATSUOKA   But Ryôanji has a universal meaning to the Japanese mind.

NINAGAWA   In fact, the garden uses perspective to add depth, although our stage equipment cannot actually represent it. The invention of perspective is a great advantage for Europeans. Unfortunately, we didn't have it in our tradition, and I think the mystery of perspective forms the basis for European philosophy. I thought that the so-called Japanese elements could be effectively conveyed by representing them within this framework of perspective.

It's not enough if we use only one style or aesthetic in the play; we have to fuse many disparate elements to create Shakespeare's world. In this *Midsummer Night's Dream*, we use a wig made from black plastic bags for the fairies. Of course, we could use real wigs, but we bought the plastic bags especially for the production. Maybe it wouldn't be noticed by foreigners that we were using plastic bags for wigs, but we needed to use modern and shiny objects in the play, and it was plastic bags this time. Otherwise, it will become too securely set in the Ryôanji garden. The production needs to have something slightly incongruous about it, and that's why I used plastic bags for the wigs. I made them myself.

TAKAHASHI   I wonder if you have already heard the story about George Steiner. When he came to Japan and visited Ryôanji, he got angry when he saw a vending machine nearby. Shakespeare, however, includes everything, from the rock garden to the vending machine.

MOTOHASHI   I think that could be one of the problems of modernization. If we consider only the Noh stage on Sado Island, the Butsudan, and the stone garden in your plays, we're considering only "good old things." When you, Ninagawa, consider these old things, however, you use a method that reflects how your personal modern ideas can be expressed through them in a Shakespeare play. The reason for using the Noh stage in your play is to show that modern elements by themselves can't express the grand scale of Shakespeare. Is that right?

NINAGAWA   Well, I certainly think so. If we can't express the large scale of Shakespeare in our productions, it means we've failed. My *Othello* failed. When I watched my *Othello* on TV, I realized, "Oh no, this is a flop!" The problem of discrimination within white society and the racial tensions between white and black people makes the play wrong for a Japanese to produce. I used blond hair to symbolize the difference of white society in the play, but I think that was a bad idea. I don't think the problem can be satisfactorily expressed by a Japanese.

MATSUOKA   I think it's interesting that you use traditional Japanese styles in your plays because you could use a modern Japanese style if you wanted. I think this must relate to the desire to evoke collective memories.

NINAGAWA   Yes. Structure triggers memory.

MATSUOKA   That means, doesn't it, that collective memory is like the DNA of the Japanese people, something deeper than one's own personal history. Without this memory, we can't describe this society as Japanese. And, to continue to maintain it, we need to bring our past culture and its aesthetics to bear on modern life. We need to cross-fertilize the past with the present. Without this procedure, we couldn't represent a modern society in a truly human way.

NAKANE   Memory is a very important factor for Ninagawa when he directs a play. It's all about his personal memories; he assumes his audiences feel like him. Then he creates the artistic circuit that relates him and them. He does not intellectually manipulate history.

NINAGAWA   When I am creating an image for a play, I don't work like a researcher or a scholar. I respond to the past just as an ordinary human being. I don't look for, or follow, historical facts in the way researchers do.

ANZAI   I think what you are describing is very close to Jung's definition of archetypes. It sounds like the collective unconscious.

TAKAHASHI   Even if we don't use the theory of Jung to explain what Ninagawa does, we can still use Zeami. If you consider the structure of Zeami's Noh, it has a similar technique for invoking memories. Memory-recall forms the basis of Mugen Noh, doesn't it?

NAKANE   Some people have analyzed Ninagawa's *Tempest* as having the structure of Noh.

TAKAHASHI   Ninagawa's *Macbeth* also uses the structure of the Butsudan to recall collective memories. And, of course, the Noh stage for *The Tempest* has the same effect in the play. If you think of it in that sense, Noh does provide a basic structure for the whole play.

MOTOHASHI   Shakespeare's plays provide challenging entertainment. *A Midsummer Night's Dream* is the first comedy you have produced, I think. There are many other Shakespeare comedies that are a lot more fun. What do you think? Is a tragic story more appropriate to produce because it has a structure to help express the collective memories in the play?

NINAGAWA   I think so. Not all of Shakespeare's plays are equally presentable. *The Merchant of Venice*, for example; we can't produce that kind of story. It wouldn't work so well for us. Speaking honestly, *Othello* would be the same. I thought *The Merry Wives of Windsor* would be interesting, and I liked the story, but I didn't think I could make a successful production out of it. I only produce a play if I can find a theme I can share. *Richard III* is another one I can't do. I thought it wouldn't work because I couldn't express its deep meaning even if I changed the situation. There are many Shakespeare plays I love, but many I can't produce because I know they can't be done my way.

CARRUTHERS   I'm fascinated by the way you are producing *A Midsummer Night's Dream*, bringing together many different kinds of performer. Do you use any special approach to training and rehearsal?

NINAGAWA   I never thought about using any kind of method. If I did, I think it would be a serious inconvenience. However, I always have to face the problem that I have to produce a play with untrained actors. Japanese theatre companies tend to be structured in peer groups, so there is less contact between different age groups, and older and younger actors don't have much vertical interaction. I feel really ashamed that we're losing the good practices of old Shingeki. We used to have established relationships in our companies, like those between grandfathers, fathers and sons – what I call vertical group structures – but they're gone now. In this situation, it is very difficult to use freelance actors and pull them together into one company. Also, it's difficult to impose my will on them in a short period of time. It often becomes a struggle in which I end up throwing and breaking things.

CARRUTHERS   How much freedom does each actor have?

NINAGAWA   In my case, I always prepare a stage set in the rehearsal studio which is very similar to the one we'll be using in performance. This is the hypothesis that the director presents to the actors. Then I ask the actors to show me their acting hypotheses in this context. Then we negotiate the possibilities in detail.

MOTOHASHI   When you are putting on a second production of a play in a short period of time, do you explain what you want to the new actors yourself?

NINAGAWA   Yes, I do. But I usually say to them they can first try out their own approaches.

MATSUOKA   In the last production of *A Midsummer Night's Dream*, Tsumiki Miho was playing Helena; this time she is playing Hermia opposite a new Helena, so there's a new dynamic.

NINAGAWA   Yes, she seems to be enjoying it. I told her, "I changed your role because I want to meet a different you."

CARRUTHERS   That must be exciting for the actors: to play different roles in the same play. I've not been lucky enough to have seen Ninagawa's work before, so I found his rehearsal today very interesting. It seems to combine the aesthetics of Chikamatsu with those of Shakespeare, and use not only Shingeki realism but different forms of traditional performance styles as well. These things seem perfectly balanced.

NINAGAWA   I want to include *everything* to reflect life!

(*Transcribed by Inazawa Shôko; translated by Yoshida Masako, Ian Carruthers, and Anzai Tetsuo.*)

18

Interview with Noda Hideki

(May 9, 1996; with Matsuoka Kazuko, Minami Ryuta, Suzuki Masae, and John Gillies.)

MATSUOKA We would like to ask you several questions concerning Shakespeare and yourself. To begin, we think Shakespearean productions in Japan can be roughly divided into three categories. The first are the rather straightforward presentations. The second are the ones localized or framed by a local setting. The third are those with drastic textual alterations. As you may be aware, yours and Suzuki Tadashi's are the ones which make the most drastic changes to Shakespeare's text. However, although Suzuki boldly cuts the original texts and stitches them together with other materials, he doesn't change characters' names. Your Shakespeare productions can be placed at the further limit of the "Shakespearean Map," or the translation–adaptation continuum. So, the first question is about your place on this continuum; the second question is about the place of Shakespeare in your career as a theatre practitioner; the third question is about your personal experience of Shakespeare.

NODA Well, I am basically different from a director like Ninagawa because I am also a writer. Ninagawa makes it a rule never to deviate from the original texts, and he gets his energy from such self-restraint. I approach Shakespeare from the opposite direction. In the first place, there is a large problem in translating western plays into Japanese. When they are translated into Japanese – though I don't mean I read them in the original language – I think they have already become something different. In the case of Shakespeare, I think his word play is almost fatally lost in translation. When I first worked on *Twelfth Night*, I was still afraid to alter his text. I was not sure how far I should go. It was like touching a lump of clay for the first time in an art class. After *Twelfth Night*, I thought I didn't work enough on it. I thought I should have adapted the play much more, drawing it closer towards my interests. The next Shakespeare play I tackled was *Much Ado About Nothing*. The fact that I didn't find it so interesting helped me to be bolder. It made me courageous enough to cut many parts, weave into it the scenes from *Othello*, and adopt the idea of the sleeping potion from *Romeo and Juliet*.

Also, in translated works, there is a problem of understanding the concepts behind the words. For example, titles like "Prince" or "Count" do not sound familiar to us, though we do have words for such terms. That is because modern Japanese are not as class conscious as the British. At least on the surface, Japan is a classless society. But I thought of several examples in Japanese culture that may suggest a sense of class distinction to a Japanese audience. One is the world of sumô wrestlers. The second is the hierarchical system of the flower arrangement, which I adopted in my *Richard III*. The third was the Japanese Imperial Family. I thought the audience would understand the implications of such examples. For *Much Ado*, I thought the world of sumô wrestlers with rankings would ring bells for us, for it is a familiar part of our culture. That was how I started drawing Shakespeare's world nearer to mine.

MATSUOKA   The fact that you are a writer clearly distinguishes you from directors like Ninagawa and Deguchi, who are faithful to the written texts. What do you think of Suzuki, then?

NODA   Well, above all, Suzuki has his own acting method. I do not know how deeply he loves Shakespeare, but it is clear that Shakespeare is only one of the many materials he uses for his plays.

MINAMI   I think you mentioned something about using other people's works as a framework to create your own plays. How much do you expect an audience to know about such things before they watch them?

NODA   Well, first of all, these are my writing habits. I never write things believing that they should be accepted in such and such a way. I don't consciously think about what I can or can't assume about the audience's knowledge. It depends on the situation.

MATSUOKA   In relation to *Half-Gods*,[1] I think you said you felt both restricted and liberated when you wrote plays based on someone else's work. So far, you have adapted *Half-Gods*, *Under the Cherry Blossoms in Full Bloom*, *The Battles of Coxinga* and *Crime and Punishment*. Do you feel any difference between adapting the works I mentioned now and adapting Shakespeare?

NODA   I must start from how I came to adapt *Half-Gods*. Before working on it, I wrote the *Nibelung Trilogy* inspired by Wagner's opera, but the plot and structure of the trilogy were still my own. And then I got stuck. Coincidentally, there was a request from my actors to make *Half-Gods* into a play. So I asked Hagio Moto to rewrite it into a play for us. But I found it rather difficult to stage her adaptation, for she was not used to writing plays. So I rewrote here and there, and it turned out quite differently. Since I loved her original comic story, I still took pains not to ruin her world. With that restriction, I experienced a pain and pleasure different from writing an original play.

MATSUOKA   When creating your *Under Cherry Trees in Full Bloom*, you made it a rule to use only Sakaguchi Ango's stories as its source materials, didn't you?[2]

NODA   Yes.

MATSUOKA   That is a kind of restriction, too. But do you feel less restricted when working on Shakespeare?

NODA   I also feel more free to change the words. I hesitate to say this in front of a translator, but I think it's acceptable to change the phraseology and word plays of translated works. Maybe I feel more free to do so because I often use

Odashima's translations. I started reading his versions after I entered the university. Before that, I read those by Fukuda Tsuneari or Nakano Yoshio in paperback.

But I am not yet sure how far I should go from the original. When I adapted *Crime and Punishment* (1994), I thought it difficult to judge how much I could add to the original. For the original work, even though in translation, is still complete within its own world. It was also hard for me to work on this text because, at that time, I had just started a workshop after coming back from one-year study in London. A workshop gives me both freedom and a restrictive framework. It binds me because I make it a rule to use what comes out of it as the basis of my work.

My present production, *Taboo*, also includes many scenes and episodes that came out of our workshop, but this time I decided I did not necessarily have to adhere to it so closely. A workshop is meaningful in itself, but I thought I shouldn't care too much even if nothing came out of it in the first two weeks or over the following two weeks.

MATSUOKA   You haven't done any workshops for Shakespeare plays, have you? Is this because all your Shakespearean productions were produced before you went to London?

NODA   Yes.

MINAMI   You created *Sandaime Richâdo* (*Richard III*) for your own company, but the other Shakespearean plays were produced for Tôhô. Did you choose actors for those Tôhô productions?

NODA   Yes, I did. Although Tôhô Company had already decided that Daichi Mao was to star in *Twelfth Night* and that Saitô Yuki was to play a principal role in *Much Ado About Nothing*, I was allowed to choose actors for other parts.

MINAMI   Were you also allowed to choose a play to direct?

NODA   Yes, but in the case of *Twelfth Night*, they first wanted me to direct a musical. I read the script, and found that it was written ages ago and was very old-fashioned. I told them I couldn't do it, and then they asked me what I wanted to do. I bragged, "Well, Shakespeare may be good enough for me." Then they said I could do Shakespeare if I wanted to, and I found myself in trouble.

I had to think of a Shakespeare play that could feature Daichi Mao. Speaking of Shakespeare, everyone thought of Ninagawa's productions at that time. So I didn't want to direct a tragedy, and I thought comedy would work well. As I wanted to direct *A Midsummer Night's Dream* some time in the future, I chose *Twelfth Night*, thinking that the play would be interesting with Daichi Mao (an ex-*otokoyaku*, male impersonator at Takarazuka Revue Company) playing both parts of the twins.

MINAMI   According to *Teihon*,[3] on the day of the first performance of *A Midsummer Night's Dream*, you wrote in your diary, "I am now sure that my decision to disband my company was not wrong." Was it when you were working on *A Midsummer Night's Dream* that you became confident in your training method and became convinced that you could work with actors outside your company?

NODA   Well, I had already thought of disbanding my company before *A Midsummer Night's Dream*. It was probably when I was directing *Much Ado About Nothing*. I had my own company, and its members knew my methods and ideas well, but I found them losing liveliness. Then I was suddenly invited to direct outside my company. When I saw Karasawa[4] in the rehearsal for *Much Ado About Nothing*, I thought, "How joyfully and straightforwardly he acts!" I started asking myself about the nature of a theatre company and the meaning of working with actors outside my company.

MINAMI   I thought that your physically expressive style of acting would be difficult for actors outside your company.

NODA   I had been aware for some time that what was extraordinary about my performances was my acting. I mean, I can't make my actors imitate my funny movements, and such an acting style cannot develop into a kind of acting method, for my acting is based on my own habits. But, if you carefully watch a person just standing still onstage, you can find a kind of truth in his or her stage existence. It does not necessarily matter whether she is standing still or moving. Kiki Kirin[5] did not move around in *Much Ado About Nothing*, but she has some truth in her acting. For example, she was very sensitive to footsteps and listened carefully to the sounds her acting partners made. I was surprised at that. I don't know about "universal truth," but I feel there was something absolute in what Kiki did. When I joined Simon McBurney's Theatre de Complicite workshop in London, I always heard them say "light foot," which means, "don't make a noise." I also heard them say "with pleasure," which is exactly what I always said to my actors. If you are tired and not acting with pleasure, however you try to hide it, it will show. I directed *A Midsummer Night's Dream* basically in the same way as I did *Much Ado About Nothing*. I mean I made use of and developed what I did in *Much Ado*.

MATSUOKA   I see. Besides physical movement, we have discovered by comparison with Shakespearean performances elsewhere in the world that visual style is another characteristic of Shakespearean stages in Japan. Do you always have a visual image of your stage from the beginning?

NODA   It depends. For *A Midsummer Night's Dream*, Horio Yukio brought me various ideas about the stage sets, but Takada Ichirô, who was the stage designer for *Twelfth Night*, didn't do anything, so the set for *Twelfth Night* was designed by me. That was when I was directing the trilogy for Yume no Yûminsha at the athletic hall in Yoyogi. I asked Takada to come and see my clay model, and told him what I wanted for my *Twelfth Night*. He just made the set after my clay model.

MATSUOKA   I see. That image of two giant faces was very effective.

NODA   Since I first got the basic directorial ideas of the play from the story of Oedipus and the Sphinx, I brought the images of that story into the stage design. In the case of *Much Ado*, I said at the preliminary meeting that I wanted a kind of embankment for the set. In *A Midsummer Night's Dream*, however, Horio brought me that design of a mountain. But he's good at guessing the director's intention, so he knew what would please me.

MATSUOKA   Did that design originate from the amusement park, Fuji-kyû Highland, because you set the play at the foot of Mt. Fuji?

NODA   Maybe. I told him in the beginning that I wanted to run a roller coaster on stage. He must have started with that image.

MATSUOKA   How about the costumes? I think Demi-san's (Demetrius) and Rai-san's (Lysander) headbands in *A Midsummer Night's Dream* came from images of matadors.

NODA   They were mostly designed by a costume designer, Naitô Kozue. I worked with her for the first time when I directed *Much Ado About Nothing*. She first came with the drawings of very plain Shingeki-like costumes.

As she also designs costumes for commercial films, she tried to guess what was expected of her, and adapt herself to circumstances. It was trial and error. These days, however, she gives me her own ideas first, for she now understands my world. Even if I hesitate to accept her plans, she pushes them forward.

MATSUOKA   Setting, then, is one way that Shakespeare starts turning into Noda. For example, you set the first scene of *A Midsummer Night's Dream* in a Japanese restaurant. Why? I understand your employing the sumô world to suggest a hierarchical system in *Much Ado About Nothing*, but that setting for *A Midsummer Night's Dream* was not clear to me.

NODA   Well, *A Midsummer Night's Dream* is a play about liking and disliking people, so I thought of presenting it as a play of "appetites," for love is an appetite, too. So I added lines like, "I want to eat you." Well, how convincing it will be depends on the extent to which I can believe in my own lies. I sometimes think I'm adding a forced meaning myself. First, I thought that setting *Sandaime Richâdo* in the world of flower arrangement was splendid, but I am not fully satisfied now about how well the flower associations worked. The Japanese people can easily understand that something like *Richard III* can happen behind the scenes in flower arrangement. In that sense, that setting played an important role in the play.

MATSUOKA   I understand why you brought in the world of flower arrangement. But why did you adapt it as a trial play?

NODA   Well, when I was thinking of adapting *Richard III*, I remembered *The Daughter of Time* and decided that the best way to make use of that novel was to make it a trial play. I also remembered *Nothing Like the Sun*, the biographical novel dealing with Shakespeare's life. Oh, I shouldn't reveal so much about the secrets of my writing, should I?

MINAMI   May I ask you about *Much Ado About Nothing*? Iago and the sleeping potion from *Romeo and Juliet* also appear in your adaptation. Did you have the idea from the beginning?

NODA   I wondered why *Much Ado About Nothing* lacks charm. Then I noticed that Shakespeare's plays are interesting when the villains are charming. Don John in *Much Ado About Nothing* lacks charm as he is. Then, I wondered who my favorite Shakespearean villain was, and it turned out to be Iago.

MINAMI   The other interesting point is that you have changed the heroines, "Hiro and Azami" (Hero and Beatrice), into sisters who are clearly contrasted.

NODA   That was just a casual idea. For one thing, I thought their relationship as "cousins" in the original might not be so appealing in contemporary Japanese society. It didn't ring a bell for me. So I thought of changing it to a sister relationship. The other thing was the casting problem. I was told to use Saitô Yuki as one of the heroines from the beginning. I thought it wouldn't work if I cast another young and pretty actress as the other heroine. Maybe I was thinking of a similar contrast in *A Midsummer Night's Dream*: I mean one heroine being pretty and the other having an inferiority complex.

MATSUOKA   Examining your works like this, I see that your *Midsummer Night's Dream* is also a collage. Why did you combine *Alice in Wonderland* with it? Was it because the amusement park is a kind of wonderland? You also had Mephistopheles in it. That was a very loaded play.

NODA   Perhaps I introduced those images because of its dream quality. In *A Midsummer Night's Dream* and *Alice in Wonderland*, what the characters believe they really saw in a forest turns out to be dreams. That's a very simple way to relate the two, but that would be the reason I had *Alice* in the play. I brought in Mephistopheles because I wanted to make the role of Puck different in nature from the one in the original.

MATSUOKA   But Mephistopheles overshadowed Oberon.

NODA   Mephistopheles took away much of his role, true. Mephistopheles deceived Puck and packed him into a bottle. Oh, wait, maybe I was reminded of *Alice* because of that bottle! Yes, maybe that's another key. The dream and a bottle.

MATSUOKA   In your work, various worlds are connected and integrated by verbal and visual associations just like a word association game.

NODA   Like wild fancies. That's right, I may be magniloquent.

MATSUOKA   You treat Shakespeare's plays as one of your source materials. It does not, however, mean that you devalue Shakespeare. We can approach his plays in many ways. Are you planning to take up Shakespeare again?

NODA   I would like to. I haven't tackled a Shakespeare tragedy yet, apart from *Richard III*.

MATSUOKA   Now, we would like to turn to your personal experiences with Shakespeare.

NODA   My first Shakespeare experience was when I was in the third year of

junior high school. I starred in *Hamlet* in my school uniform just before gradu-
ation. Once my high school teacher gave me a ticket and said, "Go and see the
Seinen-za *Romeo and Juliet*." At the theatre, I found myself among a noisy group
of high school girls out on a theatre visit. I liked the story of the play; I mean,
just as one does when one watches Kabuki, I enjoyed the production with pre-
knowledge of the story. Maybe that is the strong point of Shakespeare plays.
But I reported to the teacher that it wasn't worth seeing.

When I was sixteen, I also saw Peter Brook's *A Midsummer Night's Dream*.

MATSUOKA   By choice?

NODA   I was already a member of a theatrical group then and had seen many
interesting plays including Ninagawa's production of Shimizu Kunio's *When
We Go Down the Large River of Coldheartedness*⁶ in the same year. I was in the first or
second year of senior high school then. As it was a great year with so many historic productions, I simply thought that there were many interesting plays in
the world and that I could go on seeing more good plays like Brook's. But, as
time went by, I noticed how epoch-making Brook's *A Midsummer Night's Dream*
was. I recognized its greatness, especially when I met foreign directors of my
age. For example, Alexandre Darrie saw it when he was ten, and many more
said they had seen it.

I saw that production twice. Recently, I saw the video recording of the performance broadcast on TV. It looks rather old fashioned now. Everything about
the performance, including its acting style now appears outdated, even though
it was a revolutionary production. Theatre has changed a lot since then. What I
remember clearly are the swings, the dish-turning trick, and the scene where
an actress jumps at the exit and seals it with her body to block the actor trying to
get out. I suppose the performance did have a considerable influence on me. I
sometimes hear myself saying, "Stick yourself there!" and realize that I was
thinking of that scene where the actress stuck herself to the door.

MATSUOKA   In your younger days, you saw Shakespeare plays performed
before you read them, is that right? Except for your first *Hamlet* at junior high
school.

NODA   Yes. But I read Shakespeare's plays every time I saw them staged,
although Odashima's translation of the Shakespeare canon was not available
yet. I also saw and liked the Bungaku-za's *Hamlet* with Emori Tôru as Hamlet
and Kurano Akiko as Ophelia in 1973. But, since Brook's production was so
fascinating, I didn't enjoy later Shakespeare stagings by the Old Vic or other
English companies. I realized that, just like poor Japanese stagings, some
English performances were not worth watching, even though they might be
highly praised. Shingeki productions were very boring in those days. It was the
time when they staged plays like *The Lower Depths*, and I didn't enjoy them at all.
They were at their "lower depths" then.

MATSUOKA   Have you seen plays by the older generation of the Little Theatre
Movement such as Kara Jûrô's?

NODA   I had an instinct about Kara.[7]

MATSUOKA   That you had better not see his plays?

NODA   My friends at high school recommended the plays, saying I would surely love them, but I told them I didn't want to go because I was afraid of being influenced. All my friends were. Finally I saw his *Koshimaki Oboro* after I entered university. It was very interesting. They were enjoying great popularity at the time.

I also saw Terayama Shûji's plays,[8] like *Jashû-mon*, but I didn't like his work until I read his books and discovered that his poems were beautiful. Then I saw *A Hundred Years of Solitude* at Harumi. His plays around that time were far better than his early plays.

I was young and square then, and lacked self-confidence. So I always thought I shouldn't run across such people. Suzuki Tadashi came to see my play at Komaba when I was twenty-three or twenty-four and asked for an interview, but I refused. I didn't want to get acquainted in that way. I had seen his productions and read his book, *The Sum of the Interior Angles*, which was regarded as a Bible among students in drama societies.

MINAMI   Theatre troupes of your generation and the younger ones have recently taken up Shakespeare. What do you think of the work of young groups such as Jitensha Kinqureat or Hanagumi Shibai?

NODA   It depends. Some are good, and some are not so good. I can't make any generalizations. I think Eriko[9] is great. She still keeps her company together, while I disbanded mine.

MATSUOKA   Speaking of Eriko, would you want to see her do Shakespeare? Some writers and directors are very eloquent, and others are reticent. In creating plays, some subtract and divide, while others add and multiply. You and Eriko are the multiplying type with word plays and others, and I think so was Shakespeare. So her Shakespearean play should be interesting. She was wonderful when she appeared in your *Midsummer Night's Dream*. Have you ever felt an affinity with Shakespeare when you read his plays? I think you and Shakespeare have similar verbal dexterity and eloquence as playwrights.

NODA   Well, I read his works only in translation, and I first thought his plays were really good. But when I read his plays with the intention of staging them, I suddenly felt uneasy about his phraseology. This is probably because I have the rhythm of contemporary theatre in me. His similes and metaphors seemed to me beautiful and really absorbing when I just read them, yet when I re-read his plays for staging, they turn out to be different from the first impression I got from reading them for fun.

MATSUOKA   In an interview before *Sandaime Richâdo*, I pressed my opinion that you have similarities with Shakespeare. For example, both you and Shakespeare seem to believe it necessary to spend two or three pages even when you have only to say, "Let's go from here to there." Copiousness is something I think you share with Shakespeare.

NODA   You mean I write in a roundabout way?

MATSUOKA   No, I don't mean that. I mean you both write tens of lines full of puns and metaphors just to say, "I love you."

NODA   I see. But I'm not so sure of that myself. I can't compare myself to Shakespeare, can I?

MATSUOKA   I'm talking about the way you approach writing.

NODA   Well, I can't deny that I am under a kind of subconscious influence.

SUZUKI   When I once asked you to explain what you and Shakespeare have in common, your answer was something like, "Our love for the theatre that overcomes our grudge and hatred towards society." Can you explain this?

NODA   Well, I meant that Shakespeare's villains are attractive. If the hatred toward the society were greater, an author would think he must punish villains severely and his/her plays would be too argumentative to have charm as theatre. You will find it true of good Kabuki plays, too. Evil characters are always punished at the end of Kabuki plays, but they would not be interesting without villains.

GILLIES   I have read that the shape of your plays is related to the style in which they are acted: an intensively physical acting style, very fast, lots of puns in Japanese. Now, if that is true, is this perhaps a reason why you like adapting Shakespeare? I mean, does Shakespeare done straight not work in your acting style?

NODA   Well, if I am to honor the rhythm of his plays, I will think it necessary to rewrite his long lines. Since word plays cannot be translated as they are, I will make a free translation of his plays according to my own interpretation. So I must say that the answer to your question is "no."

GILLIES   Thank you. What does "Map" in "Noda Map" mean?

NODA   Maps are interesting. I didn't name my new organization "Noda Map" because I'm crazy about maps. But in a map you draw and see all you know about the world.

MATSUOKA   Why did you choose Theatre de Complicite among others?

NODA   Well, I thought I would be accepted only as an observer and get bored if I approached a big theatre company like the Royal National Theatre to study as a director. So, as an actor myself, I thought it would be profitable for me to join a group that runs workshops with emphasis on physical expression. I inquired about the best group of that kind, and I was told that Complicite would be the best. Ninagawa Yukio was in England at that time with his *Tempest*. He introduced me to Thelma Holt, who wrote a letter of recommendation for me.

MINAMI   Mr. Noda, in an interview just after you came back from England, you said something about realism in England. Do you think of introducing English realism into your future productions?

NODA   No. I just meant that the realism of English theatre is distinctively English. After seeing plays in England, I understood what the Shingeki actors really wanted to do. I thought that early Shingeki practitioners must have been impressed by this kind of acting, and wanted to do the same. Unfortunately, the Japanese don't have their voice and physique. We must act as Japanese without any lies. There are many ways to do so.

(*Translated by Suzuki Masae*)

NOTES

1   *Half-Gods* (*Han-shin*) is Hagio Moto's *manga* or story comic about a pair of Siamese twins. The original Japanese title, *Han-shin*, literally means "Half-gods," but it can also mean "half of a body." Noda put *Han-shin* on stage for the first time in 1986 and also presented it at the Edinburgh Festival in 1990.

2   Noda first staged his *Nisesaku: Sakura no Morio no Mankai no Shita* (A fake: under cherry trees in full bloom) in 1989. This play is primarily based upon four short stories by Sakaguchi Ango. A seminal writer after World War II, Sakaguchi Ango (1906–55) was well known for his *Daraku-ron* (An essay on decadence), short stories, and detective stories. Noda often wrote in his life history, jokingly, that Sakaguchi Ango was reincarnated in Noda's body.

3   *Teihon: Noda Hideki to Yumeno Yûminsha* (ed. Hasebe Hiroshi, Kawade Shobô Shinsha, 1933).

4   Karasawa Toshiaki has appeared in three of Noda's plays: *Much Ado About Nothing* (1990), *A Midsummer Night's Dream* (1992) and *Taboo* (1996).

5   Kiki Kirin is an experienced actress known for her carefully studied comic acting. Noda invited her to play the role of "Hero" in his adaptation of *Much Ado About Nothing* (1990).

6   Ninagawa Yukio staged most of Shimizu Kunio's plays from 1969 to 1973, including *Bokura ga Hijô no Taiga wo Kudaru Toki* (When we go down the large river of coldheartness), 1973. The collaboration of Ninagawa and Shimizu produced seminal works which influenced the Little Theatre Movement.

7   Kara Jûrô, an actor, director, and writer, represents "the first generation" of the Little Theatre Movement. His troupe called "Aka Tento" (Red tent) always presented his plays in a red tent that was readily set up anywhere.

8   Terayama Shûji (1935–83) was a poet, playwright, director, critic, scriptwriter, novelist, filmmaker, and essayist. His avant-garde plays won popularity in Europe as well.

9   Watanabe Eriko won the Kishida Drama Award in the same year as Noda did (1983). She leads her "Theatre Troupe Sanjû-Maru" as a writer, director, and actor. She played Titania in Noda's version of *A Midsummer Night's Dream* (1992).

19

Interview with Hira Mikijirô

(*July 5, 1997; with Anzai Tetsuo, Matsuoka Kazuko, Ian Carruthers, and Minami Ryuta.*)

MATSUOKA   Mr. Hira, you started your career at the Haiyû-za (Actors' Company), didn't you? Which part did you act in the Haiyû-za *Hamlet* (1965)?

HIRA   I played Horatio.

MATSUOKA   Was it your first Shakespearean role?

HIRA   It was. These days *Hamlet* gets performed somewhere in Japan every year, but when I was young, it was seldom done. A Shingeki company used to produce *Hamlet* only when it had a large enough group of talented actors and actresses, while today we feel we can stage Shakespeare with only a few. So the Haiyû-za didn't perform *Hamlet* until ten or more years after the Bungaku-za (Literary Theatre Company). I first saw Akutagawa's Hamlet when I was in the acting school of the Haiyû-za. After that, I always picked *Hamlet* as the text for my voluntary training at night.

However, in Japan there is no effective method for training Shingeki actors. Some take singing lessons to help with articulation, and others consult books such as *Kindai Haiyû-jutsu* (The Art of Modern Acting), but we have no reliable guides on how to become good performers.

MATSUOKA   Didn't you learn these things at the Haiyû-za?

HIRA   Senda Koreya wrote *Kindai Haiyû-jutsu* based on Stanislavsky's method, and put his principles into practice at the Haiyû-za. But, at this time, his theory was still in the laboratory stage and we were his guinea pigs. No one was certain if his "method" would work. I was obliged to work out a method more or less on my own. For example, I would speak Hamlet's part in several ways alone at night. "To be or not to be" was one such passage. So, when I was with the Haiyû-za, I became more and more eager to play Hamlet.

Eventually the Haiyû-za did put on *Hamlet*. In those days, the company had many able performers, from Senda on down. Ichihara Etsuko played Ophelia, Nakadai Tatsuya (who later played the Lear role in Kurosawa's *Ran*) performed Hamlet, and I acted Horatio. This was at the Nissei Theatre. I thought I would never get a chance to act in *Hamlet* at the Haiyû-za because it was likely to be put on only once every ten years. Just when I had given up on the idea, Asari Keita approached me saying, "Would you like to join our company and play Hamlet? If you do, you'll have to quit the Haiyû-za because it would be too awkward for a Haiyû-za actor to take the lead in a performance celebrating Shiki's anniversary."

At that time in the Haiyû-za, I was cast in several major roles, such as

Faust, and Vershinin in *Three Sisters*. So I was at a loss whether to quit or not. I understood that it might be my last chance to play Hamlet, but I couldn't decide. Looking back now, I had many wonderful opportunities in the Haiyû-za, so I wouldn't have quit the company if I hadn't received Asari's offer. I was caught like Hamlet – "To be or not to be, that is the question" – you know? Finally, after much thought, I gave in to the temptation and resigned from the Haiyû-za.

ANZAI   I think your decision was the right one.

HIRA   Perhaps, but I stress there was no political background to my decision. I left only in the hope of acting Hamlet.

MATSUOKA   Asari read your mind, didn't he?

HIRA   At that time, I found his attitude utterly new. His manner of directing was based on opening up the literary connotations of the drama. Because the Haiyû-za tendency was towards political activity, I felt all the more strongly interested in Shiki's principle of art for art's sake.

ANZAI   In aiming to do Shakespeare, you must have subconsciously realized that his work provides an outstanding model of extra-daily, mythical, emotional life.

HIRA   Perhaps it comes more from my own personality. When I was a child, I was very timid. I couldn't say anything in front of my classmates even if I knew the answer. I was very diffident, for I lost my father when I was nine months old. Besides, I have no brother or sister. I had only my mother and grandmother, and so found it very hard to communicate with others. Even now, I find it very hard to express my opinion in public. I was so retiring that I never dared to appear onstage at school festivals. But I think I must have had a latent desire to act.

In any case, while I was at high school, we were evacuated to the countryside. There was a theatre club there that had only a few female members because of the war. I was roped into taking part in their productions because I was a tall boy, so I got to act Yohyô in Kinoshita Junji's *Yûzuru*. I felt an indescribable pleasure at not being myself on stage, you know. Wearing a mask released me from myself. It was a wonderful moment.

I really find it very hard to reveal anything about myself. But if the drama itself requires strong emotions, I don't need to; I just get absorbed in my role. When I was a member of the Haiyû-za, I hated improvisations that required me to reveal my true self. Perhaps my style of acting is out of fashion today. Up until ten years ago I am afraid the style of my acting attracted audience attention more than the characters I played. This was because, with Asari, I was acting my roles by concentrating on the words. The approach bound me for many years.

Then I met Ninagawa. He loves to destroy such fixed ideas. However, I couldn't break out of my shell so easily. When I acted Macbeth with Bandô Tamasaburô as Lady Macbeth, the audience fixed their eyes on him, even as I spoke. I felt a deep sense of loneliness at that. Of course, his acting and charm as an *onnagata* actor were appealing to the spectators. Everyone was curious about a man acting a woman's part. It's a primitive human curiosity. Having seen how changing sex could attract audience attention, I hoped it would help me break out of my shell, although I had played the Heian poetess Komachi in Ninagawa's *Sotoba Komachi* before this.

MATSUOKA   It was a wonderful performance!

HIRA   Since I vividly remembered the experience of acting Komachi in that play, I accepted the title role in Ninagawa's *Medea*. Medea helped set me free because, of course, it was a very powerful mask.

About ten years have passed since I gave up working with Ninagawa, and, since then, while working with other directors, I've thought a lot about my style of acting. These days I realize that acting without a mask may be more comfortable. Last year, when I played King Lear, I felt I was at last able to act freely.

MATSUOKA   I found something new in your acting when I saw you in *Measure for Measure*. You appeared completely different and fresh in the role of the Duke. I realized you could be as good at comedy as you are at tragedy. Many theatre-goers tend to typecast you as a tragedian, and I have to admit that, when you announced you would perform all of Shakespeare's plays, I worried how you would manage the comedies. But after seeing you as the Duke, I'm looking forward to seeing your Malvolio – and Falstaff too, I hope!

HIRA   Looking back on my life as an actor, I think that, quite by chance, I met the right directors at the right time about every ten years. At first, I began my career as an actor under Senda at the Haiyû-za. Then I met Asari of Shiki Theatre Company and worked with him for eight years; and, when I had come to what I thought was an impasse, I met Ninagawa. He broke my die-hard mask and gave me a new life as an actor for eleven years. Next, I worked with several young directors, such as Kuriyama and Uyama. And now I have a plan to work with Ninagawa again. I really am lucky to have met such creative artists at the right time.

ANZAI   Your history as an actor reads like an omnibus of Japanese theatre for the last thirty to forty years.

MATSUOKA   And it all started when you chose "not to be" with the Haiyû-za but "to be" Hamlet. At that time, everybody thought that joining a theatre company was like joining a business company; it was for life. Looking back now, that way of thinking seems like nonsense. After all, actors don't belong to a company; they should be free to work where they choose. These days, it is not unusual to see a producer enlisting actors and actresses from various companies to present a new production. Your behavior was ahead of its time.

When did you announce that you would try to act the complete works of Shakespeare?

HIRA   When I became sixty years old – four years ago. Shakespeare is very attractive to me because he writes so much about men. In Japan these days, there are relatively few dramas covering a man's lifespan. Most of the plays presented in the Japanese theatre are about women, and men are merely supplements in such dramas. Obviously, I'm interested in male roles! As someone who devotes his whole life to acting, I'd like to perform plays that anatomize what it means to be a man. Only Shakespeare can fully satisfy this condition.

A director sometimes gives us a new point of view, a role that we never expected, for example. However exciting our collaborations with directors can be, we always have to wait for such encounters. Actors cannot mentally prepare themselves and get into physical shape by waiting passively for roles. I began to think it would be better to be proactive. With a life project, I can prepare one or two years ahead for the plays I want to perform. This is completely different from being given a play only three months before the performance. Just before I was scheduled to perform Macbeth and Medea at the National Theatre in London, the doctor told me that a malignant tumor had grown in my lung. I explained that in three months time I'd have to go to London and act two major parts, and asked to put off the operation until my return. His reply was firmly in the negative. When I asked if it was possible to have the operation at once and get to London on schedule, he agreed. But, after the operation, I recovered so quickly that it took the doctor by surprise. My firm intention of acting two title roles in London made even cancer give way. At that time, I felt acutely that I needed some concrete goal to help me live vividly for the rest of my life. This is the second reason why I announced that I would do all the plays of Shakespeare.

By another stroke of luck, even before I had announced my intention to perform, the Tokyo Globe-za asked me to join them. The production system of the Globe Company was so efficient that, besides an international program of Shakespeare productions, they were able to present their own productions two or three times a year. This guarantee of three parts a year meant that I could conceivably perform the complete works. I had already performed seven or eight, so I screwed my courage to the sticking point and declared I would perform all of Shakespeare's plays as a life work.

Alas, the management of the Tokyo Globe has now changed, and in a cash-strapped economy, their production system has faltered. Now I have to return to producing plays through my own Miki no Kai, which means we have to be on the road for two or three months just to balance our budget. Unfortunately, one stage production a year is now my limit.

The trouble is that there are still so few efficient production systems in Japan which allow that kind of creative work.

CARRUTHERS   Mr. Hira, in your international performances, did you find that you had to modify what you normally do in order to achieve audience rapport?

Put another way, did you yourself feel anything different about performing for an audience that could not directly understand what you were saying?

HIRA   I played Medea at the ancient theatre of Herod Atticus in Athens, and also at the Delacorte Theatre in New York. I didn't feel much difference between a Japanese audience and a foreign audience mainly because they all knew the story of Medea well. But if I had to act Chikamatsu abroad, I can't imagine what it would be like. Ninagawa said it was a little bit too difficult to try to perform (Akimoto Matsuyo's) *Double Suicide, After Chikamatsu* in Britain. But I could really appreciate, from the level of audience attentiveness, how well they knew the stories of *Medea* and *Macbeth*.

MINAMI   It is *Ninagawa Macbeth* to which the foreign reader may feel the greatest affinity, and it was you who played Macbeth in that unique production. How do you feel about his ideas?

HIRA   Well, first of all, I felt closer to Macbeth on account of the production's Japanese style. Ninagawa's setting of the play within a Butsudan didn't come as a surprise.

ANZAI   Were you conscious of the influence of *Throne of Blood*?

HIRA   I certainly felt that Ninagawa was under the influence of Kurosawa's work, but we never talked about it because I thought it better not to. Kurosawa's *Macbeth* was presented in a black and white, austere world. On the other hand, *Ninagawa Macbeth* was gorgeous and splendid, using rich, showy colors. I just took care to keep Macbeth a somber and weighty personality in such a magnificent setting, even though I admit I was dragged in a little. When I work with Ninagawa, I always try not to be caught up too much by his world. It's very seductive, you know! If I didn't have any concepts of my own that can offer resistance, I could never create my role. My approach may have made *Ninagawa Macbeth* rather heavy, but I believed it was necessary in order to keep Ninagawa's world from being merely magnificent.

MATSUOKA   At the end of some speeches, you seemed to strike beautifully articulated Kabuki-style *mie* freezes. If you had worn western clothes, you wouldn't have struck such flamboyant poses, would you?

HIRA   No, it would have looked too theatrical. By stylizing my way of acting, it was possible to go beyond a realist *Macbeth*, but there were some risks involved. Striking flamboyant poses increased the possibility of *Ninagawa Macbeth* being seen as merely a pastiche of Kabuki. I think it can sometimes weaken a performance. In short, style is a double-edged sword. If I strike a flamboyant pose superficially, it will convey nothing to the audience. And, if I give emotion and significance to such *mie*-like poses, it will sometimes seem too serious to the audience. When I perform, I need to find a balance, but it's very hard for me because I didn't study Japanese classical plays or dance very much. I want to strike a skilful *mie* pose, but can't do so without any classical training. And if I can do it with ease, it may appear to lack seriousness and depth of emotion.

15 *Ninagawa Macbeth*, directed by Ninagawa Yukio, Nissei Theatre, 1980. Hira Mikijirô as Macbeth in the dying moments of the play.

ANZAI   An important point. When I go to Kabuki, I look forward to seeing the beauty of the style. One of the pleasures of seeing Kabuki is the pure theatricalism of its *kata* (forms). On the other hand, we also find realism in Kabuki. Neither theatricalism nor realism is satisfactory by itself.

HIRA   When I performed in *Macbeth* and *Double Suicide*, creating mental exaltation while being realistic was indispensable to achieving a style. When you try to go beyond realism while retaining a sense of realism at the same time, some styles or *kata* are created anew, just as in the case of the suicide scene in *Double Suicide* and some of the murder scenes in *Macbeth*.

MATSUOKA   Ninagawa always visualizes his *mise-en-scène* vividly, and is a recognized master of both realism and stylization. Did his direction of *Macbeth* help you bring your Macbeth to such an intensity as to create a style or *kata*?

HIRA   Ninagawa not only accepted my way of acting, but also stirred up my passions with music and extravagant visual effects such as snowstorms. He stimulated me with the most magnificent *mise-en-scène*, and expected me to challenge him with my acting, again and again.

(*Translated by Chiba Shôko.*)

Afterword: Shakespeare removed: some reflections on the localization of Shakespeare in Japan

JOHN GILLIES

In this volume, Japanese Shakespeare appears simultaneously as a sign of the globalization of "Shakespeare" as a contemporary cultural value, and – paradoxically – as a sign of the endurance and reassertiveness of the local in the face of that global value. On the one hand – by virtue of the sheer cultural, geographical, and linguistic distance spanned – Shakespeare seems at his most imperial in Japan. As in ancient Rome, where a Triumph was celebrated by parading the scutcheons and denizens of exotic regions beneath archways symbolic of the Roman center, distance and difference function as strong signs of cultural mastery. On the other hand, however, any such assumptions are checked by the realization that in Japan, Shakespeare has become deeply local. Here, I want to ask a simple question: what does this assimilation of an imperial cultural icon amount to? What does localization mean?

In the recently concluded (or ever concluding) era of modernism, the local has not been a value to be treated with respect. Marx had thought of it as conspicuously among those previously "solid" properties which modernity "melts into air":

In place of the old local and national self-sufficiency and isolation we have a universal commerce . . . As in the production of material things, so also with intellectual production. The intellectual creations of individual nations become common currency . . . from the many national and local literatures a world literature arises.[1]

It is for such reasons, Marshall Berman suggests, that modernism – considered as an aesthetic born of the inescapably global condition of ceaseless modernization – has preferred to seek its salvation in the universal, the global and the "now."[2] The local, where noticed at all, has tended to be the preserve of nostalgia buffs, folk-revivalists, and heritage enthusiasts. To this degree, Shakespeareans of all nationalities have tended to behave as modernists. In the west, the local has characteristically seemed too contingent, too parochial, too inward-facing, too apologetic and fragile a value to serve as a basis for thinking about Shakespeare. Its unaptness for this purpose is illuminated by comparison with the "contemporary." By contrast with the local, everybody seems to know what is meant by the idea that Shakespeare is "our contemporary," and seems to find the idea intuitive, plausible, consistent, and solid – also reliably fertile in imaginative possibility. Partly as a result, the local can easily be occulted when Shakespeare is acted as "our contemporary" ("contemporary" productions of the tragedies in Australia have had a habit of being set in Europe).[3] Again, the local is commonly thought to be erased or compromised when a Shakespearean tradition establishes itself beyond the Western pale.

For this latter reason, postmodernists, postcolonialists or scholars with an orientation towards Japan or Asia rather than towards Shakespeare may now be disposed to see his presence in Japan in terms of cultural politics rather than aesthetic preference. In this view – variants of which are powerfully argued here by James Brandon and Yoshihara Yukari – the taste for Shakespeare in Japan becomes a problem of cultural authority, the roots of which lie in Meiji Japan's enthralment to modernity and the west. Neither (to put it mildly) sees Shakespeare's presence in Japan as an unmixed blessing. In Yoshihara's essay, a resourceful Meiji adaptation of *The Merchant of Venice* is analyzed as a cultural vehicle for the importation of an "Asian" inferiority complex. In Brandon's view, the foisting of "canonic" translations of Shakespeare on performance genres with which they had no resonance, contributed to the relegation of Kabuki from a position of cultural centrality in the Meiji period, to its current position of respectable marginality as a "heritage" art. While both scholars are inclined to view localized productions (adaptations) of Shakespeare more charitably than they view "canonic" productions, even these can seem suspect – aimless and abortive compromises lacking either the integrity of their local roots, or a true appreciation of the Shakespearean text which is inevitably read against an alien horizon. "Shakespeare" and "remote" (extra-European) cultures are quantities that do not sit comfortably together. For Shakespeareans the remote (literally "removed") performance site has been too long invisible, while for those more attuned to the cultural values of such sites – for those aware of them primarily as "places" – Shakespeare is simply an interloper. Originating from a seminar of the 1996 International Shakespeare Association conference, on Japanese Shakespeare Performances, the present volume can be taken as (at last) betokening a desire to bring Shakespeare and the removed locality together.[4] This preparedness is perhaps what distinguishes Yoshihara's and Brandon's essays from a slightly earlier generation of postcolonial writing on various Shakespearean diasporas, in which Shakespeare's relationship to "Other" places tends to be obliterative.[5]

Localization is not just a nascent critical proposition but a long-standing theatre practice which, however defined and taxonomized, has evolved for over a century in Japanese theatre. Apart from his essay in this volume, the most searching and challenging proposition of it in English is perhaps James Brandon's "Some Shakespeares in Some Asias."[6] While that essay is concerned with localization within an "Asian" as distinct from a uniquely Japanese context, the paradigm it offers is eminently suited to Japan, and implicitly assumed in "Shakespeare and Kabuki" in this volume. In what I shall call "the Brandon thesis," there are three Shakespeares in Asia, and hence Japan, each representing a different negotiation between the values of "Shakespeare" and the values of "place." One is the Shakespeare of the "canonic" translations stemming from the pioneering scholarship of Tsubouchi Shôyô. For Brandon, Tsubouchi's commitment to an absolute standard of translation had the effect of annulling local performance genres because so much alien content and cultural authority were "carried across" in the process of translation as to have left no room for local content and no role for local theatre practice (pp. 7–8). Thus did canonic Shakespeare fashion its own performance vehicle out of Shingeki ("new drama"): a stilted imitation of western naturalism. By contrast, the second Shakespeare is localized: "one whose plays are assimilated into indigenous theatre genres to the point of disappearance, and their own foreign origin largely erased" (p. 11). This is largely the Shakespeare of the Meiji-period adaptors, playwrights adapting existing translations of prose redactions of Shakespeare plays (such as Lamb's Tales from Shakespeare) with little or no care for Shakespeare as a master text. Here, relatively speaking, "Shakespeare" is subordinated to the interests of locality. The third Shakespeare detected by Brandon is an "intercultural Shakespeare . . . a postcolonial, postmodern phenomenon of the past forty years . . . based on confrontation of the textual values of canonical Shakespeare with the immediacy and vitality of indigenous theatre" (p. 17). This is the Shakespeare of Suzuki, Ninagawa, and the heirs to the "little theatre movement" of the 1960s: a Shakespeare who has become deeply place-conscious, yet just as deeply conscious of himself as a "canonic" western construct. While there are adaptations in this stage, they do not tend to resemble the unselfconscious Meiji adaptations. These adaptations are conscious of themselves as departing from one norm, entering another and setting each in opposition to the other.

The Brandon thesis challenges those inclined to take a more benevolent view of Shakespeare's presence in Asia/Japan to prove it wrong, and nowhere more so than in its powerful thinking through of the term "localization." Whereas this term may seem relatively innocuous – amounting to little more than the cosmetic addition of local elements to a Shakespeare script, set, or costume – for Brandon "localization" is a necessarily strategic move: a mobilization of local cultural forces in the face of an alien cultural incursion. Moreover, where only one of Brandon's Asian Shakespeares is localized, all three represent differing responses to an essentially common appreciation of the cultural tension between Shakespeare and a given Asian locality. The first is a capitulation, the second an appropriation and the third an agonized and fractured dialogue. In what follows, I want to problematize the local as category and localization as practice in ways that, while beside Brandon's purpose, are made thinkable by his work. Though localization can easily seem a kind of ur-phenomenon, persisting through aboriginal cultural traces and sustained by a kind of inviolable cultural ontology, I want to suggest that it has (particularly in more recent phases) come to articulate and evolve itself out of a continuous negotiation with the global. Two moments of this negotiation will occupy me: first, the moment at which the globalized paradigm of "Shakespeare our contemporary" impacted on local practice; and second, the moment at which localized Shakespeare becomes the object of global attention.

As a first step, I would like to discuss how the reassertion of the local is indebted to the earlier globalized practice of making Shakespeare "contemporary" (while eventually rendering that practice in some senses obsolete). Antonin Artaud's *The Theatre and its Double* was published in Japanese in 1965, Jan Kott's *Shakespeare Our Contemporary* in 1968, Peter Brook's *The Empty Space* in 1971. Kott and Brook "were regarded as bible by theatre practitioners of the *Shingeki* and the Little Theatre movement."[7] The influence of the new approach on contemporary *Shingeki* practice has already been described by Minami Ryuta (a reading of whom would imply that Brandon rather underestimates the continuance and versatility of contemporary *Shingeki* Shakespeare, particularly its responsiveness to innovation and its maturer responsiveness to western naturalism).[8] Strong traces of contemporism would also seem to persist in the philosophy of influential "Little Theatre" directors such as Deguchi Norio and Suzuki Tadashi. Deguchi seems to have been notably Kottian at the JeanJean theatre in his early commitment to minimalist staging without set or costume. As he reveals in the interview in this volume, Deguchi remains "contemporary" in his urbanism, his modernism, his preference for Odashima's prose over earlier poetic translations, and his disdain for local postmodern theatrical fusions based on what he takes to be premodern "agricultural" performance genres. As a strikingly postmodern figure, Suzuki is less obviously Kottian. However, Takahashi in this volume makes good use of Kott to unpack Suzuki, and important Kottian emphases seem present in his theatre practice. One such emphasis corresponds to what Ted Motohashi has called Suzuki's "strategic essentialism" – the tendency to reduce texts such as *Macbeth* and *King Lear* to exemplarily bleak essences.[9] Another is Suzuki's insistence on the "cruelty" of Shakespeare. A third Kottian signature is Suzuki's tendency to conjoin Shakespeare with absurdist authors such as Beckett. Peter Brook represents another conduit by which the contemporist paradigm entered Japan. *Ninagawa Macbeth* is highly Brookian in its combination of a radically counter-normative performance context with strict adherence to the Shakespeare text.[10] Noda Hideki had seen Brook's *Midsummer Night's Dream* as a schoolboy during its 1970 tour, but drew an opposite lesson from Ninagawa in combining his own highly individual performance style with a freeform localizing textual adaptation (see above, p. 266). In his *Sandaime Richâdo*, as Suzuki Masae argues in this volume, Noda treats an exemplarily Kottian text as "contemporary" but in a way that owes nothing to Kott. In place of the Kottian exemplar of nihilistic cold war politics, Noda's Richard is a youthful romantic, a sign of child-like and "wild" creativity.

Regardless of whether Kott or Brook was the more influential, and regardless of which director was the more influenced, it seems clear that the Kottian "contemporist" paradigm has been important. Paradoxically, it would appear to have been more deeply influential in Japan than in Britain for the reason that it has resulted not merely in striking isolated performance experiments, but in the institutional revolution represented by the proliferation of new theatre groupings ("little theatres") typically under the control of committed artist-directors. This compares with the situation in Britain, where though radical new groups have certainly emerged in the wake of Brook's pathbreaking Royal Shakespeare Company productions of *King Lear* (1962) and *Midsummer Night's Dream* (1970), the RSC itself has grown into a monumental theatre institution, and tended to consolidate "Shakespeare as usual" in which performance retreats to being supplementary to text and accumulated Shakespeare lore. Where there seem few *auteurs* left among British Shakespeare directors to compare with Brook, there are a number in Japan – prime among them, the interviewees of this volume. Shakespeare continues to be done "straight" in Japan of course, including under the direction of western directors (such as Gerard Murphy) working with Japanese translators, dramaturges, and actors.[11] But Japanese Shakespeare is best known for the powerfully localized productions of the *auteur* directors and also of idiosyncratically local companies (such as Takarazuka), in which Shakespeare is spoken back to as well as heard.

If it is true that this most recent phase of localized Japanese Shakespeare owes something to the precept and practice of "Shakespeare our

contemporary," then we must ask what exactly is owed. My suggestion is that
the contemporist movement did not so much show the Japanese how to make
Shakespeare "modern." The Meiji adaptors had already discovered how to do
this from around the turn of the century. (Indeed, Shakespeare was almost
inevitably "modern" for them as a corollary of his being primarily western.)
Rather, what the contemporist movement really gave the new generation of
Japanese directors was an Artaudian vision of how to unlock performance
from its supplementarity to text; how to free it from being a "rehearsal" (literally "*répétition*") of a presence "whose plenitude would be older than it, absent
from it."[12] In postcolonial terms, the "performative" becomes liberated from
the "pedagogical" in the sense that performance of this western icon is no
longer condemned to vehiculating a predictable assortment of cultural
values and institutional imperatives.[13] Thus performance is free to be local:
not merely cosmetically but strategically in something of the way that
Brandon envisages the Meiji textual adaptations ("Some Shakepeares," p. 3).
However, this vision of performance is cannier and more complex than the
appropriative vision of the Meiji adaptors. Performance is now capable not
merely of appropriating the foreign but of reflecting on its "pedagogical"
cargo, problematizing the local effects of that cargo, historicizing them and
groping towards a new synthesis. More sophisticated than the Meiji strategy,
this performance vision is also cannier than the "contemporist" paradigm
that fed it. This is because, however fertile the contemporist precept and
example may have been in Japan, its programmatic modernism was bound to
mask the gap between locality and text rather than to prise it further open.
Instead, the "contemporist" paradigm has been absorbed into Japanese performance contexts, and transvalued and surpassed in the process.

How exactly has this happened? While part of the answer lies in the wish of
Japanese directors such as Suzuki and Ninagawa to be distinctive, the other
part lies in what I have called the "programmatic modernism" of "contemporary" Shakespeare. On the face of it contemporary Shakespeare ought not to
be a generic quantity, but whatever a director chooses to make of it. To a
greater extent than is sometimes realized, however, "Shakespeare our contemporary" has tended to become formulaic. While there are various brands
of this corresponding to the various directors and companies credited with
establishing contemporism as a global theatrical phenomenon, the origins
of the tendency towards formula would appear to lie in Kott. For Kott,
Shakespeare was contemporary because of his unflinching realism, existen-
tial angst, ethical uncertainty, religious and philosophical scepticism
(amounting to nihilism), his experience of alienation and his political pessi-
mism. All the important qualities of the *avant-garde* theatre of the 1950s and

1960s were also those of Shakespeare. In particular Kott favors plays – such as the first Henriad and *Richard III* – in which the workings of what he called "the grand mechanism" of history were revealed; the mill whereby history continually ground out the same stories of "murder, perfidy, treachery" and dictatorship.[14] Machiavellian characters, such as Richard of Gloucester were thus "contemporary" *par excellence*. Also archetypally contemporary was madness and a sense of the absurd (it is no accident that the essay on *King Lear* is one of the best in the book). It is because some themes are more contemporary than others that Kott's vision of Shakespeare is at once selective and essentialist. If the selectiveness lay in preferring certain character types, certain themes and situations over others, the essentialism consisted in the syllogistic equation of Shakespeare with a particular (and in hindsight, highly periodized) vision of modernity. Though theatre-based brands of contemporism tend to be only notionally Kottian, they have nevertheless also tended to be selective and essentialist and hence ultimately formula-driven. In Japan, the best-known variant of the contemporary formula was Deguchi in his JeanJean period. These productions differed from Kott in being racily upbeat as distinct from gloomily pessimistic, and comedy-focused rather than tragedy-focused. But their very difference was formulaic. As Deguchi concedes in the interview in this volume, the JeanJean approach became a house style owing more to a particular moment of Japanese youth culture than to Shakespeare, but most perhaps to the sheer frisson of bringing these heretofore incommensurable cultural quantities together. But while the formula may have depended on the frisson, it could not outlive it. The moment that the cultural shock began to pass was the moment that the JeanJean style began to die. "Shakespeare our contemporary" has continued to survive (indeed thrive) in Japan since then, as for example in Deguchi's later work or Gerard Murphy's productions at the Globe-za. But in these productions it seems more an idiom, an ambience, a coloration, an inevitable repertoire of stylistic gestures and thematic attitudes, rather than a driving force, and as such hardly distinguishable from contemporary Shakespeare anywhere else in the world.

By contrast the localized Japanese Shakespeares have managed to be highly distinctive without being normative (a fact which may owe something to not existing as a written philosophy, a program). Whereas "contemporary" Shakespeares tend to have a family resemblance wherever they arise (Deguchi's JeanJean period would seem to have had more than a passing resemblance to the contemporary Shakespeares of Sydney's Nimrod Theatre Company in the same period)[15] there is little family resemblance between localized Shakespeares even within Japan itself. The Shakespeares of

Ninagawa, Suzuki, Noda, the Takarazuka, Jitensha Kinqureat, Hanagumi Shibai, are all different – even though each director or group might create a generic style within their own individual terms. This being so, localization would appear to be an inherently pluralist phenomenon. There is no generic form of localization, no uniform set of localizing gestures, nor even agreement on where localization might manifest itself in the production process. Thus, where for Ninagawa, localization is largely a matter of creating Japanese settings with perhaps a metatheatrical frame, for Suzuki it means creating a specific training method, a specific company culture, a specific stylization, a specific type of adaptation and dramaturgy. For Noda, on the other hand, localization occurs more at the level of writing – an irreverent, freeform type of adaptation (as distinct from Suzuki's adaptations which tend to be based on strategic excerpts blended with excerpts from Beckett and the Greeks). For Takarazuka (according to Ohtani in this volume) localization comes down to a mixture of company culture, Manga "cuteness," and cross-dressed acting.

If there is little agreement on where or how the local is to be manifested in the production process, there is equally little about what validly constitutes the local or to which audience a localized production is (or ought to be) pitched. *Ninagawa Macbeth* can be taken as a test case of such problems. Set in feudal Japan, costumed in gorgeous period robes, replete with traditional symbols (the cherry blossoms and the Butsudan) and performance conventions (the *onnagata* witches), this production has been taken as definitive of the localized approach. Equally however, it has been attacked for creating a falsely idealized image of Japan combining a nostalgic appeal to locals with an exoticized appeal to foreigners. In such a view, all that it genuinely achieves is a mutual reification of canonic text and reactive Japanism. For whom is such an imagery created? While in the interview in this volume, Ninagawa insists that the imagery was inwardly generated in a moment of spiritual reflection (while gazing on the family Butsudan) and intended for fellow Japanese, a suspicion is voiced by his interviewers that the production and the imagery were internationally driven: exoticism and nostalgia being but two sides of the same Orientalist coin. If the only defense against such a charge is ontological (Ninagawa's assertion that the symbolism was spiritually rather than box-office based), then it might well be asked what else is there separating this production from Japanized and Orientalized productions of Shakespeare directed by foreigners – such as Peter Stormare.[16] If a "Japanesque" setting can be faked up by a foreign director working in Tokyo, what – in theatrical rather than personal terms – distinguishes this from a Ninagawa Shakespeare in London or Edinburgh? In either case it is suggested that the "local" is at some stage mediated by a foreign, global, and exoticizing gaze.

A variation of the same skepticism leads to Anzai Tetsuo's provocative question in this volume as to whether "Japanese Shakespeare" can be said to exist at all in the sense of a generically identifiable body of practices and effects. If such a category is erected to explain *Ninagawa Macbeth* why, argues Anzai, should we not construct a categorically "British" Shakespeare to explain Brook's *Midsummer Night's Dream*? In a further variation of this localist skepticism, Deguchi criticizes Suzuki's choice of a tradition-based grammar of performance conventions as valorizing a pre-industrial, agricultural (and to this extent nostalgically idealized) Japan, for which reasons he refuses to localize his own Shakespeare productions:

I don't think we should emphasise our "Japaneseness." The images most people have of "Japan" at the present time derive from the period when we were an agricultural society; that is, old Japan, the "so-called Japan" . . . if we presented Japan in all its ambiguity, foreigners would not understand. It means that "Japanese Shakepeare" production cannot be recognized unless we simplify our Japaneseness. (Interview above, p. 190)

For Deguchi, localization is impossibly paradoxical. Where recognizable and definable, it has already been simplified and commodified (homogenized and pasteurized) for foreign consumption. Where genuinely deep, ambiguous, and autonomous, it is impenetrable to foreigners and hence uncommodifiable.

While a paradox however, localization so thought of may not be entirely impossible. Ironically, the best objection to this extreme skepticism is provided by Deguchi himself: notably, one of his three parallel productions of *A Midsummer Night's Dream* at the Tokyo Globe-za in 1994.[17] Set in a school, this production ran in conjunction with a second production set in a bar, and a third played in the round in which the actors wore half-masks. While the other two productions were distinguished in their own ways, the "school" production was remarkable for the depth and intimacy of its local contextualization. Here Shakespeare's play is framed within an autobiographical dream play. The production opens with a figure (the director) surrounded by a model for a theatre set.[18] He seems despondent, an impression that is heightened as a woman and child (his wife and daughter) pass by him and exit wordlessly. At this point, a winged figure dressed as a schoolboy of the immediately postwar years appears behind him. To mounting festive music, the two figures meet, and the winged figure leads the director by the hand into the play's world. The director-figure becomes Theseus (and later Oberon). The woman becomes

16 *Ninagawa Macbeth*, directed by Ninagawa Yukio, Nissei Theatre, 1980. The witches are played as *miko* (shamanesses) in Kabuki *onnagata* style.

Hippolyta and Titania. The winged schoolboy is Puck, but also the director-figure's boyhood self – a source of deep psychic energy and creative inspiration. The otherness of Shakespeare's forest has become the otherness of the director's oneiric past. Yet, this intimately remembered past is also collectively available to audience members. Thus Bottom, who is first seen in the uniform of a returned soldier – a *Yamiya*, or demobilized soldier turned black market-eer [19] – is finally seen in an American military uniform, an apparently plausible example of social mobility in the period. Much of the beauty and wit of the production consists in precisely contextualized – localized and historicized – jokes of this sort. Most significant for present purposes, however, is the emotional truth of the production: its immediacy, individuality, and depth. This was a *Dream* transposed into a particular time and place via a singular act of dream-recollection provoked (like the Shakespearean "dream") by an ontological crisis. Considered as a realization of Shakespeare's play, it is both unpredictable and excessive, an adaptation rather than an interpretation. Yet it is intimately responsive to the play's mood and symbolic architecture. Deeply personal, emphatically intended for a local audience, the production is deeply local and in no way bogus. At the same time it is not (if my own judiciously tutored reaction is anything to go by) entirely impenetrable to foreigners or incapable of impressing them – at least no less so than a production by Suzuki or Ninagawa.

Having considered something of the pluralism of localism as well as the skepticism it has invited, is there a way of defining this phenomenon that is neither needlessly exclusive nor uselessly broad? In what remains, I should like to make an attempt. First, the local cannot be reduced to a single normative value. As the arguments over Ninagawa, Stormare, and Suzuki suggest, the local can never be taken as given. Instead it is inherently unstable, contestable, and political (in sharp distinction from the "contemporary" which does not invite this degree of skepticism). While this is not to say that Ninagawa's or Suzuki's localizations are not genuine or appropriate, it is to say that contestation is to be expected as part of a localizing strategy. This said, it is probably true that some element of ontological good faith is necessary in a localized production. A Japanesque Shakespeare directed in Japan by a foreigner is too contestable. Second, and as a corollary of its political dimension, the local element is not reducible to an idea of "nation." It can be more local than this: based on a neighborhood, a class, a unit, right down to the politics of the performing company (SCOT or Takarazuka). Finally, where the local is always temporalized, it has no necessary temporal allegiance. It is not necessarily contemporary or necessarily historical. It has no exemplary period (Japan is no more feudal than it is the small-town neighborhood of Deguchi's remembered past).

At its best, however, the local can be self-historicizing in the sense of unlocking its own performative traditions and reflecting performatively upon them. In 1991 for example, a cosmetically reworked Meiji adaptation of *Othello* (originally written for Kawakami Otojirô's Shimpa troupe in 1903) was staged by the Seinen-za company. In an induction written by the director, current Shingeki actors are depicted as turning in desperation to the Meiji adaptation in preference to playing Shakespeare's script in an inevitable and bad imitation of Laurence Olivier.[20] Two of Brandon's Japanese Shakespeares – canonical and localized – are thereby played off against each other. In 1995, the same Meiji script of *Othello* furnished matter for a full-scale play by the playwright Tsutsumi Harue. In Tsutsumi's *Seigeki Osero* ("Proper Othello"), localization is more elaborately posed against the canonical, as the original script becomes a play within a larger play whose characters are a mixture of the original performers and a group of critics including the figure of Tsubouchi Shôyô who states the "canonical" position. The original Meiji script emerges from Tsutsumi's play as ironically reflecting upon the imperial Meiji politics in which it is implicated (Cyprus being transformed into Taiwan which had recently become annexed by Japan).[21] What is interesting about this scenario is the way in which this dramatized reflection on Meiji Shakespeare is simultaneously a reflection on the whole subsequent Shakespearean performance tradition. What modern performers and playwrights seem to have discovered is that strongly localized productions (particularly adaptations) of Shakespeare leave revealing historical footprints.

NOTES

1 "The Communist manifesto," in *Marx: Later Political Writings*, Terrell Carver, ed. (Cambridge University Press: Cambridge, 1996), p. 5.

2 See, Marshall Berman, *All That Is Solid Melts Into Air* (Penguin: Harmondsworth, 1988), ch. 2, pp. 87–130.

3 The Nimrod Company's *King Lear* (1985) was set in a rubble strewn European wasteland. Soldiers in the Bell Shakespeare Company's *Hamlet* (1991–93) wore World War I costumes and carried Lee Enfield rifles.

4 The full title of this ISA conference seminar was: "Japanese performances, adaptations and co-productions of Shakespeare: the values of stylization and localization" (Los Angeles, 1996).

5 Some examples are: Ania Loomba, *Gender, Race, Renaissance Drama* (Oxford University Press: Delhi, 1992); Jyotsna Singh "Different Shakespeares: the Bard in colonial/postcolonial India," *Theatre Journal*, 4, December 1989, 445–58; Susan Bennett, *Performing Nostalgia: Shifting Shakespeare and the Contemporary Past* (Routledge: London and New York, 1996), ch. 4.

6 James R. Brandon, "Some Shakespeare(s) in some Asia(s)," *Asian Studies Review*, vol. 20, no. 3, April 1997, 1–26. Minami Ryuta's "Seven phases of Shakespeare in Japan" (generously made available to the other co-editors of this volume) is not in print.

7 I am indebted to Minami Ryuta for this information regarding the Japanese publications of Kott, Brook, and Artaud.

8 "What happened to *Shingeki* Shakespeare?: from imitation to localisation" (forthcoming).

9 In his, "Strategic essentialism in Suzuki Tadashi's 'Tale of Lear,'" a paper submitted to our ISA seminar, Los Angeles, 1996. In similar vein, Ninagawa Yukio finds Suzuki's use of Shakespeare over-selective (see above, p. 215ff).

10 Ninagawa describes his approach to *Macbeth* as "rearranging the play to use visual images in a Japanese style without changing the words from the original" (see above, p. 211).

11 See above, Motohashi Tetsuya's "Interview with Gerard Murphy."

12 Steven Connor, *Postmodernist Culture: An Introduction to Theories of the Contemporary* (Blackwell: Oxford, 1997), p. 147.

13 The "pedagogical" mode is vividly evoked by Ninagawa Yukio's account of the performance culture of 1973: "When we play Shakespeare in Japan it usually has to be educational and explanatory" (see above, p. 209).

14 Jan Kott, *Shakespeare Our Contemporary*, Boleslaw Taborski, trans. (Methuen: London, 1964), p. 7.

15 Julian Meyrick, *See How It Runs: The Nimrod Theatre And The New Wave, 1970–1985*, Ph.D. Thesis, LaTrobe University, 1999. Meyrick's view of the Nimrod's Shakespeare productions as driven by "fun" and a syllogistic assimilation of Shakespeare to its own "new wave" values is highly suggestive of Deguchi. I am grateful for the use of this valuable work.

16 See above, Ted Motohashi, "Interview with Gerard Murphy."

17 See above p. 109ff.

18 As I have experienced this production on video, I will use the present tense for detailed description.

19 I am indebted to Minami Ryuta for this detail.

20 See Suzuki Masae, "Shakespeare recreated by Tsutsumi Harue," *The Review of the Osaka University of Commerce*, No. 109, December 1998, pp. 117–38, p. 120. The induction was dropped from the production itself.

21 Suzuki, "Shakespeare recreated."

INDEX

Note: Japanese names in the index follow conventional Japanese usage: the surname first, followed by the given name